The Poverty of Welfare

Helping Others in Civil Society

The Poverty of Welfare

Helping Others in Civil Society

MICHAEL D. TANNER

CATO INSTITUTE
Washington, D.C.

Library of Congress Cataloging-in-Publication Data

Tanner, Michael, 1956-
  The poverty of welfare : helping others in civil society / Michael D. Tanner.
    p. cm.
Includes bibliographical references and index.
  ISBN 1-930865-41-4 (paper : alk . paper)
  1. Public welfare—United States. 2. United States. Personal
Responsibility and Work Opportunity Reconciliation Act of 1996. 3.
Welfare state. I. Title.

HV95. T365 2003
361.6'0973—dc21   2003055298

Cover design by Amanda Elliott.
Cover Photo: © Deborah Roundtree/Getty Images.
Printed in the United States of America.

CATO INSTITUTE
1000 Massachusetts Ave., N.W.
Washington, D.C. 20001

Contents

Preface

In 1996, just as I was completing work on *The End of Welfare: Fighting Poverty in the Civil Society*, Congress passed and President Clinton signed the Personal Responsibility and Work Opportunity Reconciliation Act, the most significant overhaul of the American welfare system since the initiation of the Great Society some 30 years before.

At the time, I was skeptical, warning that many of the provisions contained more illusion of reform than substance. We have now had a chance to observe welfare reform in action for six years, and the results are mixed. Welfare rolls have declined more dramatically than even supporters of reform believed possible. Widespread warnings that welfare reform would lead to increased poverty and hardship have been proven wrong. Poverty, while still far too high, has declined, especially child poverty. For the most part, former welfare recipients are better off both financially and in nonmaterial terms.

Yet, in other areas, my fears have come true. Work requirements have not been vigorously enforced, and time limits have done little to discourage chronic or long-term welfare dependency. Out-of-wedlock childbirth remains a crisis and has not yet been seriously addressed. Most significant, many former welfare recipients remain mired in a swamp of government assistance, failing to find true self-sufficiency.

Perhaps the worst consequence of welfare reform is the way it has frozen the policy debate. Congress is now debating reauthorization of welfare reform, yet there are few new or bold proposals. Congress seems content instead to tinker around the edges of the welfare system. Democrats want more money for childcare and job training with looser work requirements. Republicans want more money for marriage promotion and tighter work requirements. The debate is both predictable and sterile.

In 1996 I argued that government welfare was a failure. Nothing since then, including welfare reform, has changed that conclusion.

Indeed, if anything, PRWORA has shown us the limits of reform. As much today as in 1996, it is time to end welfare and replace it with an invigorated system of private charity. As the pages ahead will show, civil society affords more effective and compassionate ways to help lift the poor out of poverty. After all, it should be our goal, not to preserve a welfare system, reformed or otherwise, but to create a society that ensures that all Americans have the opportunity to achieve all that they can and in which poverty is a rare and temporary condition.

This book could not have been written without the advice, support, and assistance of a great many people. In particular I want to thank Jenifer Zeigler, officially my research assistant, though that title does not do justice to either her or the work she did on this book. Routinely putting in 14- to 16-hour days, she was actively involved in developing both the ideas and the research on these pages. Without her help, there would be no book. I also have to commend Ray Patnaude and Jonathan Levy, our interns, who proved themselves first-rate researchers and valuable assistants.

Others deserving thanks include Cato's president Ed Crane and executive vice president David Boaz, as well as Elizabeth Kaplan, my copyeditor, who has done her best to straighten out my mangled syntax. Any remaining errors are mine, not hers. Finally, I must thank my dear wife, Ellen, who not only provides me with inspiration but constantly challenges my assumptions and forces me to remember that public policy is, not an abstraction, but something that ultimately affects real people.

1. "The End of Welfare As We Know It"

On August 22, 1996, leaders of both political parties gathered in the White House Rose Garden to watch President Clinton sign the Personal Responsibility and Work Opportunity Reconciliation Act, a bill that, despite its obscure title, represented the most extensive revision of federal welfare policy in more than 30 years. In the Rose Garden, there were smiles all around and an uncommon political harmony, as both Democrats and Republicans basked in the warm afterglow of their enormous undertaking. Clinton even saw it as the beginning of a new era of bipartisan cooperation. "Welfare will no longer be a political issue," he said. "The two parties cannot attack each other over it."[1]

Behind the façade of cooperation, however, welfare reform remained a contentious issue. Clinton had run for president as a "New Democrat," on a platform that called for "ending welfare as we know it." But once in office, he quickly found that the same divisions that split the Democratic Party over the issue also existed in his administration.

As a result, the Clinton administration never formulated a clear vision of welfare reform. The president's reform plan was repeatedly delayed by internal bickering.[2] When finally released in June 1994, the president's plan called for a two-year time limit for welfare eligibility. During that period, recipients would receive job training and be eligible for other educational programs. At the end of the two years, they would be required to find work. If they were not able to find jobs in the private sector, they would be required to work in publicly funded community service jobs. The administration estimated that between 500,000 and 1 million public service jobs might be required. There would be no limit on the length of time a person could remain in a public service job. In addition, there would be a significant increase in funding for childcare. The president called for a crackdown, including federal sanctions, on fathers who failed to pay child support. Unwed teen mothers would be required

1

to live with their parents in most cases, and the administration would launch a $100 million media and education campaign against teen pregnancy.[3]

The Clinton plan was not an attempt to cut welfare spending. Early versions of the plan were estimated to increase welfare spending by as much as $58 billion over 10 years. That was quickly whittled back, but the final Clinton plan would still have increased spending by $9.3 billion over five years.[4]

For better or for worse, the president's proposal was released at the height of the battle over his plans for health-care reform. As a result, it received only cursory public attention and almost no debate in Congress. Thus, welfare reform remained a hot political issue going into the 1994 elections.

The centerpiece of the successful Republican effort to capture control of Congress was the Contract with America, one provision of which called for welfare reform. The Republican plan, dubbed the Personal Responsibility Act, called for returning responsibility for many welfare programs, including Aid to Families with Dependent Children, to the states and providing them block grants.[5] The Republican welfare reform proposal had many other components, including work requirements, time limits, and provisions to deal with out-of-wedlock births. But the most important was the block grants, not because block grants themselves were an innovation, but because they would end welfare's status as an entitlement. Under an entitlement program, every individual who meets the program's eligibility criteria is automatically entitled to receive the program's benefits. Spending on the program is not subject to annual appropriation; it rises automatically with the number of people enrolled. The block grant proposal, by contrast, would provide states with a fixed amount of money and they would have the power and authority to determine welfare eligibility.[6]

Ending welfare's entitlement status would have two important effects. First, it would allow states to impose a variety of conditions and restrictions on receipt of benefits. Second, because it would make welfare spending subject to annual appropriation, Congress could assert greater control over the growth in spending.

As did most provisions of the Contract with America, welfare reform passed the House of Representatives largely intact and was significantly watered down in the Senate. The Senate added a maintenance-of-effort (MOE) requirement, ordering states to continue at least 80 percent of their previous welfare spending. That would prevent states from dramatically reducing welfare spending or benefits. The Senate also added a new child-care program and other spending increases.

President Clinton initially supported the Senate version and even indicated that he might sign the final compromise. However, he quickly became the target of a withering lobbying campaign by liberal groups, notably the Children's Defense Fund. In the end, Clinton vetoed two different versions of the welfare reform bill.

However, as the 1996 elections approached, pressure grew on both parties to pass some type of welfare reform. President Clinton changed course yet again and agreed to end welfare's status as an entitlement, if Congressional Republicans would agree to increase funding for childcare and job training and ease some of the eligibility restrictions that appeared in the original bill.[7] Republicans agreed, and welfare reform passed the House by a vote of 256 to 170 and the Senate by 74 to 24.[8]

Of course, not everyone was pleased with welfare reform. Even as President Clinton prepared to sign the bill, nearly 300 protesters marched outside the White House, chanting "One, Two, Three, Four. Stop the War on the Poor."[9] Three senior members of the administration had resigned in protest.[10]

But President Clinton was not deterred. Echoing his campaign theme, he declared, "Today, we are ending welfare as we know it."[11] And with a presidential signature, 60 years of welfare in America changed.[12]

The Personal Responsibility and Work Opportunity Reconciliation Act of 1996

Welfare reform made a number of significant changes in the way welfare was provided.[13]

Before PRWORA, when most people thought of welfare, they thought of AFDC, the country's largest cash assistance program, which provided direct cash payments to children in families where the parents were absent, incapacitated, deceased, or unemployed, as well as certain other members of the children's household, most frequently their mother. The program was funded by a combination of federal and state funds (the federal portion varied from 50 to 80 percent), with states setting benefit levels and the federal government determining eligibility requirements.

PRWORA replaced AFDC with the Temporary Assistance for Needy Families block grant. This effectively abolished most federal eligibility and payment rules, giving states much greater flexibility to design their own programs. The TANF block grant was a fixed amount for each state, largely based on the pre-reform federal contribution to that state's AFDC program. In addition, as mentioned above, the block grants eliminated welfare's "entitlement" status, meaning that no one would have an automatic right to benefits.[14] States could choose which families to help. States were however, required to continue spending at least 75 to 80 percent of their previous levels under the MOE provision.

Widespread work requirements were to be imposed on welfare recipients. States were initially to have at least 40 percent of their welfare recipients either working or participating in work preparation activities; that percentage was to have increased to 50 percent by 2002, although states were given wide discretion in designing work programs. However, states were given various credits and exemptions that significantly reduced the number of recipients actually required to work.

PRWORA also established a time limit for welfare receipt. Recipients could not remain on the rolls for longer than 60 months (five years). However, that restriction did not apply to child-only families, in which the children receive benefits but the parents do not, and states could exempt up to 20 percent of their adult recipients from time limits for "hardship" reasons. States also had the option of imposing stricter time limits or of using their own funds to continue paying benefits to families who exceed the five-year time limit.

The legislation included incentives for states to establish programs to limit out-of-wedlock births. Each year, the five states that achieved the greatest reduction in out-of-wedlock birth ratios (defined as the proportion of out-of-wedlock births to total births), while also decreasing the ratio of abortions to live births, would receive $20 million in additional federal funds. PRWORA also included other provisions targeted at out-of-wedlock births, including (1) unmarried mothers under the age of 18 are required to remain in school and to live with an adult; (2) states are allowed to prohibit additional benefits for women who conceive additional children while on welfare; (3) states are required to establish numerical goals for the reduction of teen pregnancy and out-of-wedlock births and to develop specific plans for achieving those goals; (4) the secretary of Health and Human Services is directed to implement a comprehensive program to combat teen pregnancy and to ensure that at least 25 percent of American communities have teen pregnancy prevention programs in place by 2002; and (5) states are authorized to spend unused TANF funds on teen pregnancy prevention and teen parent services.[15]

In one of the more controversial provisions, legal immigrants who arrived after 1996 and had not become citizens were made ineligible for TANF, as well as food stamps and Supplemental Security Income. (However, later legislation restored food stamp eligibility for most immigrants.)

And finally, rules were changed to encourage greater state efforts to determine paternity and to collect child support from absent parents. The federal government would also provide additional assistance in collecting child support.

Welfare Today

What does welfare look like today? First, despite welfare reform, most of the mammoth federal and state social welfare complex remains unchanged. There are still more than 70 overlapping federal anti-poverty programs.[16] For example, there are 11 different programs providing food, administered by two separate federal departments. There are 16 housing programs, administered by three separate federal agencies.[17]

In 2000, the last year for which final data are available, total welfare spending by federal, state, and local governments topped $434 billion.[18] Of this amount, roughly 72 percent came from the federal government, and the remainder was provided at the state and local levels.[19] Approximately 51 percent of all welfare spending goes to medical and health-care programs, the largest of which is Medicaid. Cash programs such as TANF, food stamps, housing, and energy programs make up 38 percent of the total, while 11 percent goes to education, job training, social services, and community aid programs.[20]

Still, when most people think of "welfare," they are thinking of the cash assistance program, formerly AFDC, now TANF. Therefore, unless otherwise stated, for the purposes of this book, when discussing "welfare" I will be referring to TANF and associated programs.

The block grant at the center of PRWORA has been held constant at $16.5 billion per year since 1996. But when combined with other TANF-related spending, TANF can be estimated to have cost more than $25.5 billion in 2001. Roughly 53 percent of that was federal money; the remainder was state funds. Just over $10 billion was for direct cash assistance; the remainder was used for childcare, education and training, work support, administrative costs, and other expenses.[21]

That is a significant change in the distribution of expenditures from prereform welfare. Prior to reform, direct cash assistance accounted for 73 percent of welfare spending under AFDC and related programs.[22] Under PRWORA, cash assistance has shrunk to 40 percent. The second largest category of expenditure, roughly 13 percent, was previously for childcare. Despite rhetoric about the importance of work to welfare reform, work-related expenditures—including those for education and training as well as subsidized employment, job search activities, employment counseling, and outreach efforts to employers—represent less than 10 percent of expenditures.[23]

It is also important to recognize that the number of welfare recipients declined dramatically after 1996, which meant that states had far fewer individuals to serve with the same size grant. As a result, on a per recipient basis, spending has increased from about $7,000 to more than $16,000.[24]

Families can receive TANF in two ways. In most cases, both the parent or parents and the children receive benefits. However, in some cases, the children may be eligible, though the parents are not. As a practical matter, that may be a distinction without a difference, but in some cases different rules apply.

Overall, roughly 2.1 million families, comprised of 1.4 million adults and a few more than 4 million children, receive TANF.[25] That number reflects postreform reductions in the welfare caseload, but it may also understate the impact of welfare on our society and the prevalence of welfare receipt. For example, more than 20 percent of all children born in the late 1960s have spent at least one year on welfare; more than 70 percent of African-American children born during those years have done so. And the situation is growing worse. More than 30 percent of children born in 1980 spent a year on welfare; more than 80 percent of African-American children did so.[26]

About 61 percent of the nearly 2.3 million adults who live in families receiving TANF benefits receive benefits in their own right. More than 90 percent of those recipients are women. The average age of adult recipients is much higher than might be commonly believed, 31 years. Seven percent of recipients are teen parents, and 19 percent are over the age of 40.[27]

Ninety-two percent of families on welfare have no father present. The average family size is 2.6 persons, down from 4.0 persons in 1969. Only about 10 percent of families have more than three children.[28]

The average age of children on welfare is 7.8 years, and about 92 percent are under the age of 16 and 38 percent under the age of 6. Roughly 63 percent live with at least one parent, generally their mother, but 22 percent live with a grandparent.[29]

The racial composition of the welfare rolls has changed significantly in the past decade, a trend that accelerated sharply in the aftermath of welfare reform. In 1992 whites were more likely to be on welfare than blacks: 39 percent of recipients were white, 37 percent were black, and 18 percent were Hispanic. However, today African Americans make up 39 percent of recipients, while whites have fallen to just 30 percent; and Hispanics have shown an exceptionally large increase to 26 percent. The rise in Hispanic welfare receipt is particularly pronounced in California, Texas, and New York. For example, Hispanics make up 49 percent of California's caseload.[30]

Although many conservatives complain about immigrants coming to this country for welfare, the reality is quite different. Fewer than 2 percent of children receiving TANF are noncitizens. And only 113,000 noncitizen adults receive TANF.[31] Noncitizen use of other welfare programs, especially Medicaid, may be much higher, however. At least one study indicates that 22.7 percent of noncitizen immigrant families have at least one member who has used a welfare program at some time. Medicaid, other government health-care programs, and food stamps were the most frequently used. On a more positive note, noncitizen families who used noncash welfare programs were more likely to have a family member working, making long-term dependence less likely.[32]

7

Divorce is the most common reason a person goes on welfare, followed by an out-of-wedlock birth. Contrary to the rhetoric, relatively few individuals go on welfare because they have lost a job or suffered a decline in wages.[33]

Although the average length of time spent on welfare is relatively short, generally two years or less, 65 percent of persons enrolled in the program at any one time have been in the program for eight years or longer. The vast majority of long-term recipients are single mothers, especially those whose entry into the welfare system was brought about by an out-of-wedlock birth. In fact, women who started on welfare because of an out-of-wedlock birth average more than nine years on welfare and make up roughly 40 percent of all recipients who are on welfare for 10 years or longer.[34]

The difference between point-in-time and beginning-spell estimates can be confusing. The probability of being on welfare at any given time is necessarily greater for long-term recipients than for those who use the program for shorter periods of time. To better understand that concept, consider hospitalization. Suppose a hospital has 13 beds. Twelve of those beds are occupied all year by chronically ill patients. The remaining bed is used for one week each by 52 different short-term patients. On any given day, a hospital census would find that 85 percent of patients (12 of 13) were in the midst of a yearlong spell of hospitalization. However, 80 percent of those who enter the hospital (52 of 64) spend only one week there.[35] The same dynamic works for the welfare population.

Understanding why people leave welfare is complicated by poor record keeping at the state level. For example, while independent studies generally estimate that between 50 and 60 percent of recipients who leave welfare do so because they have found employment, official state figures put that percentage at just 19 percent. On the other hand, states categorize fully 23 percent as leaving for "other" or "unspecified" reasons. Even the U.S. Department of Health and Human Services finds these figures unconvincing.[36]

Whatever the precise numbers may be, finding a job appears to be the most important reason people leave welfare. That represents a change since welfare reform was passed. Under the old AFDC program, marriage was the primary reason for leaving welfare.[37] Presumably the change is due, not to fewer marriages, but to an increased emphasis on work under PRWORA.

Reauthorization

President Clinton's prediction of bipartisan harmony on welfare reform proved not to be the case. Welfare reform was originally passed for a five-year period, requiring reauthorization in 2002. However, as with so many legislative issues, the Republican-controlled House of Representatives and the Democrat-controlled Senate could not reach an agreement on proposals for reauthorization. As a result, instead of being reauthorized, PWRORA was continued on a temporary basis into 2003, setting up a new debate over reauthorization.

The debate is over many of the same issues it was in 1996, including the need for and meaning of welfare reform; funding levels for TANF; whether states should have more or less flexibility in program design and operation; whether time limits and sanctions should be eased; what can be done to encourage family formation and discourage out-of-wedlock births; whether there is enough money for childcare; whether more assistance should be provided to working poor families; and whether more should be done to help mothers qualify for better jobs.[38]

The House has passed a bill reflecting President Bush's views on the issue.[39] However, support was far less bipartisan than in 1996. The measure passed by a vote of 230 to 192. Eleven Democrats joined 219 Republicans in support of the bill, while two Republicans voted with 190 Democrats in opposition.[40]

The bill would essentially reauthorize the main provisions of PWRORA, with a few key changes. In particular, the bill would strengthen the work requirements in several ways. First, the percentage of welfare recipients required to work would be increased to 70 percent by 2007. At the same time, the credit that states receive for caseload reduction would be significantly scaled back, meaning that far more states would actually be subject to the work mandate. Second, the number of hours of work per week required to meet the mandate would be raised from 30 to 40, and the number of core hours—which cannot be met by education and training requirements—would be increased from 20 to 24.[41]

The bill would continue current federal spending levels on the welfare program at $16.5 billion per year and increase child-care funding by $2 billion over five years. More important, the legislation would give states more flexibility in how they spend welfare funds.

9

In particular, it would make it easier for states to save unused funds as a "rainy day" or contingency fund to be held against future shortfalls. It would also allow states to spend their MOE funds on a wider array of support activities.[42] This includes such programs as food stamps, childcare, income supplements, and transportation assistance. Under the president's proposal, states would be given the flexibility to streamline and coordinate support programs, which now operate under different agencies, different rules, and different reporting requirements. The federal government would be given enhanced authority to grant states waivers from federal law and rules applying to several low-income programs, including food stamps, public housing and homeless assistance programs, the Child Care and Development Block Grant, the Social Services Block Grant, most workforce investment and job-training programs funded under the Workforce Investment Act, the Employment Service, adult education programs, and TANF.[43]

Finally, the president's proposal, and the House bill, would spend some $300 million on programs designed to promote marriage. Those programs include premarital education and counseling as well as research and technical assistance.[44]

Democrats in both the House and the Senate advanced several competing proposals for reauthorization, all of which differed from the president's in several important areas.[45] Not surprisingly, they would significantly increase spending, including an additional $11 billion to $15 billion for childcare.[46]

Not only would the alternative proposals fail to strengthen work requirements, in many cases they would actually weaken them. For example, legislation sponsored by Sen. Max Baucus (D-Mont.) would create so many additional credits and exemptions that virtually the entire work requirement would be eliminated. Indeed, the total number of credits and exemptions possible under the Baucus bill exceeds 100 percent of a state's caseload.[47] The alternative proposals also would weaken time limits and remove many of the sanctions for noncompliance with work and other requirements. In general, they would allow considerably more activities to substitute for work, including higher education.[48] And, they would spend far more money on childcare.[49]

Needed: A Different Debate

Those are all important issues, and the way in which they are decided will either improve or undercut PRWORA. Yet, in the end, this is not the debate that we should be having.

Rather than quibbling over the details of reform legislation, we should be asking how we can best create a country where every American can reach his or her full potential, where as few people as possible live in poverty, and where no one must go without the basic necessities of life. This is not a question of funding levels, work requirements, time limits, or child-care subsidies. Rather, it is a question of the fundamental role of government—about the balance between government and civil society.

The answer to poverty does not lie with government. If we are to be successful in fighting poverty and creating opportunity for all Americans, we must think outside the box of government programs—no matter how well intentioned, no matter how efficiently operated. We must develop a new paradigm, based not on government and political society but on civil society.

Civil society is that sphere of human behavior that lies outside of government or political society. It does not rely on force or coercion to achieve its goals; it relies on voluntary cooperation and persuasion. It provides the widest possible latitude for people to live their lives without interference, so long as they do not harm others. Civil society would not use government either to redistribute wealth or to shape poor peoples' behavior.

Neither would it be indifferent to the plight of the poor. It would, in fact, unleash our natural tendencies toward generosity and compassion. Of course, civil society would stress self-reliance and individual initiative, but it would also provide a vigorous network of private, localized, nonbureaucratic charities that were far more capable than government of actually helping those in need.

In the coming pages I will examine the American welfare system, looking at how we changed from a system that combined small, local welfare programs with private charities and civic and fraternal organizations to today's massive welfare state. I will explore the problems that the welfare state has caused: family disintegration, a diminution of the work ethic, crime, and increased poverty. I will show that, as a practical matter, welfare can never be reformed enough to eliminate its destructiveness and perverse incentives. Rather than waste more time—and more lives—on further tinkering, we should end government welfare once and for all. That step alone would reduce poverty in America. Fewer children would be born to poor single mothers unable to care for them. More poor people would find the road out of poverty through work and education.

11

Americans are already the most generous people on earth; they contribute more than $212 billion per year to organized private charity and volunteer more than 15.3 billion hours, with an estimated value of $239 billion.[50] History and the American character suggest that we would more than rise to the occasion to meet the needs of those who continue to need our help.

No matter what Congress does about reauthorizing PRWORA, there will remain work to be done. We should not be satisfied with half measures. We should continue to strive for a society in which every man, woman, and child has a chance to realize the American dream.

It is civil society, built on personal responsibility, opportunity, and genuine compassion, that offers them the best hope for the future. Let the debate begin.

2. Welfare before 1996

In looking at the future of welfare, it is worthwhile to first examine the past. How did the American welfare state develop? How did we move from a society that relied primarily on the generosity of individuals to one that depends on massive government-directed transfers of wealth?

Although some conservatives like to portray charity in this country in the early years as a purely private matter, in truth there was some degree of government involvement from the beginning. However, government activity was almost exclusively at the local level. The idea that the federal government should involve itself in charity did occasionally crop up, but it was nearly universally rejected by the Founding Fathers, who considered such action beyond the proper constitutional role of the federal government. In 1794, for example, James Madison, debating a proposed welfare bill, rose on the floor of the House to declare, "I cannot undertake to lay my finger on that article of the Federal Constitution which granted a right to Congress" to pass such a bill.[1]

That was still the attitude in 1854 when President Franklin Pierce vetoed a bill to give land to the states to allow them to build institutions for the insane. In his veto message, Pierce wrote: "I cannot find any authority in the Constitution for making the Federal Government the great almoner of public charity throughout the United States. To do so would . . . be contrary to the letter and spirit of the Constitution and subversive of the whole theory upon which the Union of these States is founded."[2]

Colonial America was influenced by the English Poor Law. That law, passed in 1601, established four basic principles for government charity: (1) care for the poor was a public responsibility; (2) care for the poor was a local matter; (3) public relief was denied to individuals who could be cared for by their families; and (4) children of the poor could be apprenticed to farmers and artisans who would care for them in exchange for work.[3] Those principles would underlie the

13

earliest American welfare programs. The early states also followed English precedent by enacting "settlement laws," which prevented the poor from moving to towns with more generous welfare benefits.

In general, public charity was administered by counties and townships through one of two methods: outdoor relief or poorhouses. Outdoor relief, which most closely resembled today's welfare programs, took a number of forms. In some cases small cash grants were given; in others contributions were "in kind," mainly food. Fuel was generally provided during the winter.[4]

Most recipients of outdoor relief were women, children, elderly, or sick. For example, a census of those receiving outdoor relief in Philadelphia in 1814 revealed that nearly two-thirds of the recipients were sick, disabled, or aged. The remaining third was made up of single mothers, the vast majority of whom were widows.[5] However, a small minority of outdoor relief recipients were able-bodied but unemployed men who engendered a considerable amount of resentment that was often directed toward outdoor relief in general. That led many communities to reduce outdoor relief in favor of poorhouses.

Poorhouses or workhouses were another carryover from England. There were poorhouses from the very earliest days of the colonies. Boston established a poorhouse in 1702, and New York followed suit in 1736. The Philadelphia poorhouse was opened in 1766.[6]

Poorhouses were seen as superior to outdoor relief both because they were less expensive and because they provided a deterrent to able-bodied people's applying for relief. Conditions in poorhouses were harsh. Long hours of work were mandatory. Whipping and other punishments were common for infractions of the rules.[7] The poor were often housed together with the insane, prostitutes, and petty thieves.[8]

The harshness was intentional, designed to "deter many intemperate wretches and lazy vagrants from seeking admission."[9] Reports of the time indicate that the policy met with some success. Typical was a report from New Bedford, Massachusetts, which said that since the town had switched from outdoor relief to a poorhouse, it had "experienced a diminution of that class of vagrants who have for years annoyed us."[10]

Starting in the 1830s, state governments began to require that cities and counties establish poorhouses.[11] For nearly a century thereafter, poorhouses would remain the central feature of government anti-poverty policy. During the early part of the 19th century, there was also a brief experimentation with "auctioning" the poor. Poor individuals would be auctioned off to people who agreed to care for them at the lowest cost. However, many bidders saw the auctions as a source of cheap labor, and abuse was rampant. In 1842 a report by Secretary of State J. V. N. Yates of New York warned that "the poor, when farmed out, or sold, are frequently treated with barbarity and neglected by their keepers."[12] As a result of abuses, the practice had largely died out by the middle of the century.

Government welfare was supplemented and generally surpassed by private charitable activities. Alexis de Tocqueville commented on the compassion of ordinary Americans and the widespread activities of private charity, contrasting the United States with European countries, where "the state almost exclusively undertakes to supply bread to the hungry, assistance and shelter to the sick, work to the idle, and to act as sole reliever of all kinds of misery."[13]

In his seminal work, *The Tragedy of American Compassion*, Marvin Olasky has detailed the astonishing breadth and variety of private charitable efforts throughout the first half of this country's existence. Most were religious in nature—Protestant, Catholic, and Jewish charitable organizations all thrived—and almost all operated on the principle of distinguishing between the "deserving" and the "undeserving" poor.[14]

The deserving poor included those who, although normally self-sufficient, found themselves suddenly in need of help because of sickness, accident, loss of employment during a recession, or similar misfortune. The deserving poor also included the elderly, orphans, and others for whom circumstances made self-sufficiency impossible. The undeserving poor were those who could be self-sufficient but were not because of personal or "moral" failings; that group included drunkards, layabouts, and profligates.[15]

Interestingly, there is evidence that the total amount of charity in a community remained relatively constant regardless of the mix of public and private sources. In 1899 Frederic Almy, secretary of the Buffalo Charity Organization Society, gathered data on public and private charitable activities in 40 cities. Almy ranked the cities in four groups from high to low in both categories of charity. He found that cities in the highest two categories of private charity had the lowest levels of public charity. Those with higher levels of public charity tended to have lower levels of private charity. Almy concluded that "a correspondence or balance between the amounts of public and private relief appears to be established."[16]

The Progressive Era and the Rise of Government Charity

By the closing years of the 19th century, both public and private charity were undergoing profound changes. For public welfare, the days of purely local control were on the way out. State, and even federal, involvement was rising.

At the same time, a significant change was occurring in Americans' attitude toward government. The rise of "modernism" and "progressivism" caused many Americans to believe that "experts" were required to solve most problems and that only government could provide the needed expertise. Previously, the purpose of government had been seen as protecting individual rights. Now, government was seen as a problem solver.

Reformers admitted that private charities had done a good job so far but thought they were now facing "a problem infinitely bigger than they can handle—a problem so big that no institution short of society itself can hope to cope with it."[17] The problem might be big, but there was no problem that was too big for government experts to fix. Owen Lovejoy, president of the National Conference of Social Work, wrote in a 1920 article of social workers as "social engineers" imposing "a divine order on earth as it is in heaven."[18]

The federal government was taking its first tentative steps into the social welfare arena. The Civil War had left a large number of disabled veterans for whom the federal government provided pensions and other benefits. In addition, the federal government provided emergency relief to victims of floods in 1867, 1874, 1882, and 1884. Farmers devastated by a locust infestation in 1875 received a special appropriation. There was also an 1879 appropriation to establish colleges for the blind.[19]

At the local level, poorhouses were on their way out. A series of reforms had removed many groups—orphans, the mentally ill, the sick—to specialized institutions, leaving the poorhouses to gradually transform themselves into old-age homes. At the same time, outdoor relief was making a resurgence. For example, between 1911 and 1925, the amount of outdoor relief dispensed in the nation's 16 largest cities increased from $1.6 million to $14.7 million.[20]

Not surprisingly, children and the elderly were at the heart of new government programs to help the poor. Certainly many children were living in miserable conditions. What became known as the Child-Saving Movement developed. The Child-Saving Movement was a broad, loose social movement that sought better conditions for children. Among the many issues embraced under the general heading of child saving were removing children from poorhouses; preventing child abuse and enacting child cruelty laws; replacing institutional care with foster care; juvenile justice reform, including the introduction of juvenile courts and the removal of juveniles from adult prisons; compulsory education; and public health measures to combat infant mortality.[21]

Not all child savers favored government action. Many supported traditional charitable activities, with a new emphasis on the problems of children. Many in the Child-Saving Movement regarded government institutions as corrupt and sought to limit government's role in helping children. That appears to have been particularly true in the East, where big-city political machines had corrupted nearly all governmental activities. For example, in New York, the Child-Saving Movement successfully fought to forbid government regulation of any children's institution that did not receive government money.[22] However, the movement gradually became dominated by pro-government reformers, and the emphasis shifted to government action.

Among the Child-Saving Movement's greatest successes was moving children out of poorhouses into orphanages. Orphanages had a long history in the United States, as both private and public institutions. Private orphanages were established in New Orleans as early as 1729 and in Savannah in 1738. The first public orphanage was probably the one in Charleston, South Carolina, established in 1794.[23]

The heyday of the orphanage came in the late 19th and early 20th centuries. Between 1900 and 1904 alone, the number of children in public institutions doubled.[24] By 1910 there were at least 1,151 orphanages in the United States. Approximately 90 percent of them were at least nominally private, but nearly all received at least some government funding.[25]

The Child-Saving Movement continued to drive government to become more involved in social welfare issues. In 1912 Congress established the Children's Bureau to study and report on "all matters pertaining to the welfare of children and child life among all classes of our people."[26] The agency had no authority and an annual budget of only $25,640 but nonetheless represented an important turning point in the growth of the welfare state.[27] The federal government was taking a direct role in social welfare policy.

Among the first state welfare programs were "mothers' pensions," small stipends to widows and other mothers to assist them in caring for their children. In part, those programs were a county-level response to the large number of widows in the aftermath of the Civil War. They were also a continuation of the Child-Saving Movement. Mothers' pensions eventually moved to state government. In 1911 Missouri and Illinois became the first states to enact mothers' pensions. Other states soon followed, and, by 1919, 39 states and the territories of Alaska and Hawaii had authorized mothers' pensions. By 1935 every state except Georgia and South Carolina provided widows' pensions.[28]

In many ways mothers' pensions foreshadowed future welfare programs, particularly Aid to Families with Dependent Children. The original recipients of mothers' pensions were intended to be almost exclusively widows. However, the program soon expanded to cover women who for a variety of reasons were "without the support of the normal breadwinner."[29] As a result, the program soon began to provide aid for divorced and abandoned women, and even unwed mothers.[30] The program grew steadily. By 1930 mothers of more than 200,000 children were receiving funds.[31]

By the 1920s most states had established a variety of child health programs and clinics. They also provided subsidized milk to mothers with young children and information and referrals to private charities. In 1921, establishing the first federally funded government health care program, Congress passed the Sheppard-Towner Act, which provided matching funds to the states to establish prenatal and child health centers. Among the purposes of those centers was to "teach expectant mothers the rules of personal hygiene and offer advice on how to maintain and improve the health of their children."[32] The program itself was short-lived—Congress stopped funding it in 1929—but the principle of federal government involvement in welfare had been firmly established.

Indeed, in 1921 Warren Harding campaigned on the idea of establishing a federal department of public welfare.[33] His proposal died in Congress, but his attitude shows how far America had come since the days of President Pierce's veto.

States also began to play a role in the care of the aged. In 1914 Arizona passed the first law establishing an old-age pension. By 1933 approximately 30 states had followed suit.[34]

The changing attitude toward government welfare can also be seen in the era's changing terminology. For example, as part of New York's 1929 Public Welfare Law, "relief" was renamed "public welfare," "almshouses" became "county homes," "superintendents of the poor" became "commissioners of public welfare," and the State Board of Charities was renamed the State Board of Social Welfare.[35]

The same reverence for experts and structure was evident in private charities, which became more structured and hierarchical. Volunteers were replaced with paid staff.[36] Social workers became increasingly specialized, styling themselves as medical social workers, visiting teachers, vocational guidance specialists, and psychiatric social workers. Schools of social work sprang up, then proliferated. By 1930 there were 30 schools of social work.[37]

As they became a professional class, social workers began to resent competition from their unschooled counterparts. Accordingly, they sought increased government regulation of social work and private charitable activities. By 1911 Frederic Almy was led to complain that "social workers, like doctors, will soon have to pass an examination before they are allowed to practice on the poor."[38]

With the changing nature of private charity and the increasing involvement of government at all levels, the stage was set for the next major expansion of the welfare state. The opportunity for that expansion came with the onset of the Great Depression.

African Americans and Fraternal Organizations

During the 19th and early 20th centuries, there developed an interesting trend in the African-American community.[39] Most public welfare programs—particularly in the South but throughout the country as well—refused to provide benefits to African Americans.[40] Many private charities also discriminated. Therefore, African Americans began to develop their own charitable institutions.

Among them were mutual aid societies and fraternal organizations.[41] Although they provided services to poor whites as well, fraternal organizations were particularly important to the African-American community. Black Bostonians had established the first African-American Masonic Lodge in 1792. Blacks in Philadelphia followed suit five years later.[42] By the 20th century there were hundreds of black lodges and fraternal groups. Some were segregated black chapters of groups like the Masons, the Elks, and the Loyal Order of Moose. Others were all-black organizations such as the autonomous Grand United Order of Odd Fellows.[43]

Membership in those organizations was enormous. In 1916 the Odd Fellows had more than 304,000 members nationwide. The Knights of Pythias had 250,000 members.[44] In Philadelphia fully 80 percent of the African-American population during the 1800s was said to belong to black fraternal groups and their women's auxiliaries.[45] Nearly 30 percent of all adult black men in southern states were thought to be members of the Prince Hall Masons.[46]

Black fraternal organizations provided a wide variety of social services both to their members and to the African-American community at large. They built orphanages and old-age homes. The Odd Fellows, for example, operated 47 homes for the elderly in 1929.[47] They provided food to the hungry, helped the unemployed find work, and provided shelter for the homeless.

One of the most important services provided by fraternal organizations was the "death benefit," a form of life insurance. Death benefits helped prevent the widows of members from falling into poverty. As a 1910 article in *Everybody's Magazine* put it: "Rich men insure in big companies to create an estate. Poor men insure in the fraternal orders to create bread and meat. It is an insurance against want, the poorhouse charity, and degradation."[48]

In addition to life insurance, fraternal organizations provided "lodge-practice medicine," an early form of health insurance. Members would pay the lodge a premium of one or two dollars per month. The lodge, in turn, would contract with a doctor who would agree, for a flat monthly or yearly fee, to treat all lodge members. In many ways, lodge-practice medicine resembled health maintenance organizations.[49]

As a result of the widespread influence of black fraternal organizations, African Americans were more likely to be insured than were whites during the early years of the 20th century.[50] A 1919 survey of African Americans in Chicago, for instance, found that 93.5 percent of families had at least one member insured.[51] The same year a survey in Philadelphia found that 98 percent of African-American families had at least one insured member.[52]

A strong network of black churches and private organizations such as the National Urban League and the National Association of Colored Women also offered a wide variety of social services, including homes for the aged, women, and children; relief funds for the feeding and care of the unemployed; and job referral services.[53]

Private charitable efforts among African Americans strongly emphasized the difference between deserving and undeserving poor. Individuals who refused work or were engaged in "immoral practices" were routinely denied benefits. Although it may have been making a virtue of necessity, African-American public opinion often appeared contemptuous of public charity. For example, the membership manual of the Colored Knights of Pythias proudly claimed, "The sick among our brethren are not left to the cold hand of public charity; they are visited, and their wants provided for . . . without the humiliation of . . . individual relief—from which the freeborn mind recoils with disdain."[54] In a similar vein, Booker T. Washington argued that "in our ordinary southern communities, we look upon it as a disgrace for an individual to be taken from that community to any institution for dependents."[55]

Immigrants and other groups that were routinely excluded from public charity developed similar private institutions, including Mexican-American Penitente Lodges; Chinese companies and tongs; and organizations in the Polish, Italian, Irish, and Slovak communities.[56]

Fraternal organizations remained a major factor in African-American charity well into the 1930s. However, as the federalization of welfare made government benefits increasingly available to blacks, the mission of the lodges was supplanted. The organizations declined in membership and influence and gave up many of their social service activities.[57]

In addition, the American Medical Association, complaining that lodge-practice medicine was undermining physicians' incomes, launched a campaign against the practice that resulted in its virtual elimination by 1930.[58] As a result, African Americans moved into the mainstream of the welfare state.

The New Deal

The Great Depression was one of the most traumatic events in American history. At its worst point, in 1933, nearly 13 million

21

Americans, 24.9 percent of the labor force, were unemployed. Among nonfarm laborers unemployment was even worse, as high as 37.6 percent. The nation's gross national product declined by half between 1929 and 1933. One-third of the nation's banks suspended operations. Businesses went bankrupt, and there were widespread mortgage foreclosures, particularly on farms.[59]

Both public and private charities were unprepared to deal with the sudden massive unemployment and poverty. The burden was huge. For example, a Bureau of the Census survey in 1929 found that an average of 334,000 families were receiving relief nationwide each month. By 1931 that number had risen to more than 1 million per month. By 1933 the number of families on relief each month had increased to 4 million, or nearly 18 million persons.[60] During the first quarter of 1932 public and private relief in New York State totaled more than $15 million compared with less than $4 million in the first quarter of 1929.[61]

Local governments found that providing relief was a serious drain on their resources and created financial crises. Several cities went bankrupt. Detroit and Chicago found themselves without enough money to pay their schoolteachers.[62] Private charities found it equally difficult to cope. In New York City alone nearly 400 private charities went under between 1929 and 1932.[63] A desperate announcement from Silas Strong, president of the U.S. Chamber of Commerce, in 1932 provides a glimpse at how severe the problem was.

> For many months the Illinois Emergency Relief Commission has been taking care of 111,000 families, or about 600,000 of the destitute. The $10.5 million fund contributed by the citizens, and the $12.5 million additional, being the proceeds of the State of Illinois notes, in all $23 million are exhausted. Accordingly, the relief stations in Chicago have been notified that all available funds having been exhausted, the stations must close tomorrow night.[64]

Local governments, not surprisingly, looked to state governments for assistance. Among the first to respond was New York's governor Franklin Roosevelt, who called a special session of the legislature to pass the Wicks Act, which created the Temporary Emergency Relief Association. TERA, which would later serve as a model for some of Roosevelt's federal anti-poverty programs, provided matching grants to localities for emergency unemployment relief.[65] In the next few months six major industrial states—New Jersey, Pennsylvania, Rhode Island, Wisconsin, Illinois, and Ohio—followed New York's lead and established unemployment relief funds.[66]

Demands for federal action began to mount. There were marches on Washington, protests, even riots. The demands were supported by the now thoroughly "professionalized" social worker class. In 1931, for example, the Rockefeller Foundation gave a $40,000 grant to the American Association of Social Workers to "educate public opinion regarding the fundamental importance of welfare work in the present government."[67]

In Congress Sens. Edward Costigan (D-Colo.), Robert La Follette (D-Wis.), and Robert Wagner (D-N.Y.) pushed hard for the federal government to intervene. In 1931 Congress passed a bill introduced by Senator Wagner that would have established a federally funded public works program, an expanded federal employment service, and unemployment insurance, but President Herbert Hoover vetoed the bill.[68]

Hoover was adamantly opposed to federal intervention. In his 1931 message to Congress, he said: "I am opposed to any direct or indirect government dole. The breakdown and increased unemployment in Europe is due in part to such practices. Our people are providing against distress from unemployment in the true American fashion."[69]

Hoover's opposition to federal government action stemmed from two important experiences. In London in the 1920s he had seen the destructive influence of England's dole on World War I veterans, whom he observed passing up available work in favor of unemployment benefits. Second, Hoover had led the massive private and religious charitable campaign that provided relief to the war's civilian victims. That instilled in him a firm belief in the ability of private charity to meet any crisis.[70]

Hoover repeatedly stressed private charity as an alternative to government action. "This is not an issue as to whether people shall go hungry and cold in the United States," he said. "It is solely a question of how hunger and cold shall be prevented. It is a question of whether the American people on the one hand will maintain the spirit of charity and mutual self-help through voluntary giving and the responsibility of local government as distinguished on the other hand from appropriations from the federal treasury for such purposes."[71]

23

Private charitable groups were indeed beginning to rally. Americans were contributing more to charity than ever before. In New York City, for example, a group of philanthropists contributed $8.5 million to put the unemployed to work.[72] In 1932, despite worsening economic conditions, the Community Chest set a record for contributions.[73]

Whether Hoover was ultimately correct that private charity would be sufficient to handle the crisis would never be known, because as elections approached and the depression deepened, he began to waver. In 1932 he signed legislation creating the Reconstruction Finance Corporation, a $300 million public works highway program.[74] He also supported federal credit guarantees to drought-stricken farmers and other limited federal programs.[75]

In November 1932 Franklin Delano Roosevelt was elected president, and an overwhelming Democratic majority was elected to Congress. Roosevelt wasted no time in expanding the federal welfare role. Just 10 weeks after his inauguration in 1933, he signed the Federal Emergency Relief Act, a $500 million program of grants to state and local governments. Half the funds were to be used as matching grants—$1 of federal money for each $3 of state or local money—for unemployment relief. The other $250 million was set aside in a discretionary fund for states that needed additional assistance in providing relief to a wide variety of needy individuals.[76]

The Federal Emergency Relief Act, the first large-scale entry of the federal government into relief spending, resulted in significant changes in the way state and local governments dispensed relief. For the first time, funds were directed, not narrowly to widows, orphans, and the disabled, but to "all needy unemployed persons and/or their dependents." The measure also covered all "those whose employment or available resources are inadequate to provide the necessities of life for themselves and/or their dependents."[77]

Though it was financed at the federal level, the Federal Emergency Relief Act routed aid through state and local governments. However, Roosevelt quickly began to seek a more direct federal role.

It is impossible within the scope of this book to discuss the whole dizzying array of welfare and employment programs that the Roosevelt administration eventually enacted. However, that administration's plans generally proceeded along three tracks: (1) public works and other programs to provide employment for able-bodied men;

(2) direct relief for women, children, and others who could not support themselves; and (3) a broad social insurance system for the middle class.

Two of the earliest public works programs were the Civilian Conservation Corps, which provided jobs in the national forests at subsistence wages for 500,000 men, and the Public Works Administration, which would eventually spend $6 billion on a variety of public works construction projects.[78] Both programs passed in 1933. Later that year, the Civil Works Administration, which would become the greatest public works experiment in American history, was created. During its brief life, the CWA would employ 4.26 million people. More than 22 percent of American households had a member working for the CWA.[79] In 1935, Congress created the Works Progress Administration, which undertook a variety of projects from road construction to recording the stories of former slaves.[80]

Although they were the most widespread of New Deal welfare programs, the public works projects were actually short-lived. The CWA, for example, lasted only four months. By 1939 nearly all were gone. A few, such as the WPA, limped through World War II with vastly reduced budgets.[81] Although cash relief was initially much smaller than the public works projects, it was destined to have a much greater and longer-lasting impact.

Roosevelt claimed to be skeptical of direct relief; in speeches he warned that the dole could become a narcotic.[82] He nevertheless continually expanded the programs. By the winter of 1934 there were 20 million people on the dole,[83] and the biggest expansion was yet to come. As part of the Social Security Act of 1935, Roosevelt created Aid to Dependant Children, a program of matching grants to the states, which essentially federalized state mothers' pensions.[84] Little remarked upon at the time, ADC would eventually become AFDC and remain the mainstay of the welfare system until it was replaced by Temporary Assistance for Needy Families in 1996.

Originally intended as a small program, ADC expanded rapidly. By 1938, 243,000 families with more than 600,000 children were participating in the program; the next year the numbers jumped to 298,000 families and 708,000 children. The program's total cost in 1939 exceeded $103 million, of which the federal portion was $34 million.[85] That amount was modest, of course, in comparison with the public works programs, but unlike those programs, ADC was not going to go away. Instead, it would continue to grow inexorably.

25

Finally, Roosevelt began the construction of a series of social insurance programs to act as a safety net for the middle class. The best known, of course, is Social Security.[86]

President Roosevelt and the New Deal forever changed the face of welfare in America. Between 1932 and 1939 welfare spending at all levels of government—federal, state, and local—increased from $208 million to $4.9 billion. In 1933 welfare programs accounted for only 6.5 percent of all government expenditures; by 1939 that figure had risen to 27.1 percent.[87]

At the same time, the New Deal dramatically increased the federal role in welfare. In 1932, 97.9 percent of all government welfare spending was at the state and local levels. By 1939 such spending had declined to just 37.5 percent.[88] The growing government role in charity under the New Deal pushed private charity to the sidelines. As historian William Brock puts it, the New Deal "brought public agencies to the center of the stage and relegated private charities to the wings."[89]

The Great Society

After World War II, during good economic times, the growth in government welfare slowed dramatically but did not stop. The genie was out of the bottle.

The massive public works programs of the New Deal were long gone, leaving direct relief, primarily ADC, as the main vehicle for welfare. ADC's original grants provided only for the needs of children. However, the program was amended in 1950 to provide an additional allowance to support the mother or another adult relative as caretaker.[90]

Despite rapid economic growth and declining levels of poverty throughout the 1950s, ADC rolls continued to grow. By 1956, 609,000 families, totaling 2,221,000 people, were receiving benefits.[91] The problems that were to plague the program in the future were fast becoming apparent. As social scientist Charles Murray explained: "By the fifties, it had become embarrassingly, outrageously clear that most of these women were not widows. Many of them had not ever been married. Worst of all they didn't stop having babies after the first lapse."[92]

Indeed, by 1956, 22.7 percent of recipients of aid originally intended for widows were unwed mothers. Widows were only 13 percent of recipients. The rest were divorced, deserted, or disabled.[93]

President John F. Kennedy took office amid renewed concern over poverty in America. Several studies in the late 1950s had argued in favor of a theory of "structural poverty." People were poor because they lacked the education, skills, and training necessary to take advantage of good economic conditions.[94]

Kennedy was aware of those studies and a growing dissatisfaction with ADC. As a result, he proposed remaking welfare programs so that they would no longer provide merely a subsistence living to poor mothers. Instead, they would provide the tools people needed to lift themselves out of poverty—in Kennedy's words, "a hand up, not a hand out."[95]

Beyond renaming ADC AFDC and expanding it to include two-parent families in which the father was unemployed, Kennedy actually took very little action on welfare.[96] But his rhetoric set the stage for Lyndon Johnson's Great Society.

After Kennedy's assassination, Johnson had a free hand in Congress, and he was determined to use it to remake government. In his first State of the Union address on January 8, 1964, Johnson announced the War on Poverty. Just eight months later, he signed the Economic Opportunity Act, which created the Office of Economic Opportunity and appropriated $947.7 million for 10 work-training programs, including Job Corps, the Manpower Development and Training Program, the Neighborhood Youth Corps, and the Work Incentive Program.[97] In addition, Johnson greatly enlarged a little-used 1961 food and commodity pilot program, making it permanent and expanding it into the food stamp program we know today.[98]

In 1965 Johnson upped the ante still further, calling for the establishment of the Great Society. Not only would the War on Poverty be waged with double its previous funding, but America's crippled cities would also be rebuilt. America had not seen such an expansion of government or such a proliferation of anti-poverty programs since the New Deal. Among the major Johnson initiatives in 1965 were Medicaid, which would pay for health care for the poor and grow to dwarf all other anti-poverty programs; Head Start; Community Action grants; the Model Cities program; and Legal Services.[99]

Johnson also created the U.S. Department of Housing and Urban Development in 1965 and in 1968, at the end of his administration, signed the Housing and Urban Development Act, which authorized HUD to construct 600,000 federally subsidized housing units over the next 10 years.[100]

Finally, Johnson followed in Roosevelt's footsteps by enlarging the social insurance safety net for the middle class, principally through Medicare, a program to provide health care for the elderly.

The proliferation of training and other noncash welfare programs did not mean a reduction in AFDC. On the contrary, its rolls continued to grow. By 1965 the number of people receiving AFDC had risen to 4.3 million.[101] By 1972 that number would more than double to nearly 10 million people. During the 1950s welfare rolls had increased by 17 percent. During the 1960s they increased by 107 percent, and three-quarters of that increase occurred between 1965 and 1968, at a time of relative economic prosperity and low unemployment.[102]

There were warnings. In his famous 1965 report, *The Negro Family: The Case for National Action,* then–assistant secretary of labor Daniel Patrick Moynihan warned of the increasing breakdown of African-American families and its likely consequences. Introducing themes that would be heard again 20 years later, Moynihan spoke of a growing black underclass and warned that if trends were not reversed welfare would become a way of life.[103] Moynihan's report was highly controversial. Both white liberals and the civil rights establishment loudly and vehemently rejected his analysis.[104]

Other voices on both the left and the right warned that Johnson's programs were not well thought out, cost too much, and were poorly targeted. Even *Time* magazine noticed that anti-poverty programs did not seem to be working, remarking on "a paradoxical trap: the more the U.S. spends on the poor, the greater the need seems to be to spend more still."[105] However, as Johnson's biographer Doris Kearns Goodwin noted, Johnson's attitude was, "Pass the bill now, worry about its effect and implementation later."[106]

Not only did Johnson greatly increase the size of the welfare state, he increasingly federalized its administration, cutting out state and local governments. Some historians suggest that Johnson's federalization of the welfare state was a deliberate political strategy. For example, historian Frances Fox Piven says that Great Society programs were specifically designed to attract black voters, bypassing local political organizations that were considered too independent or "unreliable." Johnson wanted the federal government to be clearly seen as the source of largesse for the African-American community.[107]

In the years following the creation of the Great Society, there was a consensus among both Democrats and Republicans for preserving and even expanding Johnson's legacy. Presidents Nixon, Ford, and Carter all added new anti-poverty programs. Nixon even experimented briefly with the idea of a guaranteed national income.

Johnson's legacy was further cemented by a series of court decisions that established the "rights" of welfare recipients. In *King v. Smith* (1968), the Supreme Court struck down state laws denying benefits to mothers with able-bodied men in the house.[108] The same year, a federal court struck down laws against aid to mothers whom AFDC administrators considered "employable."[109] In 1969 the Supreme Court found in *Shapiro v. Thompson* that state residency requirements for welfare were unconstitutional.[110] And, in perhaps the most important welfare rights decision, the Court held in *Goldberg v. Kelly* (1970) that welfare was an "entitlement" that could not be denied without due process.[111]

The real impact of Johnson's programs was not felt until after he had left office. Between 1965 and 1975, measured in constant dollars, spending for cash welfare programs such as AFDC tripled, medical assistance increased nearly fourfold, food aid increased more than fourfold, housing assistance increased sevenfold, and job-training expenditures rose an astounding 15-fold.[112] After 1975 the growth in welfare slowed again but nonetheless continued upward.

Ronald Reagan is often attacked by liberals for cutting welfare programs. There is no doubt that he rode into office attacking the welfare system. However, once in office, Reagan did very little to marry his rhetoric to action. In fact, welfare spending grew throughout his two terms. When Reagan took office, federal welfare spending totaled $199 billion. By the time he left office, spending had increased to $230 billion. Spending for cash, food, housing, health care, and energy programs increased under Reagan.[113]

Reagan did shift funding emphasis among programs. Thus funding for AFDC declined by 1 percent (hardly a draconian cut) during his administration, but spending for the Earned Income Tax Credit increased by 102 percent. Food stamp spending declined by 4 percent, but the Women, Infants, and Children Supplemental Food Program increased by 58 percent.[114] Reagan also attempted to tighten eligibility requirements on a program-by-program basis in an effort to restrict eligibility to only the "truly needy." States were required to set eligibility and income verification standards.[115]

If Reagan slowed the growth in welfare, it exploded again under President George Herbert Walker Bush. During Bush's four years in office, welfare spending increased by nearly $100 billion to $324 billion per year.[116]

In 1988 the growing dissatisfaction with welfare led to the last major attempt at reform prior to the Personal Responsibility and Work Opportunity Reconciliation Act, the Family Support Act of 1988. The centerpiece of that reform effort was the Job Opportunities and Basic Skills Training Program, a combination job-training and job-search program. States were allowed to mandate that individuals participate in job-search programs and could require some participants to perform community service jobs as a prerequisite for receiving benefits. The legislation's chief sponsor, Senator Moynihan, said of the legislation: "For 50 years the welfare system has been a maintenance program. It has now become a jobs program."[117]

But evidence showed that very few welfare recipients were ever put to work. It is estimated that only about 10 percent of recipients participated in work or job-training programs.[118]

The Buildup to Reform

By the time President Clinton took office, there had developed a broad national consensus that welfare, as then constituted, had failed. According to one public opinion poll in 1993, an astonishing 78 percent of Americans thought that welfare was not working well.[119] That led to a period of experimentation, with states seeking waivers from the federal government to allow them to make changes in their welfare programs.

That authority had been used to a limited extent in prior administrations, but the Clinton administration greatly expanded both the number and scope of waivers approved. Between January 1993 and August 1996, the U.S. Department of Health and Human Services approved welfare waivers in 43 states. Some of those waivers supported modest demonstration projects, limited to a few counties, but many others instituted dramatic statewide changes in the AFDC program.[120] In order to receive federal approval of waivers, states were required to conduct rigorous evaluations of the impact of their demonstrations. In most cases, they were required to randomly assign applicants and recipients to a control group, which was subject to the standard AFDC rules, or to an experimental group, which was subject to the waiver rules. By comparing the outcomes of the two groups, the states could measure the impact of the waiver provisions. States also had to show that the waivers would be cost neutral.[121]

Many of the state experiments reflected provisions that would later become part of PRWORA, particularly work requirements; time limits; and "family caps," or limits on additional benefits for additional children.[122] The implementation of waiver programs was uneven and produced mixed results, though it did start the first decline in welfare receipt since the beginning of the Great Society. Indeed, the Council of Economic Advisers estimates that 10 to 15 percent of the total decline in welfare rolls that we have seen since their peak is due to programs put in place under pre-1996 waivers.[123]

But perhaps more important, the availability and use of waivers greatly increased public debate over welfare and added to the momentum for greater reform.

The Growing Welfare State: Follow the Money

The growth of the welfare state since 1929 can be clearly seen in Figure 2.1. Federal spending on welfare was $28 million in 1929, and total federal, state, and local welfare spending was just $90 million.[124] Adjusted for inflation, that would equal $970 million today. Welfare spending grew steadily as a result of the Great Depression and the New Deal, peaking in 1939 at $58.3 billion (2000 dollars). Most of Roosevelt's programs disappeared during World War II, and welfare spending remained relatively low during the postwar period. With Lyndon Johnson's War on Poverty, welfare spending quickly reached and then surpassed New Deal spending levels. From there, it has continued steadily upward. By 1996, when welfare reform passed, welfare spending at all levels of government had reached nearly $400 billion. But, even after reform, spending continued to rise, reaching $434 billion today.[125]

The growth in welfare spending is even more dramatic when compared to the number of poor people. Figure 2.2 shows welfare spending per poor person (generously defined as the lowest quarter of incomes). Spending per poor person has increased more than 1,000 percent since 1965. Indeed, in 2000 we spent more than $13,985 for every poor man, woman, and child in this country. For a poor family of four, that amounts to more than $55,000.[126] If we simply gave poor people the money, we could raise every poor family above

31

Figure 2.1
TOTAL FEDERAL, STATE, AND LOCAL WELFARE SPENDING, 1929–2000

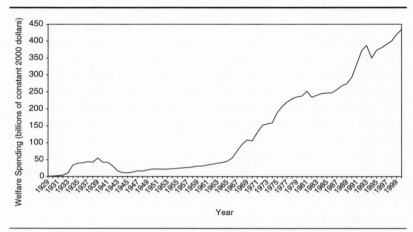

SOURCES: Robert Rector and William Lauber, *American's Failed $5.4 Trillion War on Poverty* (Washington: Heritage Foundation, 1995), Table 1; and Robert Rector, "The Size and Scope of Means-Tested Welfare Spending," Testimony before the House Committee on the Budget, August 1, 2001, Charts 1, 4.

the poverty level for less than half of what we are now spending. While that is unrealistic—there would always be some administrative cost involved—something is clearly wrong.

Moreover, note the dramatic spike in per recipient spending following welfare reform. PRWORA clearly did nothing to reduce the size and scope of the American welfare state.

Not only has the welfare state grown steadily since the New Deal; it has also become increasingly federalized. Programs such as food stamps and most of the job-training and education initiatives of the Great Society were funded and directed by the federal, not state, government. In addition, the federal government assumed a larger and larger proportion of AFDC costs. The original ADC program was one-third federally funded, with states paying two-thirds of the cost. By the time PRWORA passed, the federal government was paying 55 percent of AFDC costs.[127] Under TANF, the federal government is paying 71 percent of cash assistance costs.[128] When noncash

Figure 2.2
WELFARE SPENDING PER LOW-INCOME PERSON, 1947–2000

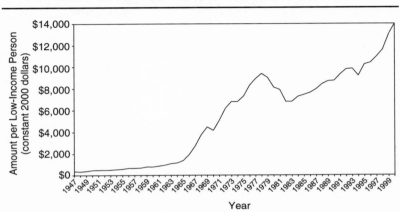

Sources: Robert Rector and William Lauber, *America's Failed $5.4 Trillion War on Poverty* (Washington: Heritage Foundation, 1995), Table 7; Robert Rector, "The Size and Scope of Means-Tested Welfare Spending," Testimony before the House Committee on the Budget, August 1, 2001, Charts 1, 4; and U.S. Bureau of the Census, *Statistical Abstract of the United States: 2000* (Washington: Government Printing Office), p. 441.

programs are considered, we can see the existence of a truly massive federal welfare state.

Conclusion

During much of this country's history, care of the poor was a function of private charity supplemented by local governments. However, beginning with the Progressive Era, those traditional sources of charity began to be pushed aside in favor of first state then federal government programs. The Great Depression gave new emphasis to the federalization of welfare and established the basic structure for the programs we have today. The final pieces of the welfare state were put in place by President Johnson's War on Poverty. Despite their anti-welfare rhetoric, neither President Reagan nor President George Herbert Walker Bush significantly slowed the growth of the welfare state. Neither did President Clinton, despite the passage of PRWORA. The result is a $434 billion per year welfare system.

Despite all this spending, the welfare state has failed. As the following chapter will show, the American welfare system has created far more problems than it has solved, problems that continue despite reform.

3. The Need for Reform—Then and Now

As we have seen, since the 1930s there has been a steady growth in the American welfare state, a growth that accelerated rapidly following creation of the Great Society and the War on Poverty in the mid-1960s. In fact, since the War on Poverty began in 1965, federal, state, and local governments have spent nearly $8.3 trillion fighting poverty in this country.[1] To put that amount in perspective, it is more than double what it cost to fight World War II. Yet, as Figure 3.1 shows, the poverty rate is actually as high today as it was in the early 1970s. Clearly, welfare, even reformed welfare, has failed to meet the goal of ending poverty. But the real failure of welfare lies not in wasted money but in wasted lives.

Welfare and the Family

Perhaps the gravest social challenge facing America today is the breakup of the American family. As Table 3.1 shows, the number of single-parent families has risen dramatically since 1960. In 1960 more than 87 percent of children lived with their mothers and fathers. By 2000 fewer than 70 percent of children lived with two parents, including stepparents or adoptive parents.[2]

There are many complex reasons for the change. However, welfare is clearly contributing to the problem. Take, for example, the most important reason for the rise in single-parent families—births to unmarried women. As Figure 3.2 shows, out-of-wedlock births have increased by more than 632 percent since 1960. In 1960 only 5.3 percent of all births were out of wedlock. Among whites, only 2.3 percent were out of wedlock, while the out-of-wedlock rate among blacks was 23 percent.[3] By 2001, 33.5 percent of all births were out of wedlock. The rate among whites had increased to an alarming 27.7 percent, and among blacks it had skyrocketed to an astonishing 68.4 percent.[4]

Figure 3.1
WELFARE SPENDING VS. POVERTY RATE, 1949–2000

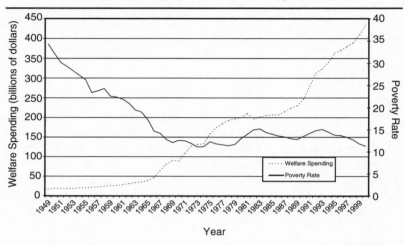

SOURCES: U.S. Bureau of the Census, Current Population Surveys, Series P60, various numbers; Robert Rector and William Lauber, *America's Failed $5.4 Trillion War on Poverty* (Washington: Heritage Foundation, 1995), Table 1, pp. 92–93; and Robert Rector, "The Size and Scope of Means-Tested Welfare Spending," Testimony before the House Committee on the Budget, August 1, 2001, Chart 3.

Table 3.1
FAMILY ARRANGEMENT FOR CHILDREN UNDER AGE 18, 1960–2000

Percentage of Children Living with	1960	1970	1980	1990	2000
Both parents	87.7%	85.2%	76.7%	72.5%	69.1%
Mother only	8.0%	10.8%	18.0%	21.6%	22.4%
Father only	1.1%	1.1%	1.7%	3.1%	4.2%
Neither parent	3.2%	2.9%	3.7%	2.8%	4.2%

SOURCES: U.S. Bureau of the Census, "America's Families and Living Arrangements: March 2000," Current Population Reports, Series P20-537; U.S. Bureau of the Census, "Marital Status and Living Arrangements: March 1984," Current Population Reports, Series P20-399, p. 8; and U. S. Bureau of the Census, *1960 Census of the Population*, PC (2)-4B, "Persons by Family Characteristics," Tables 1, 19.

Figure 3.2
BIRTHS TO UNMARRIED WOMEN (1960–2001)

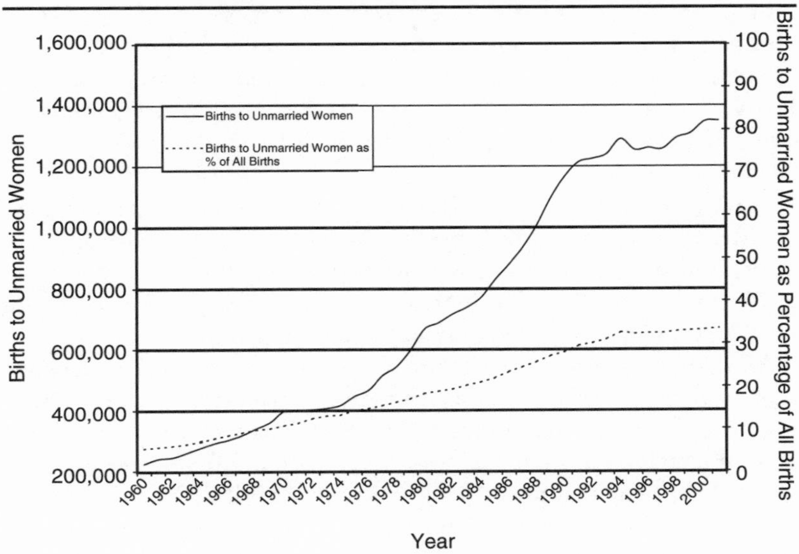

Y-axis (left): Births to Unmarried Women — 200,000 to 1,600,000

Y-axis (right): Births to Unmarried Women as Percentage of All Births — 0 to 100

X-axis: Year (1960–2000)

Legend:
Births to Unmarried Women
Births to Unmarried Women as % of All Births

SOURCES: Centers for Disease Control, "Births: Final Data for 2001," *National Vital Statistics Reports* 51, no. 2 (December 2002): Table C, p. 10; and CDC, "Nonmarital Childbearing in the United States, 1940–99," *National Vital Statistics Reports* 48, no. 16 (October 2002): Table 1, p. 17.

The rate of out-of-wedlock births to teenagers more than doubled in the two decades preceding welfare reform, peaking at 46.4 percent in 1994, before declining slightly in the years following reform. Teen mothers now account for roughly 26 percent of all out-of-wedlock births. But that figure may understate the severity of the problem. Because women who have out-of-wedlock births as teens frequently go on to have additional out-of-wedlock children, more than a third of all out-of-wedlock births involve mothers who had their first child as unwed teenagers.[5]

The concern about the increased rate of out-of-wedlock births is not a question of private morality. In 1992 Vice President Dan Quayle caused a firestorm when he criticized the television show *Murphy Brown* for portraying nonmarital childbearing as acceptable. In truth,

however, if Murphy Brown, an educated, upper-middle-class professional, were typical of unwed mothers, objections would be far more
muted. However, fewer than 2 percent of out-of-wedlock births to
white mothers are to women with a college degree, while 93 percent
of such births are to women with a high school education or less.[6]
In the United States at least, out-of-wedlock childbearing remains
overwhelmingly concentrated at the lowest rungs of the socioeco-
nomic ladder.

Having a child out of wedlock often means a lifetime of poverty.
Children living with single mothers are five times more likely to be
poor than are those living with two parents.[7] Indeed, economists
attribute nearly all of the increase in childhood poverty over the
past 30 years to the growth in single-parent families.[8]

More than 22 percent of welfare recipients start on welfare because
they have an out-of-wedlock birth.[9] They also tend to stay on welfare
for longer periods than other recipients.[10] The trend is even worse
among teenage mothers. Half of unwed teen mothers go on welfare
within one year of the birth of their first child; 75 percent are on
welfare within five years of the child's birth.[11] Nearly 55 percent of
welfare expenditures are attributable to families begun by a teen
birth.[12] This does not even take into account such other social programs as special education, foster care, and public housing subsidies.

Moreover, once on welfare, single mothers find it very difficult
to get off. While the average length of time on welfare is relatively
short, generally less than two years, women who started on welfare
because of an out-of-wedlock birth average more than nine years
on welfare and make up roughly 40 percent of all recipients who
are on welfare for 10 years or longer.[13]

The noneconomic consequences of out-of-wedlock births are
equally stark. There is strong evidence that the absence of a father
increases the probability that a child will use drugs and engage in
criminal activity. According to one study, children raised in single-
parent families are one-third more likely to exhibit anti-social behavior than are children of two-parent families.[14] Yet another study
indicated that, holding other variables constant, black children from
single-parent households are twice as likely to commit crimes as are
black children from families with resident fathers. The likelihood of
criminal activity triples if a child lives in a neighborhood with a
high concentration of single-parent families.[15] Only 30 percent of all

children being held for criminal offenses in state juvenile justice systems come from two-parent homes.[16]

Children from single-parent homes perform significantly worse in school than do children from two-parent households.[17] They are three times more likely to fail and repeat a year of school and are more likely to be late, have disciplinary problems, and perform poorly on standardized tests, even when studies control for differences in family income. They are twice as likely to drop out of school altogether.[18]

Children from single-parent families are two to three times more likely to experience mental illness and other psychological disorders than are children from two-parent families.[19] Nearly 80 percent of children admitted to psychiatric hospitals come from single-parent homes.[20] There is also evidence that child abuse occurs more frequently in single-parent homes.[21]

The problem perpetuates itself. For example, white women raised in single-parent households are 164 percent more likely to bear children out of wedlock than are white women raised in two-parent homes.[22] Moreover, children raised in single-parent families are three times more likely than are children raised in two-parent homes to become welfare recipients as adults.[23]

That is not to comment on any particular single mother. Millions of single mothers do a tremendous job against difficult odds of raising healthy, happy, and successful children.[24] Still, children growing up in single-parent homes are clearly at higher risk. Therefore, any public policy that encourages out-of-wedlock births should be viewed as a failure.

Perhaps no issue of welfare reform has been as hotly debated as the link between the availability of welfare and out-of-wedlock births. Since Charles Murray raised the issue in *Losing Ground*, experts have lined up on both sides of the issue. As Figure 3.3 shows, the overall out-of-wedlock birthrate has at least a surface correlation with welfare receipt.

As early as the 1960s it was recognized that the perverse incentives of welfare were likely to have a negative impact on the family structure of recipients: "What, after all, was the AFDC program but a family allowance for *broken* families. Generally speaking, one became eligible by dissolving a family or by not forming one."[25]

Of course, women do not get pregnant just to get welfare benefits. A wide array of other social factors has contributed to the increase

Figure 3.3
OUT-OF-WEDLOCK BIRTHS VS. WELFARE SPENDING, 1960–2000

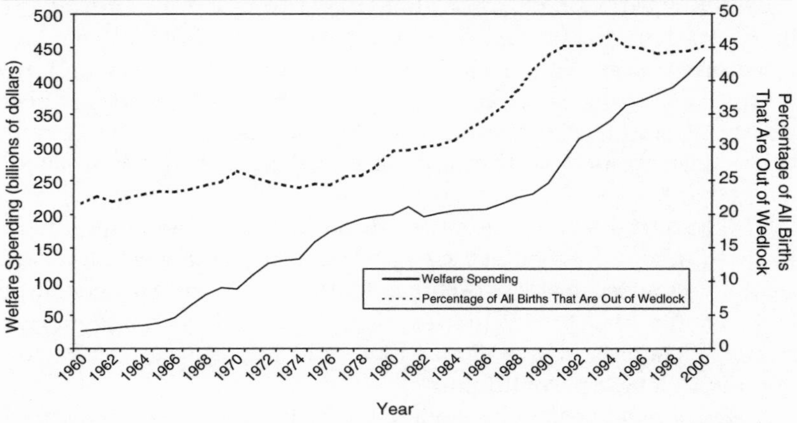

SOURCES: Centers for Disease Control, "Births: Final Data for 2001," *National Vital Statistics Reports* 51, no. 2 (December 2002): Table C, p. 10; CDC, "Nonmarital Childbearing in the United States, 1940–99," *National Vital Statistics Reports* 48, no. 16 (October 2002): Table 1, p. 17; Robert Rector and William Lauber, *America's Failed $5.4 Trillion War on Poverty* (Washington: Heritage Foundation, 1995), Table 1, pp. 92–93; and Robert Rector, "The Size and Scope of Means-Tested Welfare Spending," Testimony before the House Committee on the Budget, August 1, 2001, Chart 3.

in out-of-wedlock births. But by removing the economic consequences of out-of-wedlock births, welfare has removed a major incentive to avoid them. A teenager looking around at her friends and neighbors is likely to see several who have given birth out of wedlock. When she sees that they have suffered few visible consequences (the very real consequences of such behavior are often not immediately apparent), she is less inclined to modify her own behavior to prevent pregnancy.

As Murray explains, "The evil of the modern welfare state is not that it bribes women to have babies—wanting to have babies is natural—but that it enables women to bear children without the natural social restraints."[26] Until teenage girls, particularly those living in relative poverty, can be made to see the real consequences of pregnancy, it will be impossible to gain control over the problem of out-of-wedlock births. By disguising those consequences, welfare makes it easier for girls to make decisions that will lead to unwed motherhood.

Prior to 1996 welfare policies seem to have been designed with an appalling lack of concern for their impact on out-of-wedlock births. But, even today, combating out-of-wedlock births remains an afterthought rather than a primary focus of welfare policy. To cite just one example, Medicaid programs in three states and the District of Columbia actually provide infertility treatments for single women on welfare.[27]

Not so long ago, claims of a link between the availability of welfare benefits and rising rates of out-of-wedlock births were highly controversial. Today, however, there is a growing body of evidence supporting that link, and few academic researchers seriously dispute it.[28] More than three-quarters of the more than 20 major studies of the issue show a significant link between benefit levels and out-of-wedlock childbearing.[29]

It should be acknowledged that the connection is not perfect. For example, Louisiana and Mississippi had approximately the same rate of out-of-wedlock births as did California but had much lower Aid to Families with Dependent Children benefits.[30] That would appear to contradict the argument that high welfare benefits lead to more out-of-wedlock births. But the actual rate of AFDC payments is of far less importance than the value of the entire welfare package within the context of the local economy.[31] In that context, the welfare packages being compared were essentially equal. It is therefore not surprising that they are correlated with similar rates of out-of-wedlock births.

Some social scientists also contend that the erosion of AFDC benefits since the beginning of the 1980s has failed to reduce out-of-wedlock births. However, concentrating on AFDC ignores the total value of welfare benefits, which include food stamps, Medicaid, public housing subsidies, and other benefits. As a 1995 Cato Institute study showed, the value of the full package of welfare benefits for a mother and two children ranged from a high of more than $36,000 in Hawaii to a low of $11,500 in Mississippi, more than sufficient to provide an incentive for out-of-wedlock childbearing.[32]

Finally, it is important to note that studies showing a correlation between welfare and out-of-wedlock births generally show a stronger correlation for white women than for African Americans. One might assume that, if welfare is responsible for the increase in out-of-wedlock births, the correlation should be consistent across all ethnic groups. That is not necessarily true, however, since many other factors may contribute to the out-of-wedlock birthrate of any particular ethnic group. When studies correct for the normally high out-of-wedlock birthrates in areas with large African-American communities, the correlation does remain constant across ethnic groups.

Perhaps as a legacy of slavery, greater tolerance of out-of-wedlock births has become part of African-American culture.[33] Therefore, in areas where the black population is densely concentrated, such as the south or urban areas, out-of-wedlock births are relatively high regardless of welfare benefits. The same trend does not hold true for African Americans in areas where there is no cultural concentration, such as in Idaho or New Hampshire. Reanalyzing the data with that in mind, Murray, among others, notes, "The same data that show no relationship between welfare and illegitimacy among blacks across states suddenly show such a relationship when one controls for the size and density of the black population."[34]

The same results can be seen in studies of welfare systems in other countries. For example, a recent study of the impact of Canada's social welfare system on family structure concluded that "providing additional benefits to single parents encourages births of children to unwed women."[35] Studies in Britain have shown similar results.[36] Likewise, an Australian study indicated an increase in out-of-wedlock births as a result of the country's welfare benefits.[37]

Focusing solely on the out-of-wedlock birthrate may actually understate the problem. In the past, women who gave birth out of wedlock frequently married the fathers of their children after the birth. Marvin Olasky, for example, estimates that as many as 85 percent of unwed mothers in the 1950s ultimately married the fathers of their children.[38] Therefore, while technically born out of wedlock, the children were still likely to grow up in intact two-parent families.

However, the increasing availability and value of welfare may have made such marriages unattractive for many unwed mothers. If the father is unskilled and has few or poor employment prospects, a welfare check may seem preferable to marriage. Studies indicate that young mothers and pregnant women are less likely to marry the fathers of their children in states with higher welfare benefits.[39]

Figure 3.4
PERCENTAGE OF FEMALE-HEADED HOUSEHOLDS, 1950–2000

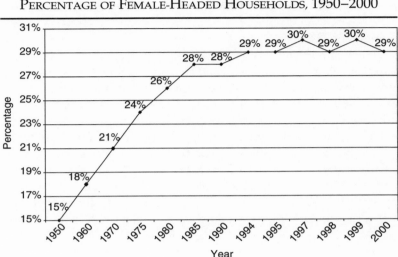

SOURCE: U.S. Bureau of the Census, Current Population Surveys, Series P60, various numbers.

Research by Robert Hutchins of Cornell University shows that a 10 percent increase in AFDC benefits leads to an 8 percent decrease in the marriage rate of single mothers.[40]

Welfare also appears to have a modest but significant impact on abandonment, divorce, and remarriage after divorce.[41] There is some disagreement about whether this is because welfare makes it easier for men to evade their responsibilities or because women are more able to leave marriages they would otherwise be financially dependent upon. Regardless, the overall result has been an increase in female-headed single-parent households, as shown in Figure 3.4.

The problem of welfare-induced family disintegration is likely to grow worse in the future. If current trends continue, the out-of-wedlock birthrate could exceed 40 percent within the next 10 years.[42]

Because the African-American family was the first to suffer from the anti-family incentives of welfare, much of the larger public has been able to remain indifferent to the consequences of those policies. They have safely watched on television as our inner cities have declined ever further into poverty, crime, and despair.

But that will not be the case much longer. As Murray has noted, the current 23 percent white out-of-wedlock birthrate is almost exactly what the black rate was in 1965, when then–assistant secretary of labor Daniel Patrick Moynihan warned of the destruction of the black family and its consequences. From that point on the black out-of-wedlock birthrate escalated sharply. Although there has been some slowing in the white illegitimacy ratio since the Personal Responsibility and Work Opportunity Reconciliation Act, there is no reason to believe that the out-of-wedlock birthrates for whites will not ultimately follow the same path as those for African Americans.[43]

That means the problems associated with single-parent families will soon be spilling out of the cities into the suburbs and rural communities. Moreover, since African Americans make up just over one-tenth of the U.S. population, if white out-of-wedlock birthrates begin to approach those of blacks, the problem will be nine times larger.

Welfare and the Work Ethic

In 1960 nearly two-thirds of Americans in the lowest income quintile were in households headed by someone who worked.[44] In 2001 only about 35 percent lived in such households, and fewer than 14 percent were in households headed by a person who worked full-time year round.[45]

Contrary to stereotypes, there is no evidence that people who receive welfare are "lazy." Indeed, surveys of recipients consistently show that they express a desire to work.[46] Yet, at the same time, more than 65 percent of welfare recipients report that they are not actively seeking work.[47]

The choice of welfare over work is often a rational decision based on the economic incentives presented.[48] Most welfare recipients, particularly long-term recipients, lack the skills necessary to obtain the types of jobs that pay more than entry-level wages.[49] Those individuals who do leave welfare for work most often start employment in service or retail trade industries, generally as clerks, secretaries, cleaning persons, sales help, and waitresses.[50] While it would be nice to increase the wages of entry-level workers to the point where work pays better than welfare, government has no ability to do so. (Attempts to mandate wage increases, such as minimum wage legislation, chiefly result in increased unemployment.) For those individuals, welfare simply pays better than work.

As far back as the 1960s experts warned that welfare would discourage work. A panel investigating the Watts riots concluded that welfare was damaging the work ethic. The report noted that a minimum wage job paid about $220 per month in 1965 ($1,269 in 2003 dollars), out of which had to come such work-related expenses as clothing and transportation. In contrast, the average welfare family in the area received from $177 to $238 per month ($1,021 to $1,373 in 2003 dollars), out of which came no work-related expenses.[51]

Studies confirm that welfare is a disincentive for work. The Seattle Income Maintenance Experiment and the Denver Income Maintenance Experiment were a series of controlled experiments conducted between 1971 and 1978 to examine the effect on the poor of guaranteed income supports. Researchers concluded that every dollar of subsidy reduced labor and earnings by 80 cents. The number of hours worked declined by 43 percent for young unmarried males and 33 percent for males who later married. Unmarried women with children reduced work by 25 percent. The length of time spent outside the workforce during unemployment increased by 9 weeks (27 percent) for unmarried men and 56 weeks (60 percent) for single mothers. [52]

An analysis of interstate variation in labor force participation during the 1980s by Richard Vedder, Lowell Gallaway, and Robert Lawson found that such participation declined as welfare benefits increased.[53] Likewise, a study by Sheldon Danziger, Robert Haveman, and Robert Plotnick concluded that the cumulative impact of welfare payments reduced the U.S. labor supply by 4.8 percent.[54]

Robert Moffitt of Brown University reviewed the available literature on welfare and work in 1992 and concluded that welfare does discourage work among recipients. Moffitt found that the work effort of welfare recipients was reduced as much as 30 percent. Moffitt commented that was "[n]ot surprising given that the average benefit is approximately equal to the earnings a woman would receive if she worked full time at a minimum wage job."[55] Research abroad has reached similar conclusions.[56]

Most of the studies probably understate the work disincentive of welfare since they consider only a small portion of the total package of welfare benefits available to recipients. For example, a 1998 study shows that education and training programs available under Temporary Assistance for Needy Families may induce people to go on welfare.[57] Other benefits, not available to the working poor, may be available to people in the welfare system, creating an incentive to go on welfare and remain in the program once enrolled.[58]

Other studies show that as welfare benefits increase, women are more likely to leave the labor force and enroll in welfare programs. For example, Hill and O'Neill found that a 50 percent increase in monthly AFDC and food stamp benefit levels led to a 75 percent increase both in the number of women enrolling in AFDC and in the number of years spent on welfare.[59]

As one group of prominent economists recently put it, "The price of generosity to those with low-incomes is a system that strongly discourages work."[60]

Welfare also appears to have the indirect effect of reducing by as much as 50 percent the work effort of young men in communities with high levels of welfare participation, even though the men themselves do not receive benefits. Hill and O'Neill attribute that to the facts that (1) high benefits reduce the probability of marriage, thereby reducing the necessity for young men to support a family; and (2) many single young men who are boyfriends of single mothers on AFDC are indirectly sharing in the mothers' welfare benefits.[61]

Perhaps most troubling of all is the psychological attitude toward work that appears to be developing among those on welfare. In his excellent book, *The Underclass*, Ken Auletta reports on interviews with a wide variety of inner-city men and women. He found little indication that the poor felt they needed to take charge of their own lives or find work to become self-sufficient. On the contrary, he found that most felt that the government had an obligation to provide for them and their children.[62]

Other reports increasingly show young men and women in the inner city refusing to work for the "chump change" of low-wage jobs. No doubt that attitude stems in part from our general "get it now" culture. But another cause is the realization that there is no *need* to work for low wages. Welfare will always be there as a safety net.

Confirmation can be seen in a study of inner-city poor in Chicago. While nearly all those who were unemployed expressed a desire for work, most also said they expected a job that paid well above the minimum wage. When they were asked how much a job would need to pay for them to take it, answers ranged from $5.50 to $10.20 per hour.[63]

Welfare recipients themselves are not the only ones to develop a prejudice against work. Evidence suggests that anti-work attitudes trickle down to their children. As a recent report by the Maryland NAACP puts it, "A child whose parents draw a welfare check without going to work does not understand that in this society at least one parent is expected to rise five days of each week to go to some type of job."[64] As a result, children raised on welfare are likely to have lower incomes as adults than children not raised on welfare. The more welfare received by a child's family, the lower that child's earnings as an adult tend to be, even holding constant such other factors as race, family structure, and education.[65] The conclusion that welfare reduces self-sufficiency and work should hardly come as a surprise. As the Chinese philosopher Lao-Tzu said in 500 B.C., "The more subsidies you have, the less self-reliant people will be."[66]

Welfare and Crime

A decade ago, the Maryland NAACP released a report concluding that "the ready access to a lifetime of welfare and free social service programs is a major contributory factor to the crime problems we face today."[67] The NAACP's conclusion is confirmed by additional academic research. For example, Hill and O'Neill's research showed that a 50 percent increase in the monthly value of combined AFDC and food stamp benefits led to a 117 percent increase in the crime rate among young black men.[68]

Welfare contributes to crime in several ways. First, as already noted, children from single-parent families are more likely to become involved in criminal activity. Recent research indicates a direct correlation between crime rates and the number of single-parent families in a neighborhood.[69] As welfare contributes to the rise in out-of-wedlock births, it concomitantly contributes to associated criminal activity.

As Barbara Whitehead noted in her seminal article for the *Atlantic Monthly*,

> The relationship [between single-parent families and crime] is so strong that controlling for family configuration erases the relationship between race and crime and between low

47

income and crime. This conclusion shows up time and again in the literature. The nation's mayors, as well as police officers, social workers, probation officers, and court officials, consistently point to family breakup as the most important source of rising rates of crime.[70]

Second, welfare leads to increased crime by contributing to the marginalization of young black men in society. As George Gilder, author of *Wealth and Poverty*, has noted, "The welfare culture tells the man he is not a necessary part of the family," a process Gilder describes as being "cuckolded by the compassionate state."[71]

Marriage and family have long been considered civilizing influences on young men. Whether or not strict causation can be proven, it is certainly true that unwed fathers are more likely to use drugs and become involved in criminal behavior than are other men.[72]

Finally, boys growing up in mother-only families naturally seek male influences. Both clinical and anthropological studies agree that boys need adult males to emulate. In his groundbreaking book on the issue, *Fatherless America*, David Blankenhorn explains the "irreplaceable" role of fathers in teaching boys about what it means to be a man in our society.[73] Unfortunately, in many inner-city neighborhoods, desirable male role models may not exist. In *There Are No Children Here*, one of the most moving books on inner-city poverty, Alex Kotlowitz describes the lives of two brothers, Lafayette and Pharro Rivers, growing up in a Chicago public housing project in the 1980s. He describes a world virtually devoid of responsible adult men. It is also a world of unremitting violence, crime, and murder—a world where mothers purchase funeral insurance for their young children.[74]

It is not an exaggeration to describe some communities as overwhelmingly dominated by single mothers and their children. According to a study by the National Research Council, nearly 70 percent of families with children in high-poverty areas consist of an unmarried mother and her children.[75] Yet we know that when welfare-induced pathologies are concentrated within a single community, the crime problem increases still further. Perhaps Moynihan summarized it best back in 1961 when he warned:

> From the wild Irish slums of the nineteenth century Eastern seaboard, to the riot-torn suburbs of Los Angeles, there is one unmistakable lesson in American History: a community

that allows a large number of young men to grow up in broken families, dominated by women, never acquiring any stable relationship to male authority, never acquiring any set of rational expectations about the future—that community asks for and gets chaos. Crime, violence, unrest, disorder—most particularly the furious, unrestrained lashing out at the whole social structure—that is not only to be expected, it is very near to inevitable.[76]

Intergenerational Dependence

The failures of welfare today are likely to entrap the next generation as well. Although it is true that the majority of children raised on welfare will not receive welfare themselves, the rate of welfare dependence for children raised on welfare is far higher than for their nonwelfare counterparts. For example, according to the most commonly cited study, by Greg Duncan and Martha Hill, nearly 20 percent of daughters from families that were "highly dependent" on welfare became "highly dependent" themselves, whereas only 3 percent of daughters from non-AFDC households became "highly dependent" on welfare.[77]

An earlier study by Martha Hill and Michael Ponza showed similar results, although the intergenerational impact was more significant for white children than for black.[78] Studies also show that, if they go on welfare as adults, children who were raised on welfare stay on the program significantly longer than do those who were not raised on welfare.[79]

The degree to which welfare dependency has become an intergenerational problem was brought home vividly in a study by scholars at the University of Tennessee. Profiling welfare recipients in that state, the study found that 29.3 percent of recipients had parents who received welfare as children. Even more troubling, 7.5 percent of recipients were actually third-generation recipients. Their parents *and* their grandparents had been on welfare.[80]

That should not come as a surprise. We know enough about childhood development to understand that a variety of pathologies, from alcoholism to child abuse, are transmitted from parent to child. Indeed, how a child is raised is one of the most important factors in how that child will behave as an adult. The attitudes and habits that lead to welfare dependency are transmitted the same way other parent-to-child pathologies are. Therefore, unless something is done quickly to change the current welfare system, we can expect to see yet another generation trapped in the system.

Conclusion

Nearly 150 years ago Alexis de Tocqueville called for abolishing government welfare programs, warning that "the number of illegitimate children and criminals grows rapidly and continuously, the indigent population is endless, the spirit of foresight and of saving becomes more and more alien."[81]

Tocqueville could easily have been describing our government welfare system today.

Welfare may have started with the best of intentions, but it has clearly failed. It has failed to meet its stated goal of reducing poverty. But its real failure is even more disastrous. Welfare has torn apart the social fabric of our society. Everyone is worse off. The taxpayers must foot the bill for programs that don't work. The poor are dehumanized, seduced into a system from which it is terribly difficult to escape. Teenage girls give birth to children they will never be able to support. The work ethic has eroded. Crime rates soar. Such is the legacy of welfare.

In 1996 we recognized the failures of welfare, which led to the most significant changes to the program in more than a quarter century. But as we shall see, welfare's failures are far deeper and more endemic than any reform can fix. They are characteristic of the welfare state itself.

4. The Results of Reform

When welfare reform passed, critics warned that "wages will go down, families will fracture, millions of children will be made more miserable than ever."[1] One frequently cited Urban Institute study predicted that more than 1 million children would be thrown into poverty.[2]

However, the results do not appear to have borne out those warnings. Poverty rates declined every year between 1996 and 2001. Despite a small uptick in 2002, caused by a slowing economy, poverty rates remain well below those before welfare reform was enacted.[3] The reduction in poverty cuts across demographic groups, even those generally considered most at risk: women, children, and minorities. Child poverty rates declined from more than 20 percent in 1996 to 16.2 percent in 2000, the lowest level in more than 20 years.[4] Perhaps even more impressive, the poverty rate among black children has fallen since welfare reform at the fastest rate since figures have been recorded.[5] Dependent single mothers, the group most heavily impacted by welfare reform, account heavily for this decline. Since the enactment of welfare reform, the poverty rate for female-headed families with children has fallen from 46 to 32.5 percent.[6] The decline in poverty for female-headed households has been greater than for any other demographic group, although women with children remain six times more likely to be in poverty than two-parent families with children.[7]

There is, of course, anecdotal evidence that in some areas some individuals have suffered hardships because of welfare reform. A 10-state study by Catholic Charities found that one client in eight at food pantries or soup kitchens had left welfare during the previous two years, while a survey of families in Atlanta homeless shelters found that nearly half had left welfare in the previous year. One national study found that 11.8 percent of former welfare recipients reported that they sometimes did not have enough money to buy food, while 38.7 percent reported that at least once since leaving welfare they had not been able to pay housing costs or a utility bill.[8] The U.S. Conference of Mayors reports a 17 percent increase in the number of people seeking food assistance and a 15 percent increase in the number of people needing shelter.[9]

In considering those reports, however, there are several reasons for caution. First, such surveys tend to be self-selective and therefore overrepresentative of a certain highly afflicted segment of those who have left welfare. While they do provide evidence of a problem, they do not provide enough of a foundation for generalization across the broad population. Second, the premise of such reports is that reliance on private charity rather than public assistance is necessarily a bad thing. In reality, given the consistent record of success exhibited by private charities, there is reason to believe that individuals receiving those services are having their needs adequately met. Finally, there is an assumption that welfare reform itself is responsible for the continued need or poverty of former recipients. However, there is no clear evidence to that effect, and given the fact that many former welfare recipients remain eligible for food stamps, Medicaid, public housing, and other forms of government assistance, it is certainly reasonable to believe that factors other than welfare reform are responsible for the problems encountered by at least some former recipients. A Fraser Institute survey of available literature on the subject concluded that the "problems of homelessness, separation of children from their parents, or hunger were not more prevalent after the time limit or welfare receipt termination."[10]

As a study by the Committee for Economic Development noted:

> We recognize that every vulnerable family that ends up in such circumstances is cause for concern. However *no* affordable public assistance program can eliminate every case of distress, and certainly the previous welfare system did not do so.[11]

There are several reasons why predictions of increased poverty failed to come true. First, most former recipients found employment after leaving welfare. A national Urban Institute survey of those leaving welfare found that 61 percent were employed, two-thirds of them full-time.[12] A broader survey found that employment among single mothers in general has increased significantly since the implementation of welfare reform, rising from 48 to 62 percent.[13] June

O'Neill, former director of the Congressional Budget Office and a long-time expert on welfare policy, finds this particularly significant, since the fact that employment is increasing fastest among the group with the highest degree of welfare participation suggests that "welfare reform is likely to have played an important role in the rise of work participation."[14] That would also seem to be borne out by a 1999 Heritage Foundation study that found that those states with the largest decline in Temporary Aid for Needy Families rolls also had the largest decrease in child poverty.[15]

It is also worth noting that 5 to 10 percent more of the people leaving welfare are finding employment than prior to welfare reform, another indication that welfare reform has had a positive impact on moving people from welfare to work.[16]

Not surprisingly, those leaving welfare and finding employment are increasing their income. There is no better route out of poverty than a job. In 2000 the poverty rate among full-time, full-year workers, ages 16–64 was only 2.4 percent. Even part-time work helped. For part-time workers, the poverty rate was 12.7 percent. But for those who did not work at all, the poverty rate was 25 percent.[17] For single mothers, the link between working and getting out of poverty is even stronger. Approximately 12 percent of single mothers who worked full-time were poor, compared with 49 percent of part-time workers and an astounding 74 percent of those who did not work at all.[18]

It is true that most first jobs found by those leaving welfare are entry-level positions and primarily concentrated in six occupational categories (cashiers, nursing aide/orderly, waiter/waitress, janitorial services, secretarial, sales clerk) requiring relatively little education, experience, or job skills.[19] But once they have found a job, former welfare recipients tend to stay employed longer than typical low-skilled, minimum wage workers. There remains a significant problem of job retention, with former recipients cycling in and out of the job market, and even on and off welfare. About one-third of former recipients return to the welfare rolls within a year.[20]

However, there is evidence that the situation is improving, that newly employed workers are retaining their jobs for longer periods, finding new jobs, and increasing their earnings over time.[21] For example, a U.S. Department of Health and Human Services study of former recipients in eight states found that in every state former welfare recipients who worked increased their earnings over the course of the year following their employment.[22] In addition, access to employer-provided benefits also appears to increase over time.[23] This bears out previous research by Richard Vedder and Lowell Gallaway that indicated that poor individuals who work are nearly twice as likely to be out of poverty within a year as are similar people on welfare.[24]

For those working, wages are low but higher than many might suspect. The General Accounting Office estimated that annual earnings of former welfare recipients ranged from $9,512 to $15,144.[25] The Manpower Demonstration Research Corporation found that the median hourly wage of former welfare recipients was between $7.50 and $8.74, which is well above the minimum wage.[26] While this remains slightly below the poverty line, it is important to realize that former welfare recipients remain eligible for a wide variety of noncash government benefits. Indeed, those benefits may actually have been enhanced under state programs designed to encourage work.[27]

In particular, former welfare recipients may benefit from a major expansion in the Earned Income Tax Credit, which rose from a maximum of $950 in 1990 to $2,428 in 2001 for a low-income family with one child and $4,000 for a family with two or more children, and possibly from state child health insurance programs established in 1997 to help provide health insurance to children in low-income families. Many states have also significantly increased child-care benefits.[28] David Ellwood of Harvard's Kennedy School of Government estimates that a woman who leaves welfare and goes to work full-time at the minimum wage would have increased her net income by only $2,005 per year in 1986 but by $7,119 a decade later.[29]

A study by the Poverty Research and Training Center at the University of Michigan found that women who left welfare for work had lower poverty rates than those who were nonworking welfare recipients (43 percent vs. 88 percent) and had much higher average incomes (112 percent of the poverty level vs. 56 percent).[30]

Clearly, however, conditions are not as sanguine for the 30–40 percent of former recipients who do not find work. Actually, "not finding work" may be something of a misnomer because only 15 percent of unemployed former recipients report inability to find a job as their primary reason for being unemployed. More frequently cited reasons are "disability or illness" (27 percent) and "taking care of family" (26 percent). Other reasons include lack of childcare or transportation (12 percent) and attending school or training (9 percent).[31] While such self-reported explanations should be regarded with a certain degree of caution, clearly some former welfare recipients face serious medical, family, or personal barriers to employment. Moreover, those problems may not be transitory. Roughly half of nonworking former welfare recipients have been unemployed for two years or longer.[32]

There is relatively little information available about how people who leave welfare but do not find jobs support themselves and their families. Many have simply transferred to another government program, continuing to receive government benefits but considered "off welfare." For example, an Urban Institute study found that between 4 and 12 percent of former welfare recipients reported that they or a family member were receiving Supplemental Security Income benefits.[33] In some states, that number may be much higher. A Wisconsin study found that 47 percent of nonworking former recipients in that state were receiving SSI.[34] Others may be receiving benefits through Social Security, unemployment insurance, or other programs. Many continue to receive food stamps, Medicaid, subsidized housing, and other benefits. After all, sanctions and time limits under welfare applied to only 4 of more than 70 government welfare programs.

Others may be relying on family members, working "off the books," or receiving help from private charities. For example, studies show that there is a high degree of cohabitation among welfare recipients, with many unmarried mothers living with the father of their children or another man.[35] It can be presumed that those men are providing at least some income to the household. In addition, there has always been unreported employment by individuals receiving welfare and working "off the books."[36] While in some cases welfare reform is assumed to have caused recipients to formalize their employment, others may simply have dropped out of welfare while continuing their work in the underground economy.[37] And unemployed former recipients can be assumed to make up the bulk of any increase reported in individuals seeking private charitable assistance. But, in the end, it may just be that, in the words of Rep. Mike Castle (R-Del.): "Some people fall off the rolls altogether. We don't know what happened to them."[38]

There is some indication that individuals who have left welfare without finding work have experienced economic hardship. For example, while overall child poverty has declined, the number of children categorized as living in "extreme poverty," defined as less than half the poverty level, increased by 26 percent.[39] However, that may be only indirectly due to welfare reform. The most authoritative study on the subject, by Arloc Sherman of the Children's Defense Fund, attributes the increase in extreme child poverty to a loss of food stamps, not simply a loss of cash benefits. However, in many cases, the families remained eligible for food stamps yet had stopped receiving them for a variety of reasons not related to eligibility.[40]

Similarly, while total income for those in the second quintile of American incomes, the group most likely to contain women who have left welfare for work, has increased by approximately 1 percent following reform, the lowest quintile, which would include those who left welfare but did not find work, saw total income decline by 6.7 percent.[41]

Overall, although problems clearly exist for some groups of former welfare recipients, particularly those who are sanctioned out of the program and others who fail to find work after leaving the rolls, the widespread increases in poverty, hunger, and homelessness predicted by critics have not occurred. On the contrary, the income of poor families with children increased significantly over the 1990s, thanks, at least in part, to welfare reform. In fact, the income of poor families with children actually increased slightly faster than that of nonpoor families with children. Moreover, the greatest increases occurred in states that adopted strong work incentives as a part of welfare reform. Only a very small number of families at the very bottom of the income scale showed declines in income or worsening economic situations.[42]

However, if welfare reform has not been the disaster claimed by critics, neither has it been quite the success claimed by supporters.

Declining Caseloads

Much of the claim for welfare reform's success rests on declining caseloads. During a roughly 30-year period from the mid-1960s to the mid-1990s, the number of people receiving welfare rose dramatically. By 1995 more than 5 million Americans were receiving welfare benefits. Nearly one of every seven children lived in a family

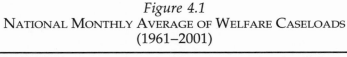

Figure 4.1
NATIONAL MONTHLY AVERAGE OF WELFARE CASELOADS
(1961–2001)

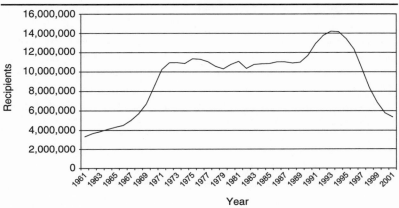

SOURCE: U.S. Department of Health and Human Services, "Average Monthly Families and Recipients for Calendar Years 1936–2001," May 2002, www.acf.dhhs.gov/news/stats/3697.htm.

receiving welfare. More than 20 percent of all children born during the late 1960s and the 1970s, and as many as 30 percent of children born in the 1980s, spent at least a year on welfare. Among African-American children the numbers were even higher. Between 70 and 80 percent of all African-American children born between 1965 and 1990 would spend a year on welfare.[43]

The trend slowed in the 1990s as the federal government began to allow states to experiment with welfare reform. Some states actually began to see a slight decline in their rolls. Following the passage of welfare reform in 1996, the caseload decline continued rapidly, with nearly every state seeing a significant drop in the number of people receiving benefits. By December 2001 caseloads were 58 percent below their 1994 peak.[44] That was the fewest recipients since 1961[45] (Figure 4.1).

There are many reasons for this decline in welfare receipt, not all of them related to welfare reform, and there has been considerable debate over which factor has been most responsible.

Welfare reform fortuitously coincided with a period of substantial economic and job growth. The question therefore is whether caseload

57

declines are due to reform or to the improved economic climate. Supporters of reform tend to credit the former, while opponents cite the latter. The reality is somewhere in between.

Certainly the impact of economic growth and the increased availability of jobs cannot be dismissed. One study found that in states where unemployment fell below 4 percent the welfare participation of single mothers was 65.5 percent lower than in states where unemployment was above 7 percent.[46] On the other hand, unemployment declined at a faster rate in the early 1990s than it did in the years following welfare reform, suggesting that caseload declines following the enactment of reform were not caused solely by the strong labor market. In fact, a 1999 report by the Council of Economic Advisers suggests that only about 10 percent of the caseload decline following reform was due to the economy. In contrast, about 30 percent of the caseload decline between 1993 and 1996 was brought about by economic growth. The study concludes that welfare reform was responsible for roughly a third of the caseload decline after 1996. Previous state reform efforts contributed to about 26 percent of pre-1996 declines.[47]

As is so often the case, different studies have reached different conclusions, often determined by the criteria that were used to measure various factors. For example, a 1999 study by the Heritage Foundation used changes in a state's average unemployment rate to measure the strength of a state's economy and its impact on caseloads and concluded that there was no statistically significant relationship between the two.[48] However, Michael New, studying the issue for the Cato Institute, used the growth in real per capita income as a measure of a state's economy and found that there was a relationship between economic growth and caseload decline, although a modest one (about a 5 percent difference between states with a strong economy and states with a weak one).[49] Douglas Besharov of the American Enterprise Institute finds an even larger correlation between the economy and caseload declines; he estimates that as much as 35–45 percent of the reduction was related to the economy.[50] Besharov speculates that it was not just a growing economy that was responsible but an employment situation that was particularly "favorable to low-skilled, single mothers."[51]

Both the Heritage and New studies found that it was not just welfare reform in the abstract but the sanction policies of the states that had the most significant impact on caseloads. Sanctions are penalties imposed on welfare recipients for failing to meet work requirements or other violations of the state's welfare policy. The most severe sanction policy withheld the entire TANF check at the first violation. A somewhat more modest policy imposed lesser penalties for the first infraction but withheld the full TANF check for multiple violations. States with the most lenient sanction policy withheld only the adult portion of TANF, allowing recipients to retain the bulk of TANF benefits regardless of the number of violations.[52]

The Heritage study found that, in general, states with more stringent sanction policies experienced a larger caseload decline than did those with more modest sanction policies.[53] New, relying on more recent data, generally confirmed the Heritage findings, concluding that as much as 20 percent of a state's caseload reduction can be attributed to its sanction policy.[54] In addition, New found that the relationship between sanctions and caseload declines is not a short-term phenomenon but is stable over longer periods of time.[55]

That is not to say that large numbers of recipients are being "thrown off" welfare. Only about 6 percent of those leaving welfare have done so as a result of sanctions, though this does represent a significant increase in the past few years. Another 16 percent were reported to have left the rolls as a result of "state policies," which may include sanctions as well as time limits and other administrative regulations.[56] However, this low nationwide average masks a wide variation by state, with more than 30 percent of case closures in Arkansas, Mississippi, and Florida due to sanctions, while 2 percent or fewer of closures are sanction related in New Hampshire, Montana, and Alabama.[57] The same is true of time limits. Time limits account for only 6 percent of case closures in Massachusetts but fully a third in Connecticut.[58]

Those removed from the rolls through sanctions, however, may experience more severe financial difficulties than other former recipients. For example, sanctioned former recipients are less likely to find employment. Nationally, employment of sanctioned former recipients runs between 20 and 50 percent.[59] In all likelihood, the same problems that led to the sanction contributed to a relative lack of employability.

Two other factors should also be considered in assessing the reasons for declining caseloads. First, research suggests that there is a link between the overall level of welfare benefits and caseloads. A 1996 study by William Niskanen found that increases in welfare benefits led to statistically significant increases in the number of welfare recipients.[60] That, basically, is the point made by welfare reformers, at least since Charles Murray wrote *Losing Ground*.[61] New's study, however, may be the first to look at benefit levels in the context of caseload declines. He found that a decline equal to 1 percent of state per capita income in the level of welfare benefits led to a nearly one-half percent decline in welfare caseloads. On a more general level, states with low levels of welfare benefits have enjoyed far more success in reducing caseloads than their more generous counterparts.[62]

Second, along with welfare reform there was a concurrent increase in the EITC and other government assistance to low-income working families. Besharov suggests that the availability of this assistance increased the attractiveness of work compared to welfare. He credits this increase in aid with as much as 20 to 30 percent of the welfare decline.[63] Certainly, we have long known that most welfare recipients have said that they would prefer to work.[64] At the same time, prior to welfare reform, relatively few reported that they were actively looking for work.[65] This was, at least in part, explainable because most entry-level jobs paid less than the combined level of all welfare benefits.[66] There are two obvious ways to change this equation: (1) increase the amount paid for work, which occurred both because of increased wages during the 1990s and because of the increased benefits to the working poor cited by Besharov; or (2) decrease welfare benefit levels, as noted by New. Thus, both Besharov and New may be correct. That is essentially the conclusion reached by Rebecca Blank and Robert Schoeni of the University of Michigan, who found that states that had strong work incentives, such as allowing recipients to retain a portion of benefits while working, combined with strong penalties for women who do not move into work made employment more valuable and had the most success at increasing both work participation and the income of welfare recipients and former recipients.[67]

In the end, it was likely a combination of factors—welfare reform, the economy, declining benefits, and the availability of other programs—that led to declining caseloads. Those factors worked in combination with one another to produce a "perfect storm," leading to unprecedented results. In this regard it is interesting to note that "employment" has now become the most frequent reason why a person leaves welfare, replacing marriage, the most prevalent reason prior to reform.[68]

Whatever the underlying reason, the largest decline in caseloads occurred in the first two years after the enactment of welfare reform. However, the steep initial decline could not be sustained. By 1998 caseloads were beginning to level out in most states, and some of the states that had experienced the biggest declines were seeing the number of recipients inch back up. For example, New Mexico cut its rolls nearly in half during the first two years after reform but saw a nearly 25 percent increase in 1999. Hawaii, Wisconsin, and Indiana also saw caseloads begin to increase again.[69]

The era of declining caseloads came to a close once and for all as the economy slowed in 2001 and 2002. By 2002, 26 states had higher caseloads than they had a year earlier, though still considerably below prereform levels[70] (Table 4.1).

One reason that early rates of caseload declines have not continued is that those early declines were, to at least some degree, brought about by "creaming" the easiest, most-employable people who were most able to take advantage of improving economic conditions. Those remaining on the rolls are a hard core of long-term unemployed and difficult-to-place recipients.

The welfare system serves two very distinctive populations. One group uses welfare as a temporary safety net, and the other remains stuck in long-term dependence. The latter group consists heavily of single mothers who have given birth out of wedlock. Thus, while the average length of time that most welfare recipients are on the program is less than two years, single mothers average 9.33 years on the program and are 39.3 percent of individuals on welfare for 10 years or longer.[71] This group is far more likely to lack education and job skills and an employment history, is more likely to have substance abuse or other problems, and, in general, presents more difficulties in transitioning from welfare to work.[72]

Studies of people leaving welfare since reform suggest that the majority are part of the easiest-to-place, least-dependent group of recipients. While they may have left more rapidly under reform, they were not the people most at risk for long-term dependence. As a group, the first wave of those leaving welfare have had better education, higher levels of basic skills, and more previous experience

Table 4.1
MONTHLY WELFARE RECIPIENTS BY STATE (1996–2002)

State	Jan. 96	Jan. 97	Jan. 98	Jan. 99	Jan. 00	Jan. 01	Jan. 02
Alabama	108,269	91,723	61,809	48,459	57,522	55,478	43,902
Alaska	35,432	36,189	31,689	26,883	24,576	17,292	18,344
Arizona	171,617	151,526	113,209	88,456	87,964	80,143	90,906
Arkansas	59,223	54,879	36,704	29,284	30,544	28,071	28,404
California	2,648,772	2,476,564	2,144,495	1,845,919	1,330,163	1,258,019	1,174,208
Colorado	99,739	87,434	55,352	40,799	29,589	27,042	31,148
Connecticut	161,736	155,701	138,666	88,304	68,717	59,977	54,891
Delaware	23,153	23,141	18,504	15,891	11,514	12,518	12,254
Dist. of Col.	70,082	67,871	56,128	52,957	48,030	43,932	43,042
Florida	575,553	478,329	320,886	220,216	170,084	129,201	128,083
Georgia	367,656	306,625	220,070	167,400	133,815	124,019	131,111
Guam	7,634	7,370	7,461	8,270	9,598	9,506	10,692
Hawaii	66,690	65,312	75,817	45,582	44,299	37,100	31,640
Idaho	23,547	19,812	4,446	3,061	2,347	2,309	2,368
Illinois	663,212	601,854	526,851	388,334	264,175	186,937	140,474
Indiana	147,083	121,974	95,665	105,069	96,551	110,216	135,643
Iowa	91,727	78,275	69,504	60,380	53,466	53,342	53,275
Kansas	70,758	57,528	38,462	33,376	31,614	32,624	35,545
Kentucky	176,601	162,730	132,388	102,370	91,323	83,272	79,014
Louisiana	239,247	206,582	118,404	115,791	79,520	68,014	63,682

Maine	56,319	51,178	41,265	36,812	28,946	26,590	25,789
Maryland	207,800	169,723	130,196	92,711	73,688	68,147	67,593
Massachusetts	242,572	214,014	181,729	131,139	105,954	96,364	107,373
Michigan	535,704	462,231	376,985	267,749	214,255	192,115	211,277
Minnesota	171,916	160,167	141,064	124,659	117,554	111,407	93,201
Mississippi	133,029	109,097	66,030	42,651	34,014	34,539	39,972
Missouri	238,052	208,132	162,950	136,782	123,947	124,911	122,897
Montana	32,557	28,138	20,137	16,152	14,663	14,891	16,613
Nebraska	38,653	36,535	38,090	35,057	24,476	23,753	25,650
Nevada	40,491	28,973	29,262	21,753	14,759	18,032	27,439
New Hampshire	24,519	20,627	15,947	15,130	14,097	13,398	14,470
New Jersey	293,833	256,064	217,320	164,815	135,436	116,688	105,181
New Mexico	102,648	89,814	64,759	80,828	75,082	57,014	49,939
New York	1,200,847	1,074,189	941,714	822,970	752,006	641,129	416,517
North Carolina	282,086	253,286	192,172	145,596	102,124	93,659	95,955
North Dakota	13,652	11,964	8,884	8,260	8,690	8,818	8,293
Ohio	552,304	518,595	386,239	311,872	255,375	205,294	197,566
Oklahoma	110,498	87,312	69,630	61,894	38,786	35,300	38,347
Oregon	92,182	66,919	48,561	44,219	43,310	40,562	41,855
Pennsylvania	553,148	484,321	395,107	313,821	245,218	218,969	214,780

(Continued)

63

Table 4.1
MONTHLY WELFARE RECIPIENTS BY STATE (1996–2002) (Continued)

State	Jan. 96	Jan. 97	Jan. 98	Jan. 99	Jan. 00	Jan. 01	Jan. 02
Puerto Rico	156,805	145,749	130,283	111,361	95,537	75,103	69,150
Rhode Island	60,654	54,809	54,537	50,632	45,753	42,286	40,157
South Carolina	121,703	98,077	73,179	45,648	38,175	39,948	54,463
South Dakota	16,821	14,091	10,514	8,759	6,894	6,529	6,836
Tennessee	265,320	195,891	139,022	148,781	145,561	153,317	162,622
Texas	714,523	626,617	439,824	325,766	339,678	358,094	340,968
Utah	41,145	35,493	29,868	30,276	22,862	21,987	20,306
Vermont	25,865	23,570	21,013	18,324	16,577	14,942	13,430
Virgin Islands	5,075	4,712	4,129	3,541	3,530	2,695	2,317
Virginia	166,012	136,053	107,192	91,544	75,798	65,713	67,198
Washington	276,018	263,792	228,723	177,611	158,151	144,457	146,094
West Virginia	98,439	98,690	51,348	32,161	32,911	38,929	43,446
Wisconsin	184,209	132,383	44,630	47,336	37,619	38,206	45,428
Wyoming	13,531	10,322	2,903	1,886	1,330	1,034	912
U.S. Total	12,876,661	11,423,007	9,131,716	7,455,297	6,108,167	5,563,832	5,242,660

SOURCES: U.S. Department of Health and Human Services, "TANF Total Number of Families and Recipients January–March 2002," November 2002, www.acf.dhhs.gov/news/stats/jan_mar2002_rev.htm; HHS, *2001 TANF Annual Report to Congress* (Washington: Government Printing Office, 2002), Table 2:2; and HHS, *1998 TANF Annual Report to Congress* (Washington: Government Printing Office, 1999), Table 1:1.

in the labor market than those remaining on the rolls.[73] As Charles Murray points out, "The reduction in caseloads is occurring disproportionately among women who wouldn't have spent much time in the system anyway and are not part of the underclass."[74]

On the other hand, those remaining on the welfare rolls are most likely to be families headed by unmarried women under the age of 30, increasingly concentrated in high-poverty areas.[75] Roughly 30 percent have less than a high school education, and 21 percent lack basic job skills.[76] Nearly half have inadequate transportation, and 30 percent have substance abuse or mental health problems.[77] Approximately two-thirds of those remaining on the rolls face two or more "barriers to work" as defined by HHS (problems with child care, disabilities, domestic violence, emergency financial needs, housing instability, lack of health insurance, substance abuse problems, and lack of transportation.)[78] And, as an Urban Institute study has demonstrated, the more obstacles they encounter, the less likely welfare recipients are to leave welfare for work.[79]

Thus, even as caseloads decline, the proportion of long-term recipients in the system is increasing. For example, while the percentage of welfare recipients who have been on the program for one year or less has declined slightly, from 36 to 33 percent, the percentage of recipients on the program for five years or more has increased from 19 to 24 percent.[80]

The Well-Being of Former Recipients

Of course, the success of welfare reform should not be judged by declining caseloads alone. For example, the well-being of those both leaving welfare and remaining on the program should be considered every bit as important as the number of people receiving checks.

As we have seen, the results of welfare reform on this score are mixed but modestly positive. Those former recipients who have found work after leaving welfare have slightly improved their economic conditions. Those former recipients who have not found work are struggling, but there has been no widespread increase in poverty or economic hardship.

Surveys of former recipients indicate that they themselves believe their quality of life has improved since leaving welfare. Studies of former recipients in South Carolina and Wisconsin, for example, found that a majority of former recipients *disagreed* with the statement, "Life was better when you were on welfare."[81] In fact, in Wisconsin, 70 percent *agreed* that "getting a job was easier than living on welfare."[82]

Even among those still on the welfare rolls, there appears to be a generally positive feeling toward the reforms. A survey by the Manpower Demonstration Research Corporation found that a majority of welfare recipients thought that their lives would be better one to five years in the future. Many of those recipients actually praised welfare reform as a stimulus for their beginning to look for work, an opportunity for a fresh start, and a chance to make things better for themselves and their children.[83] As one woman put it:

> It is just going to make me strive to get a job more so than I would have if they didn't . . . have welfare reform. I might sit back a couple more months. I might say to myself, "Well, he's going to school next year." I might sit back and wait for that, but it is making me more ready.[84]

In general, the children and families of former recipients appear to have benefited as well. When welfare reform passed, many critics predicted that it would lead to increased child abuse and neglect and family disintegration, because parents would be required to work. However, the most comprehensive study of former recipients conducted to date found a quite contrary result. Not only were no negative consequences found among children of parents who left welfare for work, but in some cases the transition off welfare appears to have resulted in an improvement in the children's mental health.[85]

A study by the General Accounting Office found no evidence of increased abuse or neglect of children of former recipients. There was no increased involvement with child protective services and no increase in placement of children in foster care.[86] Indeed, in many cases welfare reform has had a beneficial impact on children. As the Urban Institute puts it, "Children in certain subgroups will benefit from welfare reform to the extent that new policies succeed in moving parents into jobs and increasing economic resources for families; bringing about greater and more positive father involvement (both economic and social) in children's lives; placing children in care settings that are safe, stimulating, and supportive; and reducing family size."[87]

As in other areas, families leaving welfare because of sanctions seem to be an exception.[88] An Illinois study found that families sanctioned off welfare were 53 percent more likely to have a child placed with the state welfare agency than recipients leaving welfare for other reasons.[89] Again, the same factors that contributed to the family being sanctioned are likely to contribute to family problems after leaving welfare, particularly substance abuse, mental or physical illness, and domestic violence.[90] As the *Washington Post* put it: "New welfare rules have exacerbated problems for families whose lives were already chaotic. . . . The same regulations that are pushing some families toward self-sufficiency are causing other, more troubled families to unravel."[91]

There may also be long-term benefits to the families of those leaving welfare, since several studies have demonstrated the negative consequences for children of growing up on welfare. For example, women who grew up in families receiving welfare are nearly twice as likely to drop out of school as are women who grew up in families that did not receive welfare but were otherwise identical in terms of race, family income, family makeup, and childhood residence characteristics. They also spent twice as much time on welfare themselves and were nearly 50 percent more likely to have an out-of-wedlock child.[92] For men raised on welfare, studies have found a negative impact on both levels of long-term employment and earning capabilities.[93] Children whose families spent more than two years on welfare were found to be less prepared for school than children whose families spent less time on welfare or none at all.[94] One study even found that the longer a child spends on welfare, the lower his or her scores on standardized IQ tests.[95] Another indicated that children with mothers currently on welfare scored lower on letter-word achievement tests.[96]

There is little information on whether moving families off welfare will reduce the problems of current recipients, though at least one study found that children of former welfare recipients have higher math achievement scores, especially if their mothers earn higher wages.[97] It is reasonable, though, to assume that employment provides structure and consistency to families, while increasing self-esteem and self-efficacy, leading to improved family well-being.[98] Of course, others point to the strain and anxiety of leaving welfare for unfamiliar labor markets that may initially cause increased problems for families.[99] Reviewing the body of evidence, the Manpower

Demonstration Research Corporation suggests that welfare reform results in strong improvements, both psychological and behavioral, for young children, although there may be some increase in behavioral problems among adolescents, perhaps due to a lack of supervision by working parents.[100]

Overall, the evidence indicates that welfare reform has been a positive experience for recipients. Especially for those leaving welfare for work, there have been economic gains. But the most important benefits are not those measured in dollars. As Representative Castle put it: "If you get beyond the numbers, you are teaching responsibility and self-respect. I think that is improving family situations."[101]

Reducing Out-of-Wedlock Births

By several other measures, the success of welfare reform has been more limited. For example, many proponents of reform have long argued that one of the leading causes of poverty and welfare dependence is out-of-wedlock birth. The Personal Responsibility and Work Opportunity Reconciliation Act itself specifies one of its objectives as "prevent[ing] and reduc[ing] the incidence of out-of-wedlock pregnancies."[102]

An overwhelming body of research has shown a correlation between the availability of welfare benefits and the rise in out-of-wedlock births. This occurs both because prereform welfare provided economic support for out-of-wedlock childbearing (and a corresponding bias against supporting childbearing by low-income married couples) and because the welfare system contributed to an attitudinal shift on the part of the American public that removed much of the social disapproval associated with out-of-wedlock births.[103]

PRWORA contained few specific programs aimed at reducing out-of-wedlock births.[104] Nevertheless, welfare reform could be expected to reduce out-of-wedlock births by reducing the incentives to become a single mother and increasing the incentives to marry. In particular, work requirements, time limits, sanctions, and other restrictions all make it more difficult for single mothers to receive public assistance. Certainly it becomes difficult to receive assistance on the same terms as under the old Assistance to Families with Dependent Children program.

Moreover, PRWORA gave the states both incentives and flexibility to develop their own programs targeted at reducing out-of-wedlock births. Many states took advantage of this opportunity and imposed requirements that teen mothers continue to live at home with their parents and established "family caps": refusing to increase benefits for women already on welfare who have additional children out of wedlock. States, however, did not appear to enact any new programmatic initiatives aimed at reducing out-of-wedlock births. The Center on Budget and Policy Priorities estimates that states are spending only about one-half of 1 percent of TANF funds on reducing out-of-wedlock births.[105]

As Figure 3.2 (see p. 37) shows, the out-of-wedlock birthrate, which had been rising steadily since the expansion of welfare in the mid-1960s, began to stabilize in the early 1990s (about the time some states began to receive waivers allowing them to experiment with initial versions of welfare reform) and has now actually begun to decline, albeit slightly.[106] Further, despite a continuing national trend toward an increasing number of families with children headed by never-married women, the growth in the number of low-income families fitting this description has slowed since the passage of welfare reform.[107] More significant, the number of African-American children in families headed by single mothers declined dramatically in the late 1990s.[108]

More good news can be found in the modest decline in the rate of out-of-wedlock births to teenagers, those most at risk for long-term welfare dependence, although the gains are muddled somewhat by the wide variation from state to state.[109] For example, Vermont has reduced teen pregnancy to just 11 births per 1,000 teens, while Mississippi remains stuck at 58 births per 1,000 teens.[110] There was also a decline in even more problematic second births to teenage mothers. However, initial gains in this area have leveled off at about 22 percent.[111] Given the problems associated with teen pregnancy, there is certainly reason to cheer this good news.

However, a look behind the statistics gives some reasons for continued concern. For example, even as the total number of teen pregnancies inches downward, the percentage of teen pregnancies for unmarried teen mothers continues to rise.[112] In short, the decline in total teen pregnancies is largely attributable to a decline in pregnancies of *married* teens, rather than unmarried teens. In fact, the percentage of births to unmarried teenagers has risen in nearly every state.[113]

There is also considerable debate about whether welfare reform has had anything to do with the changes that we have seen in out-of-wedlock birthrates. There have been relatively few studies on the impact of specific reform measures on family formation and out-of-wedlock birthrates, and even a staunch proponent of the link between welfare and out-of-wedlock births, Charles Murray, admits, "Virtually nothing is known about many aspects of the PRWORA's effect on family formation."[114] Moreover, as with much of welfare reform, progress has been inconsistent across the states. The District of Columbia, Arizona, Michigan, Alabama, Illinois, and Oregon have done the best at reducing out-of-wedlock births, while Maine, Oklahoma, Montana, and North and South Dakota have been the least successful.[115] There is no program or approach common to successful states, which makes it difficult to generalize.[116]

Still, the few studies that are available provide some encouragement, suggesting small but positive gains.[117] Isabel Sawhill of the Brookings Institution, who has studied this issue for years, notes that the slowing of out-of-wedlock births during the first part of the 1990s was largely due to a decline in second out-of-wedlock births to women who had already had one child out of wedlock. She attributes this decline to the availability of new and more popular methods of birth control. However, since welfare reform, we have started to see a decrease in first-time out-of-wedlock births as well, and Sawhill believes that welfare reform may be a factor.[118]

Work Requirements

The response to PRWORA's work requirements has also been mixed. Under PRWORA states are required to have at least 40 percent of eligible welfare recipients from single-parent families participating in work activities.[119] For two-parent families, the participation requirement is 90 percent.

As of 2000, every state, the District of Columbia, and Puerto Rico had technically met the mandate for single-parent families. Of the jurisdictions subject to the work participation mandate, only Guam and the Virgin Islands fell short. Eight states failed to meet two-parent requirements.[120]

However, looking behind the raw numbers, we can see that far fewer welfare recipients are working than supposed. States are given a credit based on their caseload reductions, meaning that states with large numbers of people leaving welfare do not have to meet the same levels of work participation for those remaining on the rolls. Without these credits only 19 states would have met their participation requirements for single parents and only two states would have met the requirement for two-parent families.[121] In fact, for 31 states, the credit reduced the actual work requirement to *zero*. In addition, roughly 14 states have continuing waivers under the old AFDC program that may override work requirements under TANF.[122] Vermont, in fact, claims that existing waivers exempt it from *all* work requirements.[123] Exemptions make it possible for states to meet federal work participation mandates and make it seem that far more welfare recipients are working than actually are.

Given the real-world weakness of the work requirement, few states have made real efforts to require welfare recipients to participate in work activities, and nearly all states have carved out large exemptions from their work requirements. The states also vary in how quickly they require welfare recipients to work. In 30 states, recipients are supposed to begin work immediately upon receipt of benefits. However, eight states do not require work for at least six months after an individual starts to receive benefits. Twelve states allow individuals to receive benefits for up to two years before they are required to participate in work activities. And Vermont exempts recipients from work requirements for 30 months.

All but three states exempt parents of young children from work requirements. The next largest groups of exemptions are for the disabled, with 34 states exempting those who are disabled or temporarily incapacitated and 34 states exempting those who care for a disabled household member. Just over half of states (28) exempt the elderly. In addition, 30 states exempt victims of domestic violence; 28 states exempt parents who cannot find adequate childcare; 21 states exempt pregnant recipients; 28 states exempt individuals who lack transportation, people living in remote areas, or people with "other" barriers to work[124] (Table 4.2).

After all the credits, waivers, and exemptions are taken into account, fewer than 30 percent of welfare recipients are working.[125] While this is low, it does represent a substantial improvement over prereform welfare. Under the old AFDC program, only about 10 percent of recipients were working.[126] As with so much of postreform welfare, there is wide variation among states. Barely 6 percent of

71

Table 4.2
EXEMPTIONS FROM STATE WORK REQUIREMENTS BY STATE

State	Parents of Young Children	Disabled/Temp. Incap.	Disabled Household Member	Advanced Age	Domestic Violence	Inadequate Childcare	Pregnant	Other
Alabama	✓	✓	✓	✓	✓	✓	✓	✓
Alaska	✓	✓	✓		✓	✓		✓
Arizona	✓	✓	✓		✓	✓	✓	✓
Arkansas	✓	✓	✓	✓	✓	✓	✓	✓
California	✓	✓	✓	✓	✓	✓		✓
Colorado								
Connecticut	✓	✓	✓	✓	✓			✓
Delaware	✓	✓	✓		✓		✓	✓
Dist. of Col.	✓	✓	✓		✓	✓	✓	
Florida	✓	✓	✓	✓		✓	✓	
Georgia	✓							
Hawaii	✓	✓	✓	✓	✓	✓		✓
Idaho	✓			✓		✓		
Illinois	✓							
Indiana		✓	✓	✓	✓	✓	✓	
Iowa		✓						✓

State							
Kansas	✓	✓	✓	✓	✓		
Kentucky	✓	✓	✓	✓	✓	✓	
Louisiana	✓	✓	✓	✓	✓		
Maine	✓	✓	✓	✓	✓		
Maryland	✓	✓	✓	✓	✓	✓	✓
Massachusetts	✓	✓	✓	✓	✓		✓
Michigan	✓	✓	✓	✓	✓	✓	✓
Minnesota	✓	✓	✓	✓	✓	✓	✓
Mississippi	✓	✓	✓	✓	✓	✓	✓
Missouri	✓	✓	✓	✓	✓	✓	✓
Montana	No automatic categorical exemptions. Waivers allow flexibility.						
Nebraska	✓	✓	✓	✓	✓	✓	✓
Nevada	✓	✓				✓	
New Hampshire	✓	✓	✓	✓	✓	✓	✓
New Jersey	✓	✓	✓	✓	✓	✓	✓
New Mexico	✓	✓	✓	✓	✓	✓	✓
New York	✓	✓	✓	✓	✓		✓
North Carolina	✓	✓	✓	✓	✓		
North Dakota	✓	✓				✓	
Ohio	✓	✓	✓			✓	

(Continued)

73

Table 4.2
EXEMPTIONS FROM STATE WORK REQUIREMENTS BY STATE (Continued)

State	Parents of Young Children	Disabled/ Temp. Incap.	Disabled Household Member	Advanced Age	Domestic Violence	Inadequate Childcare	Pregnant	Other
Oklahoma	✓							✓
Oregon	✓						✓	✓
Pennsylvania	✓	✓		✓				✓
Rhode Island	✓	✓	✓				✓	✓
South Carolina	✓	✓	✓		✓	✓		
South Dakota	✓	✓	✓		✓	✓		
Tennessee	✓	✓	✓	✓	✓	✓	✓	
Texas	✓	✓	✓			✓	✓	✓
Utah	No automatic categorical exemptions. Waivers allow flexibility.							
Vermont	✓	✓	✓	✓	✓	✓	✓	✓
Virginia	✓	✓	✓	✓			✓	✓
Washington	✓	✓		✓	✓	✓	✓	
West Virginia	✓	✓				✓	✓	
Wisconsin	✓		✓			✓		
Wyoming		✓		✓	✓			✓
Total States	47	34	34	28	30	28	21	28

SOURCE: U.S. Department of Health and Human Services, 2001 TANF Annual Report to Congress (Washington: Government Printing Office, 2002), Table 13:3, pp. 356–57.

recipients in Maryland and 7 percent in Massachusetts are working, but nearly 60 percent are in Wyoming, and a phenomenal 73 percent are in Wisconsin[127] (Table 4.3).

It is also important to realize that the fact that a recipient is partici- pating in "work activities" does not mean that the individual is actually working. Indeed, it sometimes seems that a person engaged in "work activities" may be doing almost anything except working. For example, in all 50 states, "job search," or simply looking for work, constitutes a work activity. Some states limit the amount of time that can be spent in job search, generally to six or eight weeks of any 12-month period, but 29 states have no limit to the amount of job search a recipient can substitute for actual work. Nearly all states (47) count vocational education or training as a "work activ- ity," and in 6 states there is no time limit on the training. In 12 other states, between 24 and 36 months of training can be substituted for work. In addition, 47 states consider adult education or the study of English as a second language to meet work activity requirements, and in at least 35 states there is no time limit on those activities. Going to college or other postsecondary education serves as a work activity in 38 states. Training in "job readiness skills," such as com- pleting a job application, writing résumés, interviewing skills, "life skills," career goal setting, and workplace expectations, count as work in 48 states. Finally, 4 states include alcohol and drug abuse treatment as a work activity.[128]

A great many welfare recipients are taking part in those nonwork "work activities." In fact, of all the people states consider "working," only about 31 percent are in jobs, either subsidized community service jobs or private-sector employment.[129] Those individuals are working "at least one hour" a week. There are far fewer working full-time, since about 18 percent of those with jobs are participating in other work activities as well.[130] Therefore statistics regarding work participation may be extremely misleading.

That is particularly troubling because the evidence strongly indi- cates that the most successful form of "work activity" is work itself. There have been several studies that compared "work-first" pro- grams that attempt to push recipients into jobs as fast as possible with programs that emphasize education and training. The work- first programs increased earnings and decreased welfare depen- dency far more quickly than did the education- and training-based

Table 4.3

PERCENTAGE OF WELFARE RECIPIENTS WORKING (ABSENT CREDITS, WAIVERS, AND EXEMPTIONS) BY STATE, FY 2000

State	Absent Waiver	State	Absent Waiver
Wisconsin	73.4	Minnesota	29.3
Illinois	59.2	Utah	27.9
Wyoming	59.0	California	27.5
Ohio	52.8	Kentucky	25.6
Washington	52.8	Rhode Island	25.0
Kansas	49.0	South Carolina	25.0
Idaho	47.7	Tennessee	24.9
South Dakota	46.5	Virginia	24.6
Alaska	42.1	Hawaii	24.5
Iowa	41.8	Dist. of Col.	24.4
Indiana	40.8	Arkansas	20.8
Maine	40.0	Puerto Rico	20.0
Arizona	39.7	North Carolina	19.2
New Jersey	37.8	Mississippi	17.8
Alabama	37.7	West Virginia	17.1
Nevada	37.4	Delaware	16.8
New Mexico	36.9	Nebraska	15.8
Colorado	36.6	Georgia	12.2
Michigan	36.4	Vermont	11.6
Montana	36.2	Pennsylvania	11.2
North Dakota	35.7	Oregon	10.6
Oklahoma	33.9	Texas	7.8
Louisiana	33.5	Massachusetts	7.1
Connecticut	33.2	Maryland	6.3
New York	33.2	Virgin Islands	6.1
Florida	33.0	Guam	0.0
Missouri	30.4		
New Hampshire	30.0	U.S. Total	29.7

SOURCE: General Accounting Office, "Welfare Reform: With TANF Flexibility, States Vary in How They Implement Work Requirements and Time Limits," GAO-02-770, July 2002, pp. 11–12.

alternatives.[131] In particular, the "National Evaluation of Welfare to Work Strategies," a comprehensive review of 11 welfare-to-work programs conducted by HHS, followed former welfare recipients over a five-year period and found that employment-based programs were more successful at moving recipients into jobs and did so at far less cost than education and training programs.[132] An even more telling study by Bruce Meyer of Northwestern University and Dan Rosenbaum of the University of North Carolina–Greensboro actually found a negative correlation between education and training programs and employment.[133] Welfare recipients who participated in training programs were actually less likely to find work.

Moreover, while many labor economists have suggested that education and training would lead to greater long-term gains, there is little evidence that such programs actually lead to higher incomes or increased hours even two to three years after a worker enters the labor force.[134]

The work component of welfare reform, therefore, seems exaggerated. Because of exemptions and credits built into the law, most states are not really required to make large numbers of recipients work. And few states have chosen to do so on their own. Rather, states have exempted many recipients from work requirements altogether and, in other cases, substituted nonwork "work activities" for actual jobs (subsidized or otherwise). That would seem to run contrary to what people believe welfare reform is and may ultimately reduce the program's success at moving people "from welfare to work."

Time Limits

Under the old AFDC system, a small hard-core group of welfare recipients seemed trapped in almost permanent dependency on government aid. To combat this, welfare reform established time limits to prevent welfare from becoming a way of life. PRWORA set a federal limit of five years but allowed states to set shorter time limits if they wished. Although this sounds fairly strict, it was undercut somewhat because states were allowed to exempt up to 20 percent of their caseloads from time limits and were also allowed to use their own funds, including maintenance-of-effort (MOE) funds to continue benefits for families that have exceeded the federal time limit.[135] In addition, so-called children-only cases, where the child is eligible for welfare benefits but the adult parent is not, are not subject to federal time limit requirements.

It is still far too early to really assess the effectiveness of time limits. In most states, the first recipients did not start running up against the five-year limit until late 2001 or early 2002.[136] However, it is fair to presume that relatively few families will be removed from the welfare rolls as a result of time limits.

First, the majority of welfare recipients use welfare as a short-term safety net. Those individuals can generally be expected to leave welfare on their own long before time limits apply. Welfare reform itself appears to have speeded the exit of those individuals from the rolls. At the same time, the group of long-term, hard-core recipients most likely to face time limits is also the most likely to be sanctioned for other violations of the welfare program.[137] Therefore, many of the individuals who would have faced time limits may already have been removed from the program through other sanctions.[138]

States are expected to use either their own funds or the 20 percent federal exemption to exclude families that have been on welfare for five years from the limits. In addition, some 18 states have prereform waivers that allow them to exclude all or part of their caseloads from time limits. Some 46 states have put in place exemptions for parents or caretakers of children with disabilities and others caring for a disabled family member. Forty-two states exempt women in cases of domestic abuse, and 26 states exempt elderly recipients. Other states grant exemptions for individuals making a "good faith effort" to find work (23 states), parents with young children (22 states), recipients engaged in "work activities" (22 states), recipients enrolled in educational or training programs (21 states), and families in areas of high unemployment (19 states).[139]

As of the fall of 2001, about 42 percent of all welfare recipients were exempt from time limits; the vast majority were child-only cases.[140] However, as more families reach the five-year limit, states are expected to increase the number of exemptions, particularly through the use of state funds. For example, officials in California and New York already have suggested that they will attempt to exempt virtually all recipients. Indeed, of the 44,000 families that reached the five-year time limit in New York by December 2001, roughly 65 percent were immediately switched to state-funded benefits, while another 22 percent were exempted from the time limits under federal provisions.[141]

Studies of previous attempts to impose time limits on welfare receipt provide little cause for optimism, for whatever the talk of time limits in theory, "experience suggests that states may respond quite differently when recipients actually reach time limits."[142] Indeed, there is evidence that states will go to great lengths to avoid actually imposing time limits.[143]

As more individuals bump up against the five-year time limit, we will have an opportunity to see if PRWORA is successful in preventing welfare from becoming a way of life. Initial evidence, however, is not encouraging.

Welfare Spending

If anyone thought that welfare reform would lead to a reduction in welfare spending, he was sadly mistaken.[144] In 1996, the last full year of federal funding under the old AFDC program, welfare spending was $16.3 billion.[145] Under PRWORA, states were given an annual block grant of $16.5 billion, an amount that was frozen through 2002. Of course, some critics have complained that freezing the grant at $16.5 billion for six years was the same thing as reducing the overall grant if one factors in the annual level of inflation. (For FY03, President Bush has requested a slight increase in the block grant to about $17 billion.)[146]

However, it is also important to recognize that the number of welfare recipients was declining dramatically after 1996, so states had far fewer individuals to serve with the same size grant. As a result, on a per recipient basis, spending has increased from about $7,000 to more than $17,000 per recipient per year.[147] In addition, under MOE provisions, states must continue to spend on welfare at 80 percent of prereform levels, even if the number of recipients falls. Therefore, states are continuing to appropriate substantial funds for welfare, and state spending on a per recipient basis is rising.[148] Total welfare spending for FY 2000 (the last year for which figures are available) actually topped $25.5 billion. Roughly 53 percent of that was federal money, the remainder state funds.[149]

The composition of welfare spending has changed, however. Prior to reform, direct cash assistance accounted for 73 percent of welfare spending under AFDC and related programs.[150] Under PRWORA cash assistance has shrunk to 37 percent. The second largest category of expenditure was for childcare, roughly 13 percent. Despite rhetoric about the importance of work to welfare reform, work-related expenditures, including those on education and training, as well as subsidized employment, job search activities, employment counseling, and outreach efforts to employers, account for less than 10 percent of expenditures.[151]

Most state governments are now encountering severe budget problems as a result of both the economic downturn and their own overspending during the 1990s.[152] They are now seeking additional funds from Washington. Several advocacy groups and Democrats in Congress have also advocated increases in the size of the federal block grant. Given the enormous increase in per recipient spending that has taken place, it is not at all clear that new or increased spending is necessary. Indeed, there has been no comprehensive effort to justify current spending. In any case, welfare reform has certainly not saved the taxpayers any money.

The Big Question: Self-Sufficiency

Welfare reform's biggest failure comes in the area of preparing former recipients for self-sufficiency, or as the legislation itself puts it, "end the dependence of needy parents on government benefits by promoting job preparation, work, and marriage."[153] After all, the goal of welfare reform was always more than simple caseload reduction. The long-range goal was to end the cycle of welfare dependency by moving recipients into jobs and making them self-reliant.

Many supporters of welfare reform seem to believe that caseload declines mean that that has happened. As President Bush puts it, "Welfare reform helped to move 4.7 million Americans from welfare dependency to self-sufficiency within three years of enactment."[154]

In reality, however, self-sufficiency appears to be eluding the grasp of many, if not most, former recipients.[155] As one welfare caseworker put it, "If success is measured in client self-sufficiency, then my caseload suggests we have a way to go."[156] According to the Urban Institute, at least one-third of former welfare recipients used one or more of the following government services during their first three months off welfare: childcare, Medicaid, transportation assistance, "emergency assistance," or other forms of assistance in meeting work-related expenses.[157] An even higher level of reliance on government-provided services was found by the University of Wisconsin's

Institute for Research on Poverty, with two-thirds of former recipients receiving some type of government benefit during their first year off welfare.[158] Use of supplemental benefits does decline, however, the longer a family remains off welfare; only 35-45 percent of recipients still receive government benefits five years later.[159] Still, that means a significant number of former recipients are still dependent on government even after formally leaving welfare. Or in the words of another critic, "Replacing one open-ended entitlement with another does not serve self-sufficiency, welfare reform's real goal."[160]

Former recipients are most likely to turn to government assistance for health care, generally Medicaid and the Children's Health Insurance Program. PRWORA "delinked" Medicaid and welfare so as to make it possible for individuals to continue receiving Medicaid regardless of their eligibility for cash assistance. In addition, the law permits former welfare recipients to continue to receive Medicaid benefits for up to a year after they begin work, even if their incomes would otherwise disqualify them.

Overall, slightly more than 60 percent of former welfare recipients receive Medicaid during their first year off the rolls.[161] The other half are divided about equally between those with employer-provided health insurance and those who are uninsured.[162] Children are particularly likely to continue coverage under Medicaid, with 80–90 percent enrolled in the program at some point during the first year after leaving welfare.[163] Reliance on Medicaid drops off sharply in subsequent years, and after three years only about 15 percent of former recipients are still receiving Medicaid, compared with 38 percent who are privately insured and 47 percent who are uninsured.[164] The decline in Medicaid participation appears to be, not the result of any concerted policy by either the federal government or the states, but a combination of lack of information on the part of those eligible for benefits and various administrative and bureaucratic problems.[165] The number of former welfare recipients who are uninsured three years after leaving the rolls is particularly troubling and another telling reason why we need to overhaul our health insurance system.[166]

About half of former welfare recipients also continue to receive food stamps.[167] That is about a one-third decline in food stamp usage since January 1996 and may well be considered a partial success of welfare reform.[168] Indeed, the Department of Agriculture estimates that roughly one-third of the decline is attributable to recipients escaping poverty and becoming more self-sufficient.[169] However, there remain a sizeable number of former welfare recipients who are eligible for food stamps but fail to claim them.[170] Again, this seems less a matter of conscious public policy than a result of lack of information combined with bureaucratic impediments.[171]

There has been an effort at both the federal and the state levels to provide former welfare recipients with greater child-care assistance. As a result, between 15 and 25 percent of former recipients are receiving some degree of subsidy for childcare.[172] The amount of the subsidy as well as the number of recipients varies widely across the states, with only about 5 percent of former recipients receiving child-care subsidies in the District of Columbia but nearly 43 percent claiming assistance in Massachusetts.[173] The variation reflects differences in the way states earmark and allocate funds for childcare, as well as the cost and availability of local childcare.

Housing assistance is less common among former welfare recipients than it is among those still receiving cash benefits. Yet approximately 25 percent of those leaving welfare continue to live in public housing or receive some other form of housing subsidy.[174] It is difficult, however, to draw conclusions about whether this relatively low level of continued reliance on housing benefits represents increased self-sufficiency or simply a lack of availability of housing assistance. Only about 23 percent of people on welfare receive housing assistance, although the longer a person remains on welfare the more likely she is to receive housing assistance. Post-TANF housing assistance appears to continue at about the same rate as for those still on welfare. As with childcare, the assistance rate varies widely from state to state, ranging from more than 53 percent of former recipients in Massachusetts to just 14 percent in Illinois.[175]

Finally, we should recognize the importance of the EITC to those leaving welfare for work. The EITC expanded dramatically during the 1990s, leading to a substantial increase in income for the working poor, including many of those leaving welfare. The result has been a substantial positive work incentive, especially when combined with welfare reform.[176]

Bear in mind, however, that when the program was established in 1975, it was designed to offset the payroll taxes paid by low-income workers; in that sense the program should not be considered a welfare program or form of government assistance. Rather, it is a mechanism for undoing the way government taxation can penalize work. However, subsequent expansions of the program have turned it into a tax rebate scheme under which workers can receive back far more than they pay in both payroll and income taxes. A large portion of the EITC, thus, becomes simply another income transfer mechanism.[177]

Several states have also begun experiments under which welfare recipients can continue to receive a portion of their cash benefits after beginning to work. Under the old AFDC program, if a recipient earned a dollar working, her benefits were reduced by a dollar, clearly a disincentive to work. However, under income-disregard programs, the reduction in benefits is less than one for one, allowing the recipient to increase her income by working. Generally, the programs with income disregards also include other benefits, such as childcare, designed to make work more attractive.

Perhaps the best known of these is the Minnesota Family Investment Program, which allows welfare recipients to earn up to 140 percent of the poverty line while still receiving a portion of their welfare benefits.[178] Similar programs have been put in place in Connecticut and Vermont, and Florida and Iowa have smaller income-disregard programs.[179] Initial results of these programs show, not surprisingly, that they increase incomes of welfare recipients and also that they increase the likelihood that recipients will work.[180] Blank and Schoeni suggest that such programs are particularly successful when coupled with strong sanctions for failing to work.[181]

It should not come as a surprise that many former welfare recipients continue to rely on government assistance. Most of the young mothers who head welfare families have limited education and job experience and several young children to raise on their own. Job coaching and low-paying employment aren't going to offer any miracle cures. As far back as 1995, a Cato Institute study pointed out that, for an individual receiving the full range of welfare benefits, leaving welfare for an entry-level job would likely produce a significant initial drop in income.[182] Studies indicate that reducing the value of welfare benefits compared to work increases the likelihood that recipients will leave welfare for work, but so does increasing the value of work compared to welfare.[183] States have generally chosen the latter.

Not surprising, but also not self-sufficiency. Indeed, the increasing level of services available for former welfare recipients in particular and for the working poor more generally has led Douglas Besharov of the American Enterprise Institute to worry that America may be slipping toward the creation of a European-style welfare state, which would "saddle the economy with immense transfer systems that create troubling distributional inequities, stifle business investment, create huge work and marriage disincentives, and lock political parties into bidding wars to win over the middle class with yet more government subsidies."[184]

It is premature to accept Besharov's fears as a given, but we should remain vigilant. For, if that turns out to be true, welfare reform will turn out to have been no reform at all.

Conclusion: The Limits of Reform

Looking back at more than six years of welfare reform, we can see that it has been neither the stunning success claimed by its supporters nor the unmitigated disaster feared by its detractors. It has not resulted in increased poverty or caused significant hardship for current or former recipients. But its success in moving people from welfare to work has been largely confined to the most easily employable recipients, and much of the reduction in caseloads is a result of this group profiting from the booming job market of the 1990s. Indeed, as the economy has slowed, caseloads have begun to edge upward again. And judging from the states' recent willingness to go soft on time limits and work requirements, it is unlikely that recidivism will be effectively prevented when jobs start to disappear.

Most of those who have left the rolls and found work still remain deeply entangled in the public safety net. Few former recipients are earning enough to support their families on wages alone. In fact, two-thirds of former welfare families continue to turn to government for assistance in meeting their health-care, food, child-care, transportation, and housing needs. That's hardly self-sufficiency.

As the reauthorization debate moves forward, lawmakers should look realistically at both the successes and the failures of welfare reform. In particular, they should understand the limits of reform and the dangers of continuing to believe that the government can or should provide for the poor.

It is time to begin a new debate, not about how to reform welfare, but about how to end it.

5. Welfare: End It, Don't Mend It

We have seen the limits of welfare reform. Welfare rolls have declined—significantly—but millions of Americans remain on welfare, in many cases for years. Despite our best efforts, we have not found a way to move hard-core, truly dependent welfare recipients off the rolls. Most former welfare recipients are better off in the wake of the Personal Responsibility and Work Opportunity Reconciliation Act, but true self-sufficiency remains elusive. Only a small minority no longer needs or uses government assistance. Rather than the independence envisioned by PRWORA's authors, we have a new welfare state of people who work but remain dependent on supplemental government services.

That does not mean that reform should be abandoned or that we should pay no attention to whether reauthorization strengthens or weakens current efforts. Reauthorization should not loosen work requirements or spend billions of dollars for expanded training or child-care programs.[1]

But we should understand that no amount of tinkering around the edges of our social welfare system will solve the problems of poverty or of welfare itself. Welfare reform is, therefore, a second-best solution. Truly remaking our approach to helping the poor—to establish a social welfare system that actually does lead from dependence to self-sufficiency and offers hope for the future—will require far more radical thinking.

Short-Term Advances

There are some short-term steps that will move us in the right direction. For example, just as PRWORA devolved much of the responsibility for welfare from the federal government to the states, states should devolve responsibility to local governments. Eleven states have already taken this step, giving primary administrative responsibility under Temporary Aid to Needy Families to counties and in some cases cities.[2] In some cases this was done by building on existing local authority under the old Aid to Families with Dependent Children program, and in some cases it was done by taking advantage of increased flexibility under TANF.[3]

In general, states retain uniform policies for eligibility, benefit levels, work requirements, time limits, and sanctions. Local governments are given responsibility for administering the system, developing programs for meeting work requirements, and preparing recipients for work. There are financial incentives rewarding localities that successfully reduce their caseloads or meet work requirements.[4]

Even in states without formal devolution policies, local governments are being given greater responsibility for administering welfare programs. According to a recent survey by the National Association of Counties, 70 percent of counties have been given greater flexibility in the administration of TANF funds, half have been given more flexibility in designing work programs, and nearly 20 percent have increased flexibility with regard to issues such as eligibility and sanctions.[5]

At least one state, North Carolina, has gone even further by allowing counties to opt out of the state welfare system altogether. Counties that do so can change any or all welfare rules—including time limits, eligibility standards, benefit levels, and work requirements. To do so, the counties must submit plans to the state welfare department, which will then put together a state plan indicating which counties can opt out. The plan will be submitted to the general assembly, which has the final say. The statute also builds in considerable monitoring of the county plans by the state welfare department and an independent evaluator to determine whether the county option should continue, expand, or be terminated. County plans include goals for the program, and counties that meet the goals are allowed to reduce their share of funds.[6]

Continued devolution makes sense for a variety of reasons. One of the motivating factors for welfare reform was that states were closer than the federal government to the economic and social conditions that influence welfare and therefore better able to adjust their programs to meet those conditions. Likewise, localities differ both economically and socially. Programs well suited to the inner city may not be nearly as effective in a suburban or rural county. Local officials are far better situated than are state officials to recognize the unique economic and social problems of their community. They are also more likely to understand and be in communication with employers, providers, charities, and other resources in their locality. Finally, they provide an even larger number of laboratories in which to experiment with various approaches to welfare reform.

To date, there has been little research completed on the effectiveness of further devolution, and, in fact, the wide variation in local circumstances makes comprehensive evaluation extremely difficult. The perception of local county welfare administrators has been mixed, with some claiming that they have been given more responsibility without the resources or training to match it.[7] However, there does not appear to be any evidence that further devolution has led to any increased hardship or poverty. In fact, where research does exist, it indicates that local welfare authorities often offer more, rather than fewer, services and are more innovative in dealing with applicant problems.[8]

Therefore, states should be encouraged to continue devolving both responsibility and authority for welfare programs to local governments. In doing so, they should ensure that local authorities are properly trained and have resources equal to their responsibility. In many cases, this may mean returning tax sources and powers to local governments.

As a second short-term step, states should increase local efforts to divert potential recipients from the welfare rolls. Since PRWORA eliminated the "entitlement" to welfare, states are free to put conditions on the receipt of benefits. Approximately 30 states have used this authority to establish "diversion" programs, designed to keep potential welfare recipients, particularly those considered "job ready" or who have another potential source of income, from ever entering the system.[9]

Generally, diversion programs fall into one of three categories. The most common, at least on paper, are programs to provide "lump sum payments" in lieu of welfare benefits.[10] Those programs are designed to assist families facing an immediate financial crisis or short-term need. The family is given a single cash payment in the hope that, if the immediate problem is taken care of, there will be no need for going on welfare. The size of the grants varies from state to state, but in slightly more than half the states with this type of program the maximum payment is equal to three times the monthly TANF benefits. Most other states provide smaller amounts, although Minnesota provides payments equal to as much as four months' worth of both TANF and food stamps, and Maryland allows payment of up to a year's worth of TANF benefits.[11] In practice, the actual grants may be quite a bit smaller. One study of five county-wide lump sum payment programs found payments ranging from $300 to about $1,350.[12] In exchange for the lump sum payment, welfare applicants give up their eligibility for TANF for a period ranging from a couple of months to as long as a year.[13]

Most often, there is no restriction on how lump sum payments may be used. In practice they have been used to pay off back debts, as well as for childcare, car repairs, medical bills, rent, clothing, and utility bills. They have also been used to help individuals with work-related expenses, such as purchasing tools, uniforms, and business licenses. A few states actually restrict the use of lump sum payments to job-related needs, although that definition can be interpreted broadly. For example, childcare, transportation to work, or even moving expenses to a new job may qualify.[14]

The second most common diversion approach is "mandatory applicant job search," used by 16 states. Under this approach, welfare applicants are required to seek employment before they become eligible for benefits. In most cases the state will assist with job search in some way, such as providing job contacts and leads, providing access to a "resource room" where applicants can prepare résumés and conduct job searches, and offering classes in job search skills such as résumé writing and interview skills. They may also provide childcare and transportation assistance.

The length of time between application for welfare benefits and actual eligibility for the benefits, the time frame during which the applicant is required to search for work, varies from as little as two weeks in South Carolina to as long as six weeks in Alabama and Georgia. In many cases, however, this is not really a delay in receiving benefits but a requirement for job search during the period normally required to process the welfare application. Some states treat the job search requirement quite seriously. For example, Indiana, Missouri, and Nevada require applicants to apply for at least 10 jobs per week over a four-week period. Other states barely make an effort. Alabama requires only two job applications over a six-week period.[15] Likewise, most states do not require any sort of documentation or proof of job search activities.[16]

Finally, seven states have programs designed to encourage welfare applicants to use "alternative resources" before receiving TANF benefits. Those programs generally do not have specific guidelines but amount to caseworkers encouraging individual would-be applicants for welfare to seek help from family, private charity, or other government programs.[17] Even in states with alternative resource referral programs, this approach is the least used, possibly because it is poorly understood and requires extensive involvement by caseworkers.

There is overlap, of course; some states use more than one of these approaches, but only six states have implemented all three types of diversion strategies.[18] Table 5.1 provides a look at which states are pursuing diversion strategies.

The success of state diversion plans has been somewhat difficult to gauge, in part because even in states with diversion programs there has been limited implementation and in part because states are not set up to track diversion program participants. State TANF systems are, after all, designed to track people participating in TANF, not those diverted from it. There is a greater effort to track lump sum recipients, if only because they involve a cash expenditure, but tracking of applicants referred to charity or other alternative resources is almost entirely at the discretion of local authorities. Applicants required to participate in prebenefit job search programs are likely to be tracked only if they subsequently receive TANF. Without a comprehensive reporting system, diverted applicants may show up on TANF reports as "denied," "incomplete," "withdrawn," or "other."[19]

However, the limited data available provide reason for optimism. In Utah and Virginia, states that have the most extensive tracking information, between 81 and 85 percent of those going through the diversion program do not subsequently reapply for TANF.[20] The *Washington Post* suggests that

> the combination of these and similar [diversion tactics] explains a significant portion of the decline in welfare caseloads. . . . One noted researcher believes the policies are responsible for one-third of the . . . drop in caseloads since the nation's welfare system was overhauled in 1996. . . . The new tactic is critical to understanding the remarkable decline in the number of Americans receiving welfare over the past

Table 5.1
STATE DIVERSION PROGRAMS

State	Lump Sum	Job Search	Alternative Resources
Alabama		√	
Alaska	√		
Arizona	√	√	
Arkansas	√	√	
California	√	√	
Colorado	√		
Connecticut	√		
Delaware			
District of Columbia	√	√	
Florida	√	√	√
Georgia		√	
Hawaii			
Idaho	√	√	√
Illinois			
Indiana		√	
Iowa	√	√	
Kansas		√	√
Kentucky	√	√	
Louisiana			
Maine	√	√	
Maryland	√	√	√
Massachusetts			
Michigan		√	
Minnesota	√		
Mississippi			
Missouri		√	
Montana	√	√	√
Nebraska			
Nevada	√	√	
New Hampshire			
New Jersey	√	√	
New Mexico			
New York		√	√
North Carolina	√	√	
North Dakota			
Ohio	√	√	

State	Lump Sum	Job Search	Alternative Resources
Oklahoma	✓	✓	
Oregon		✓	
Pennsylvania			
Rhode Island	✓		
South Carolina		✓	
South Dakota	✓	✓	
Tennessee			
Texas	✓	✓	✓
Utah	✓		
Vermont	✓		
Virginia	✓		
Washington	✓		
West Virginia	✓		
Wisconsin	✓	✓	✓
Wyoming		✓	
Total	29	29	8

SOURCE: Kathleen A. Maloy et al., "Description and Assessment of State Approaches to Diversion Programs and Activities under Welfare Reform," George Washington University Center for Health Policy Research, August 1998, Table I-1.

two years. While many poor families have moved off public assistance and into jobs, many others simply have never gone on the rolls.[21]

The most extensive federal look at state diversion programs, a 1999 study by the General Accounting Office, concludes that "states diverting eligible families from receiving cash assistance may have contributed to the large decline."[22]

The federal government can encourage state diversion programs by ensuring that states receive the same credit for diverting welfare recipients as they do for moving people off welfare after they have enrolled in the program. The exact mechanism for accomplishing this will undoubtedly be complex and require careful consideration, but it makes little sense to give states credit for enrolling a welfare recipient and then helping the person get off welfare but not for keeping the person off welfare altogether.[23]

Looking to the states themselves, we can see that where diversion programs have not been effective their failure appears to stem from local welfare authorities being either unenthusiastic about diversion or unaware of the options available to them.[24] This means states must make an active effort to train local welfare authorities and provide them with clear guidance that diversion is an appropriate— indeed, a preferred—policy.

Long Term: Don't Mend It, End It

Continued devolution and expanded diversion programs are good first steps, but as June O'Neill, former director of the Congressional Budget Office and a professor at Baruch College in New York, told Congress, "The ultimate efficacy of welfare reform is going to turn on the extent to which it will have changed the incentive structures in the program, and whether that change is sufficient to deter young women from entering in the first place."[25]

Charles Murray has called for at least one state, possibly one with a small caseload and a history of effective nongovernmental welfare, to cut off all benefits to women under the age of 21.[26] But in the long run we should aim even higher. Our ultimate goal should be to eliminate the entire welfare system for individuals able to work. That means eliminating not just TANF but also food stamps, subsidized housing, and all the rest. Individuals unwilling to support themselves through the job market should have to fall back on the resources of family, church, community, or private charity.

As both a practical matter and a question of fairness, no child currently on welfare should be thrown off. However, a date should be set (for symbolic reasons, I like nine months and one day from now) after which no one new would be allowed into the welfare system. As we have already seen, there are two distinct populations of welfare recipients. Those who currently use the system as a temporary safety net will be out of the system relatively soon. Immediately ending their eligibility would have only a minor impact on the system but would risk flooding the job market and private charities without allowing for a transition.

We have seen that there are serious problems with expecting hard-core, long-term welfare recipients to be able to find sufficient employment to support themselves and their families. When we established the incentives of the current system, we may have made a Faustian bargain with those recipients. Now it may be too late to change the rules of the game. We should do whatever we can to move those people out of the system but recognize that success may be limited. It is far more important to prevent anyone new from becoming trapped in the system. That will be possible only if the trap is no longer there.

What would happen to the poor if welfare were eliminated? First, without the incentives of the welfare state, fewer people would be poor. There would probably be far fewer children born into poverty. We have seen that the availability of welfare leads to an increase in out-of-wedlock births and that giving birth out of wedlock leads to poverty. If welfare were eliminated, the number of out-of-wedlock births would almost certainly decline. Studies suggest that women do make rational decisions about whether to have children and that a reduction in income (such as a loss of welfare benefits) would reduce the likelihood of their becoming pregnant or having children out of wedlock.[27]

The magnitude of the reduction in out-of-wedlock births is a matter of conjecture. Some social scientists suggest that the decline would be small, though statistically significant; others suggest that it would be much larger.[28] Whatever the number of out-of-wedlock births, it would almost certainly be smaller than it is today.

In addition, some poor women who did still bear children out of wedlock would put the children up for adoption. Civil society should encourage that by eliminating the present regulatory and bureaucratic barriers to adoption.[29] Other unmarried women who gave birth would not be able to afford to live independently; they would choose to live with their families or their boyfriends. Some might even choose to marry the fathers of their children. Already, there is evidence that even the limited restrictions and sanctions under PRWORA have increased the likelihood of such behavior.[30]

People forced to rely on themselves will find a variety of ways to get out of poverty. Richard Vedder and Lowell Gallaway of Ohio University examined the movement of poor individuals out of poverty. They found that 18.3 percent of poor people receiving welfare moved out of poverty within one year. However, 45 percent of poor people who did not receive welfare were able to escape poverty within a year.[31]

Of course, many people will still need help. As the Bible says, "The poor always you will have with you."[32] Civil society will not turn its back on those people. Instead, they will be helped through a newly invigorated system of private charity.

Replacing Welfare with Private Charity

Private efforts have been much more successful than the federal government's failed attempt at charity. America is the most generous nation on earth. Americans already contribute more than $212 billion annually to charity.[33] In fact, more than 85 percent of all adult Americans make some charitable contribution each year.[34] In addition, about half of all American adults perform volunteer work; more than 15.5 billion hours were worked in 2000.[35] Putting a dollar value to that volunteer work would add another $239 billion in charity.[36] Volunteer work and cash donations combined bring American charitable contributions to more than $450 billion per year, not including the countless dollars and time given informally to family members, neighbors, and others outside the formal charity system.

Private charities are more successful than government welfare for several reasons. First, private charities are able to individualize their approach to the circumstances of poor people in ways that governments can never do. Government regulations must be designed to treat all similarly situated recipients alike. Glenn C. Loury of Boston University explains the difference between welfare and private charities on that point. "Because citizens have due process rights which cannot be fully abrogated . . . public judgments must be made in a manner that can be defended after the fact, sometimes even in court."[37] The result is that most government programs rely on the simple provision of cash or other services without any attempt to differentiate among the needs of recipients.

Take, for example, the case of a poor person who has a job offer but can't get to the job because her car battery is dead. A government welfare program can do nothing but tell her to wait two weeks until her welfare check arrives. Of course, by that time the job will be gone. A private charity can simply go out and buy a car battery (or even jump-start the dead battery).

The sheer size of government programs works against individualization. As one welfare caseworker lamented, "With 125 cases it's hard to remember that they're all human beings. Sometimes they're just a number."[38] Bureaucracy is a major factor in government welfare programs. For example, a report on welfare in Illinois found procedures requiring "nine forms to process an address change, at least six forms to add or delete a member of a household, and a minimum of six forms to report a change in earnings or employment."[39] All that for just one program.

In her excellent book *Tyranny of Kindness*, former welfare mother Theresa Funiciello describes the dehumanizing world of the government welfare system—a system in which illiterate homeless people with mental illnesses are handed 17-page forms to fill out, women nine months pregnant are told to verify their pregnancies, and a woman who was raped is told she is ineligible for benefits because she can't list the baby's father on the required form. It is a world totally unable to adjust to the slightest deviation from the bureaucratic norm.[40] In addition to being better able to target individual needs, private charities are much better able to target assistance to those who really need help. Because eligibility requirements for government welfare programs are arbitrary and cannot be changed to fit individual circumstances, many people in genuine need do not receive assistance, and benefits often go to people who do not really need them. More than 40 percent of all families living below the poverty level receive no government assistance. Yet more than half of the families receiving means-tested benefits are not poor.[41] Thus, a student may receive food stamps, while a homeless man with no mailing address goes without.

Private charities are not bound by such bureaucratic restrictions. Indeed, surveys of recipients themselves indicate a higher level of satisfaction with private charities than with government welfare agencies and a belief that private charities more responsively meet their needs.[42]

Private charity also has a better record of actually delivering aid to recipients. Surprisingly, little of the money being spent on federal and state social welfare programs actually reaches recipients. For example, John Goodman of the National Center for Policy Analysis points out that in 1992 the total income for poor people excluding welfare was approximately $94 billion short of the income necessary to lift them out of poverty. But the government spent more than $300 billion that year on social welfare programs.[43] If even a third of welfare spending had reached the poor, we should expect that most if not all of them would not have remained poor. In reality, however, the money is siphoned off by the bureaucrats, administrators, service providers, and others who make up the social welfare system.[44] Robert Woodson, president of the National Center for Neighborhood Enterprise, reports that in 1965, 70 cents of every dollar spent by the government to fight poverty went directly to poor people. Today, 70 cents of every dollar goes, not to poor people, but to government bureaucrats and others who serve the poor.[45] Few private charities have the bureaucratic overhead and inefficiency of government programs.

Second, in general, private charity is much more likely to be targeted to short-term emergency assistance than to long-term dependence. Thus, private charity provides a safety net, not a way of life.

Moreover, private charities may demand that the poor change their behavior in exchange for assistance. For example, a private charity may reduce or withhold benefits if a recipient does not stop using alcohol or drugs, look for a job, or avoid pregnancy. Private charities are much more likely than government programs to offer counseling and one-on-one follow-up rather than simply provide a check.

By the same token, because of the separation of church and state, government welfare programs are not able to support programs that promote religious values as a way out of poverty. Yet church and other religious charities have a history of success in dealing with the problems that often lead to poverty.[46]

Finally, and perhaps most important, private charity requires a different attitude on the part of both recipients and donors. For recipients, private charity is not an entitlement but a gift carrying reciprocal obligations. As Father Robert Sirico of the Acton Institute says: "An impersonal check given without any expectations for responsible behavior leads to a damaged sense of self-worth. The beauty of local [private charitable] efforts to help the needy is that . . . they make the individual receiving the aid realize that he must work to live up to the expectations of those helping him out."[47]

Private charity demands that donors become directly involved. Former Yale University political science professor James Payne notes how little citizen involvement there is in government charity:

> We know now that in most cases of government policy making, decisions are not made according to the democratic ideal of control by ordinary citizens. Policy is made by elites, through special interest politics, bureaucratic pressures, and legislative manipulations. Insiders decide what happens

shaping the outcome according to their own preferences and their political pull. The citizens are simply bystanders.[48]

Private charity, in contrast, is based on "having individuals vote with their own time, money, and energy."[49] The essence of private charity is voluntariness, individuals helping one another through love of their neighbor. In fact, in the Bible, the Greek word translated as charity is *agapeo*, which means love.[50]

There is no compassion in spending someone else's money—even for a good cause. True compassion means giving of yourself. As historian and social commentator Gertrude Himmelfarb puts it, "Compassion is a moral sentiment, not a political principle."[51] Welfare allows individuals to escape their obligation to be truly charitable. As Robert Thompson of the University of Pennsylvania said a century ago, government charity is a "rough contrivance to lift from the social conscience a burden that should not be either lifted or lightened in that way."[52]

That is the essence of civil society. George Washington is reported to have said that "government is not reason, it is not eloquence—it is force." He was making an important distinction. Government relies on force and coercion to achieve its objectives, including charity. In contrast, civil society relies on persuasion—reason and eloquence—to motivate voluntary giving. In civil society people give because they are committed to helping, because they believe in what they are doing.

Thus private charity ennobles everyone involved, both those who give and those who receive. Government welfare ennobles no one. Alexis de Tocqueville recognized that 150 years ago. Calling for the abolition of public relief, Tocqueville lauded private charity for establishing a "moral tie" between giver and receiver. In contrast, impersonal government relief destroys any sense of morality. The donor (read taxpayer) resents his involuntary contribution, while the recipient feels no gratitude for what he receives and inevitably believes that what he receives is insufficient.[53]

Perhaps the entire question of government welfare versus private charity was best summed up by Pope John Paul II in his encyclical *Centesimus Annus*:

> By intervening directly and depriving society of its responsibility, the welfare state leads to a loss of human energies

> and an inordinate increase in public agencies, which are dominated more by bureaucratic ways of thinking than by concern for serving their clients, and which are accompanied by an enormous increase in spending. In fact, it would appear that needs are best understood and satisfied by people who are closest to them and who act as neighbors to those in need. It should be added that certain kinds of demands often call for a response which is not material but which is capable of perceiving the deeper human need.[54]

Better yet, consider this simple thought experiment: If you had $10,000 available that you wanted to use to help the poor, would you give it to the government to help fund welfare or would you donate it to the private charity of your choice?

Big Charity and Big Government

Interestingly, some of the biggest critics of replacing welfare with private charity are some of the country's biggest charitable organizations. Their attitude has been summed up by Brian O'Connell, president of Independent Sector, an organization that represents most of the large charitable groups. "We lose our perspective on the voluntary sector and society when we exaggerate the importance of private philanthropy and volunteer organizations, particularly when we put them ahead of our responsibility to democratic government."[55]

At first, such an attitude seems surprising for organizations that should be cheerleading for private charity. But a closer look shows that large charitable foundations are no longer private charities; they have become virtual arms of the government.

Most large nationwide charities now derive much of their income, not from private donations, but from government. For example, federal, state, and local governments provide nearly two-thirds of the funding Catholic Charities USA uses to operate its nearly 1,400 programs.[56] Goodwill Industries receives half of its funding from government.[57] The Jewish Board of Family and Children Services receives 75 percent of its funding from the government. Many other prominent charities receive similar levels of government funding.[58]

A newspaper investigative report described those organizations as "transformed from charitable groups run essentially on private donations into government vendors—big business wielding jobs and amassing clout to further their own agendas."[59]

Not only does government provide most of the funding for those organizations, but their bureaucratic structure and lack of accountability frequently resemble those of government agencies. Writing for the Philanthropy Roundtable, Payne compares large, bureaucratic charities with small, community-based organizations.[60] According to Payne, the large organizations are generally managed and directed by a class of permanent, professional social workers. That is the final result of the professionalization of social work that began in the early part of the 20th century.

Payne says that the big charities "are best understood as commercial charities, entities that rely on mass-marketing techniques to sell a charitable concept to distant, rather uninformed donors."[61] As a result, there is little or no direct donor supervision and a lack of volunteers in supervisory roles. In contrast, Payne notes:

> In the task-oriented local voluntary organizations, those who supply cash and labor are well-informed about its problem-solving activities. The group is run by an inner core of several dozen volunteers who carry out operational duties. They are the managers and policy makers of the group. If the organization has paid employees, the active volunteers work with them, and are in a position to observe and evaluate their performances. Beyond this core group, the organization has several hundred less active supporters, individuals who occasionally volunteer, and who also provide financial support.[62]

Like government, big charities have become an instrument of the elites. Professional social workers prescribe the correct policies. Direct citizen involvement is unneeded and unwanted.

That situation produces three results. First, an increasing amount of the charitable dollar is eaten up by bureaucratic overhead and salaries. Less and less reaches the poor. Before his conviction for embezzling funds from the organization, William Aramony of the United Way had a salary of $390,000, a $4.4 million pension, an apartment in New York paid for by the charity, and a personal chauffeur and car.[63] His successor earns $195,000 plus benefits.[64]

Second, the organizations become more and more distant from the poor they serve. The United Way, for example, does not even operate anti-poverty programs of its own. It simply collects funds and then farms them out to other organizations, such as the National

Council of Churches and the Council of Jewish Federations, that, in turn, farm the money out to other agencies.[65]

Third, it becomes extremely important for the organizations to protect their flow of government money. As Kimberly Dennis, executive director of the Philanthropy Roundtable, complains, the big foundations "have been more interested in expanding government's responsibilities than in strengthening private institutions to address social concerns."[66]

Many charities actually maintain lobbyists on Capitol Hill to seek more of the taxpayers' money. Private donors may be surprised to find that their contributions go, not to help the poor, but to influence votes in Washington.

Private Charity in Action

The type of charity that will make a difference in civil society will not be the large bureaucratic monsters described above. Rather, it will be local, individually based operations, capable of close interaction between donors and recipients. For example, the Millionair Club has been helping Seattle's homeless since 1921. In that time it has served more than 8 million meals and found work for 700,000 people. The club offers both a day labor program and a longer-term employment assistance program. Homeless workers are paid directly by the employer, receiving $8 to $10 per hour. The program has an extraordinary level of support within the community. Last year alone, more than 8,000 people and organizations contributed to the club.[67]

Another private charity, which assists New York's homeless, is the Doe Fund's Ready, Willing, and Able program. Since its founding in 1990, the program has helped more than 1,100 homeless men and women become drug free, secure full-time employment, and obtain their own self-supported housing. In addition to receiving shelter, counseling, and drug treatment, program participants are required to work, whether around the shelter, in private-sector jobs, or helping to clean up the local community. They are paid a market wage for their work but are required to pay for their shelter and meals and must put a portion of their pay in a savings account. Upon successful completion of the program, the Doe Fund adds up to $1,000 to the individual's savings account, and that money is used to help the person find nonsubsidized housing.[68]

A similar program, the St. Martin de Porres House of Hope in Chicago founded by Sister Connie Driscoll, specializes in helping homeless women.[69] Women staying at the shelter are required to be drug free. Those who don't work must perform chores around the shelter.[70] Sister Connie describes the program's philosophy: "Giving people a bag of food and a pat on the head is not the answer anymore. Once people stop thinking of help as a right, they'll understand they have to work."[71] The shelter is not a big-budget charity. It spends less than $7 per person per day, compared to an average of more than $22 per person per day in government-funded homeless shelters. Yet it has a phenomenal success rate. Fewer than 6 percent of women who go through its program end up back on the street.[72]

Strategies to Elevate People operates in Richmond, Virginia's, largest public housing project, linking poor mothers to services from some 30 local churches and faith-based organizations. The program offers a wide range of services, including mentoring, job training, and welfare-to-work assistance. Although many of the women participating in the program face severe barriers such as substance abuse, pregnancy, and disabilities, STEP has achieved a remarkable 70 percent job placement rate, and its graduates earn as much as $11 per hour. STEP's youth outreach and mentoring programs are successfully reducing drug use, crime, and racial tensions.[73]

Not only has STEP benefited the recipients of its services, it has stimulated greater community involvement and activism. As Paul Coles, pastor of Sharon Baptist Church, explains: "[STEP] made me realize that I am right on the back door of [the housing project]. Awareness is the key. Sometimes we get so accustomed to a condition that we get 'turned off' from it, like living near the airport and you don't notice the sound of the planes anymore. That's what happened to Sharon. We were right in the middle of poverty, but we were overlooking it."[74]

One of the most successful private charities in Washington, D.C., is the Gospel Mission, which has been operating since 1906. The mission operates a homeless shelter for 150 men, a soup kitchen and food bank, and a drug treatment center. The mission operates on the principle that no one should receive something for nothing. Therefore, the homeless must pay $3 a night or agree to perform one hour of work around the mission in exchange for their lodging. The mission tries to address the full range of its clients' needs, providing not only food and shelter but also education classes, job placement assistance, and spiritual advice. Recipients must demonstrate their desire to improve their lives.[75]

"Sometimes we have to put a time limit on a guy," says Rev. John Woods, the mission's former director. "I had one guy tell me, 'Reverend, the best thing you ever did for me was kick me out.' He was using the mission for a crutch. Compassion is lifting people out of the gutter, not getting down there with them and sympathizing. These people need responsibility."[76]

The Gospel Mission has had extraordinary success at helping its clients put their lives together and return to mainstream society. For example, nearly two-thirds of the addicts completing its drug treatment program remain drug free. In contrast, a government-supported drug treatment facility just three blocks away has only a 10 percent success rate yet spends nearly 20 times as much per client.[77]

In Grand Rapids, Michigan, an organization called Faith, Inc. provides job training to the homeless and others without jobs. During the daytime, Faith, Inc.'s director, Verne Barry, seeks out homeless people, welfare recipients, and otherwise discouraged individuals and offers them a chance to help themselves. In the evening, Faith, Inc. uses a portion of a 100,000-square-foot manufacturing warehouse owned by Hope Network (a work facility for the developmentally disabled) to teach these individuals to perform light assembly and packaging jobs. At the end of the week, each employee receives a paycheck, many for the first time in years.

The key to Faith, Inc.'s success, according to Barry, is that its clients work. He questions government programs that spend millions of dollars annually to teach and train people "how to work" in lieu of the real thing. "At Faith, we don't send them to 'assessment school' for six months to decide what career they would like," he said. "We help them start working immediately. It's essential to enhancing their self-worth."[78]

A similar approach is used by St. Paul's Community Baptist Church in one of the most poverty stricken sections of Brooklyn. The church has purchased a number of small businesses that it uses to provide jobs for neighborhood poor people. If people are willing to work—and only if they are willing to work—St. Paul's will help them get a job at one of the church-run enterprises.[79]

The church has also purchased and refurbished a number of houses and is offering them to poor families for mortgages as low as $400 per month. Still, the poor are always required to pay at least something. As the church's pastor, Rev. Johnny Ray Youngblood, explains, St. Paul's philosophy is, "Never do unto others what they can do for themselves."[80]

This is only a tiny sampling of civil society in action, a few drops in an ocean of genuine—rather than government-mandated—compassion. All across America tens of thousands of small local charities like these are achieving real results in helping the poor. Such charities will form the vanguard of civil society's fight against poverty.

Will There Be Enough Charity?

People who oppose replacing welfare with private charity often argue that there will not be enough charitable giving to make up for the loss of government benefits. That criticism is based on some serious misunderstandings. First, it assumes that private charity would simply recreate existing government programs. All that would change would be the funding source. But the government programs have failed. Why would private charities want to replicate them? All the charities described above have far smaller budgets and operate far more efficiently than do their government counterparts.

Second, it assumes that private charity would have to care for the same number of poor as the government does today. However, as discussed above, without the incentives of today's welfare system there would actually be fewer people requiring assistance.

Finally, there is every reason to assume that charitable giving will increase in the absence of welfare. As we have already seen, welfare crowds out private charitable giving. As Charles Murray explains: "If government is not seen as a legitimate source of intervention, individuals and associations will respond. If instead government is permitted to respond, government will seize the opportunity, expand on it, and eventually take over altogether."[81]

A number of studies have demonstrated such a "displacement effect."[82] That effect can be seen in Figure 5.1, which shows charitable giving as a percentage of personal income since 1970. Giving declined dramatically during the 1970s, as the Great Society programs of the 1960s took hold and the public began to accept a growing welfare state. That decline leveled out in the 1980s, as the rise in welfare spending began to flatten out and the public was deluged with media stories warning of cutbacks in government

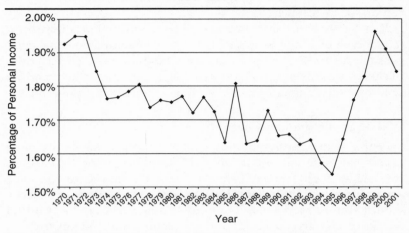

Figure 5.1
CHARITABLE GIVING AS A PERCENTAGE OF PERSONAL INCOME,
1970–2001

SOURCE: AAFRC Trust for Philanthropy, "Giving USA 2002," Indianapolis, Ind., 2002, p. 32.

programs (although, as we have seen, such cutbacks were more in the minds of the public and the media than in reality). More telling, however, is the massive spike in private giving following the passage of welfare reform in 1996.[83]

It is also important to note that Figure 5.1 shows all private charitable giving, only a portion of which goes to social welfare programs.[84] But, as Figure 5.2 shows, the same post–welfare reform spike can be seen for purely social welfare giving.[85] Indeed, there is evidence that giving shifts from educational and cultural institutions to social services as the perception of need increases. For example, in the wake of the Great Society, the proportion of charitable giving dedicated to social welfare declined from 15 to 6 percent. Following the perceived welfare cuts of the Reagan years, that percentage increased to 11.6 percent. During the Clinton administration, the proportion declined again to 9.9 percent.[86] That is a natural reaction. If people believe that their contributions are not needed to help the poor, they will contribute instead to the symphony or the Friends of the Earth. When convinced that their contributions are needed, they give more to the poor.

Figure 5.2
CHARITABLE GIVING TO HUMAN SERVICES, 1970–2001

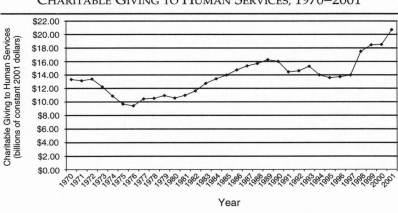

SOURCE: AAFRC Trust for Philanthropy, "Giving USA 2002," Indianapolis, Ind., 2002, p. 38.

It might be argued, of course, that increased giving in the late 1990s stemmed primarily from the booming economy. However, recent research suggests that this is not the case.[87] Rather, Americans are rationally motivated to give when they perceive both that there is a need and that their contribution will be effective. There is also evidence available from the private charitable sector, with studies showing that when charities receive government funds there is a decrease in private donations. This crowding out effect is estimated to range from as little as 2 cents to as much as 53 cents in lost contributions for every dollar of government money received.[88]

That is not a new phenomenon. There is evidence from Frederic Almy's study of outdoor relief in the 1890s (see Chapter 2) that private giving increased as government programs decreased and decreased as government programs grew more generous, leaving the overall amount of charity in society (both public and private) relatively constant.[89] Similarly, Stephen Ziliak reports that in the 1870s and 1880s, when a dissatisfaction with "outdoor relief" resulted in a reduction in government welfare, private charitable giving increased by almost exactly the same amount.[90] If government welfare disappears, there is no reason to believe that Americans will not respond, as they have in the past, with increased giving.

105

Still, if lack of funding is a concern, there are several things that the government could do to encourage giving. For example, President Bush has proposed that individuals who do not itemize on their tax returns should nonetheless be allowed to deduct their charitable contributions.[91] Approximately two-thirds of all tax filers are non-itemizers and thus are not allowed to claim tax deductions for their charitable contributions. Allowing nonitemizers to deduct their charitable contributions would help increase support for charitable organizations by rewarding and encouraging giving by all taxpayers. A PricewaterhouseCoopers report indicates that the charitable deduction for nonitemizers could increase giving by $14 billion per year and could stimulate 11 million new givers.[92]

Another option is a proposal, supported by the National Center for Policy Analysis and others, to provide all taxpayers with a dollar-for-dollar tax credit for private charitable contributions. This would be a tax credit, not a tax deduction. That is to say, if an individual gave one dollar to charity, she could reduce her tax liability by one dollar. Since current federal welfare spending is equal to approximately 41 percent of personal income tax revenue (for all means-tested programs), the amount of the credit could be capped at 41 percent of total tax liability.[93] The Massachusetts-based Beacon Hill Institute estimates that this could generate as much as $125 billion per year in additional giving.[94]

President Bush has discussed allowing married couples to claim a credit for up to half of the first $1,000 of their charitable contributions; single taxpayers could claim up to half of the first $500 of charitable contributions. In theory, the credit would be only for increased or new charitable contributions, although establishing a baseline for such determinations would appear to be difficult.[95]

These approaches are not perfect of course. At their heart, they remain a coercive mechanism for financing charity. Still, they would give individuals greater control over where their charitable dollars go and put day-to-day operation of charity in private hands. Unlike direct government funding of private charitable organizations (see Chapter 6), the funds would not come with strings or government control that could undermine the effectiveness or character of the charity. Nor would the government be in the position of deciding which charities are worthy of funding. Individuals would be contributing their own funds to the charity of their—not the government's—

choice. Government policy would simply be providing them with an incentive to do so. As an interim measure, this would certainly be preferable to the current welfare system.

Conclusion

Welfare has failed and cannot be reformed. Although there are some short-term steps we can take to improve the system, such as continuing devolution and increasing use of diversion programs, tinkering around the edges of welfare will do little to lift people out of poverty. It is time to recognize that welfare is not the solution but part of the problem. In short, end it, don't mend it.

That means an eventual end to all means-tested government transfer programs, including cash payments, commodities, and services. It does *not* mean replacing them with more efficient or somewhat less destructive programs than we have today. It is time to dismantle the American welfare state.[96]

In its place, civil society would rely on a reinvigorated network of private charity. An enormous amount of evidence and experience shows that private charities are far more effective than government welfare programs. While welfare provides incentives for counterproductive behavior, private charities can use their aid to encourage self-sufficiency, self-improvement, and independence. Private charities can individualize their approaches and target the specific problems that are holding people in poverty.

Most important, private charity is given out of a true sense of compassion, which forms a moral bond between giver and receiver. Private charity enriches the lives of everyone involved and helps to nurture the true tendrils of community.

Eliminating welfare does not mean turning our backs on the poor. It does mean finding a more effective and compassionate way to help them.

6. The Dangers of Government-Funded Charity

Given the success of private charity and the failure of government welfare, it is not surprising that some observers have suggested using government funds to subsidize private charities.[1] Particular attention, in this regard, has been focused on faith-based charities, in large part because those groups have not historically been as likely to receive government funds as other more secular charitable organizations.

As we saw in Chapter 2, faith-based organizations have had a major role in providing social services since the earliest American colonies. For most of our history those organizations operated without significant access to government funds.[2] Indeed, there has traditionally been a suspicion of government funding of religious institutions, even charitable ones. James Madison spoke eloquently for the Founders' opposition to an established national church and government funding of religion, saying, "The appropriation of funds of the United States for the use and support of religious societies, [is] contrary to the article of the Constitution which declares that Congress shall make no law respecting a religious establishment."[3]

That was a prohibition on federal aid to churches, however. Prior to the adoption of the Fourteenth Amendment, the Bill of Rights was not generally held to apply to state governments; several states had official churches and provided direct government funding of religion. The last such provision was repealed in 1833, with the abolition of Massachusetts's general assessment for support of Christian churches.[4]

Thereafter, there was little government funding of religious activities. The federal government was largely uninvolved in charitable activities, so the question of federal funding for religion seldom arose.[5] And the states, fueled in part by the virulently anti-Catholic Know Nothing movement of the 1840s, turned actively hostile to religious funding. In fact, by 1930, 26 states had constitutional prohibitions on government funding of religious activities.[6]

As the federal government's involvement in social welfare increased dramatically, the opportunities for faith-based charities to participate in government funding increased correspondingly, especially after the Johnson and Nixon administrations began widespread funding of community organizations in the 1960s. Still, government agencies struggled to reconcile funding of faith-based programs with concerns about church-state separation. Most grants came with conditions such as requiring the central religious body to form a separate nonprofit organization to administer the program; prohibiting the use of funds for the purchase or improvement of real estate that would also be used for sectarian purposes; prohibiting the provision of services in buildings that had religious symbols or fixtures; prohibiting the use of funds for training or education for a religious vocation; and prohibiting the use of funds in religious instruction, worship, prayer, or other inherently religious activities.[7]

Some of the efforts of government to distance itself from involvement with religion were almost comic in their extremism. In one perhaps apocryphal story, reported by columnist George Will, an official with the U.S. Department of Housing and Urban Development wrote to the bishop in charge of the St. Vincent de Paul Housing Center in San Francisco asking him to rename the building the *Mister* Vincent de Paul Center.[8] In another case, a city agency notified the local branch of the Salvation Army that it would be awarded a contract to help the homeless, but only on the condition that the organization remove the word "Salvation" from its name. Could the organization, perhaps, be known as some other kind of army, a government official wondered.[9] As late as 1986, HUD proposed a total ban on grants to churches and other religious organizations.[10]

Throughout the 1990s there was increased agitation on the part of Christian activists and inner-city churches who wished to participate in government social welfare initiatives. As a result, a provision was added to the Personal Responsibility and Work Opportunity Reconciliation Act to allow states to contract with religious organizations, or to "allow religious organizations to accept certificates, vouchers, or other forms of disbursement . . . on the same basis as any other nongovernmental provider without impairing the religious character of such organizations, and without diminishing the religious freedom of beneficiaries of assistance funded under such program."[11]

That provision became known as Charitable Choice and applied to four government programs: (1) Temporary Assistance for Needy Families, (2) Supplementary Security Income, (3) Medicaid, and (4) food stamps.

Specifically, states could involve faith-based organizations in the provision of subsidized jobs, on-the-job training, job search and job readiness assistance, community service positions, vocational educational training, job skills training, and GED programs. Faith-based organizations could provide meals and run food pantries. In addition, states could place unmarried minor mothers and expectant mothers who could not remain with their parents in maternity homes, adult-supervised residential care, second-chance homes, or other facilities operated by faith-based organizations. And, last, faith-based groups could provide abstinence education and drug counseling and treatment and operate health clinics.[12]

Charitable Choice went much further, however, than simply making faith-based organizations eligible for government funding. It explicitly attempted to eliminate many of the restrictions and conditions that had previously been imposed on government grants to religious organizations. Specifically, it permits

- provision of government services in actual houses of worship;
- contractors to display religious "art, icons, scripture, and other symbols" in areas where government services are provided; and
- religious contractors to discriminate against employees on the basis of their religious beliefs.

The legislation, however, continues to ban the use of government funds for "sectarian worship, instruction, or proselytization." It also requires states to provide an alternate secular provider for any aid recipient who does not wish to receive services through a religious institution.

President Bush has sought to build on Charitable Choice in several ways. First, he has established a White House Office of Faith-Based Initiatives, as well as operational centers for faith-based initiatives in five federal agencies: the Department of Justice, the Department of Health and Human Services, the Department of Labor, the Department of Education, and the Department of Housing and Urban Development.[13] Second, he would expand Charitable Choice to virtually all government programs. And, third, he has asked Congress to fund a "compassion capital fund" to highlight best practices and provide technical assistance and start-up capital to promising faith-based programs.[14]

The states' response has been mixed; some have embraced the concept enthusiastically while others have held back. Approximately 19 states have created their own office of faith-based initiatives or appointed an official liaison to the faith-based community. Overall, 38 states provide some form of outreach program to educate churches and faith-based charities about the opportunities available under Charitable Choice and other faith-based initiatives. Those outreach activities may include workshops on grant writing; conferences that bring together government officials and leaders of the faith-based community; and workbooks, websites, brochures, and other informational materials.[15]

The rationale behind Charitable Choice and the faith-based initiatives is clear enough. We saw in the last chapter the desirability of moving away from government welfare programs and toward private charity. Private charity is more effective, both on the basis of cost-effectiveness and in terms of results. But as President Bush is reported to have said, "Not every good idea needs to be a government program."

In this case, allowing the government to directly fund private charitable activities, especially faith-based organizations and programs, raises a great many troubling questions.[16]

First Amendment Complications

The phrase "separation of church and state" does not occur in the U.S. Constitution. That language comes from a letter that Thomas Jefferson sent to a group of Baptist ministers in 1802. However, the Constitution does say that "Congress shall make no law establishing religion, or prohibiting the free exercise thereof," and the courts have long held that that prohibits government funding of sectarian religious activities. The law surrounding government funding of secular activities by otherwise religious organizations is much less clear.[17]

The general legal rule is known as the "Lemon Test," after the 1971 Supreme Court decision in *Lemon v. Kurtzman*.[18] Under the Lemon Test, government may provide aid to a religious organization, provided it meets three criteria: (1) the government program must have a secular purpose; (2) it must not have a primary effect of either advancing or inhibiting religion; and (3) it must not foster "excessive entanglement" between church and state.

Most jurisprudence surrounding government funding of religious activities has centered around aid to religious schools. However, the courts have occasionally addressed government funding of charitable activities. The Supreme Court first ruled on the issue in 1899, in the case of *Bradfield v. Roberts*, holding that the District of Columbia could use public funds to subsidize the construction of a hospital that was owned by the Catholic Church, since, despite the religious affiliation of the ownership and corporate board, there was to be no direct connection between the hospital and the church. "The property and its business were to be managed in its own way, subject to no visitations, supervision or control by any ecclesiastical authority whatever."[19]

But if purely secular activities can be funded by the government even when conducted by religious organizations, the question of what happens when there is a less distinct separation of secular and religious activity has been more murky. In *Raemer v. Board of Public Works* (1976), the Court ruled that no federal funds can go to an institution that is so "pervasively sectarian" that religious activities cannot be separated from secular ones.[20] However, the Court said that if secular activities can be separated out, they may be funded. This was reaffirmed in the 1988 case of *Bowen v. Kendrick*, in which the Supreme Court ruled that government may fund social service agencies with religious ties, again provided that those agencies are not "pervasively sectarian."[21] The Court failed to define "pervasively sectarian," but a clue may be found in the earlier case of *Hunt v. McNair*, in which the Court concluded, "Aid may normally be thought to have a primary effect of advancing religion when it flows to an institution in which religion is so pervasive that a substantial portion of its functions are subsumed in the religious mission or when it funds a specifically religious activity in an otherwise substantially secular setting."[22] That has been generally taken to mean that such activities as prayer, bible study, and proselytizing may not be conducted with government funds, but the provision of social services—food, clothing, shelter, education, counseling—may be.

Given the unsettled state of the law and the vagueness of terms such as "pervasively sectarian" and "excessive involvement," government grants to faith-based charities are an open invitation to litigation. Diana Etindi, an analyst with the Welfare Policy Center at the Hudson Institute, points out the many ambiguities: "If the pastor of a church, where a new government job readiness class is starting, stops by to welcome the new group of job seeking welfare recipients and offers a prayer on their behalf, is that sectarian worship? If God or a biblical principle is mentioned during the course of counseling, is that sectarian instruction? If a client suffering a bitter divorce is invited to attend one of the church's regular support groups, is that proselytizing?"[23]

There are also issues raised about the fungibility of money provided to religious charities. If faith-based organizations are able to use federal funds for their "secular" charitable activities, money that they had previously used for those activities will be freed to be used for religious activities, essentially taking money out of one pocket and putting it into the other. In a real sense, the effect would be the same as the federal government's directly funding the religious activities, what the Supreme Court has called "a legalistic minuet."[24] In fact, this is the same logic that President Bush used in barring government funds for organizations that provide abortion counseling overseas.[25]

While critics of Charitable Choice point to the Establishment Clause of the First Amendment, supporters cite the Free Exercise Clause, arguing that government should not discriminate against faith-based organizations in giving out government grants and contracts.[26] John DiIulio, the first director of the president's Office of Faith-Based Initiatives, called it "leveling the playing field." He says that the Bush initiative expanding Charitable Choice would simply "end discrimination against religious providers" and allow "religious organizations that provide social services [to] compete for support on the same basis as other non-governmental providers of these services."[27]

Supporters are in essence making an equal protection claim, and it is not a trivial argument. When the government decides to issue a contract or grant, it should do so on a neutral basis. All applicants who meet the criteria for providing that service should be allowed to compete for the government contract. The government should not be able to refuse to give a grant to an otherwise qualified organization *simply because it is faith based.*

The 1995 case of *Rosenberger v. Rector and the Visitors of the University of Virginia* provides a useful parallel. In that case, the U.S. Supreme Court held that the University of Virginia, having decided to subsidize a wide variety of student publications, could not refuse to subsidize a Christian publication that otherwise met university criteria.[28]

However, the equal protection argument would seem to fall short on two grounds. First, prior to the adoption of Charitable Choice, faith-based organizations were not categorically barred from receiving federal funds. Rather, restrictions were placed on the receipt of those funds that forced the organizations to strictly segregate their religious and secular functions. It seems clear that government can impose conditions for the receipt of its funds, although the degree to which the government may restrict a recipient in the exercise of otherwise protected constitutional rights is an area of highly unsettled law.[29] For example, in *Rust v. Sullivan* (1991), the Supreme Court struck down a prohibition on abortion counseling by agencies receiving federal family planning funds.[30] On the other hand, the Court has upheld the imposition of government "decency standards" on artists receiving grants from the National Endowment for the Arts.[31]

Second, there is the question of whether supporters of Charitable Choice actually intend for federal grants and contracts to be awarded on a strictly neutral basis. Although President Bush has been careful to insist that faith-based initiatives will be funded without regard to denomination, recent history provides ample cause for concern. For example, many observers believe that one of the most effective organizations in addressing substance abuse and criminal behavior is the Nation of Islam. Yet, when it was revealed in 1995 that the Nation of Islam had received contracts from HUD to provide security in public housing projects, there was an uproar in Congress. The organization's history of anti-Semitism and discrimination against whites disqualified it from receiving federal contracts, critics claimed.[32]

During the 2000 presidential election campaign, then-candidate Bush was asked if he would be willing to provide public funds to the Nation of Islam. He replied, "I don't see how we can allow public dollars to fund programs where spite and hate is the core of the message."[33] Of course "hate" is a subjective term. Some people have accused Catholics and evangelical churches of preaching hatred of gays and even Jews. Recently several conservative religious leaders have claimed that Islam, as a religion, preaches hate and violence. In the wake of September 11, 2001, it is not difficult to imagine that there would be considerable objection to federal funds going to mosques and Islamic charitable organizations, especially those that were associated with criticism of American Middle East policy.

The Regulatory Burden

Regardless of how the First Amendment questions are ultimately decided, there are ample reasons to question the wisdom of Charitable Choice. Indeed, while most discussions of the separation of church and state see it as a way to protect government from religion, Yale law professor Steven Carter notes that "it also protects religion from government."[34]

Government standards and excessive regulation intended to ensure accountability and quality care inevitably come attached to government grants and contracts. Those regulations can take one of two forms. First, there are regulations that are specifically attached to the law or policy, most of which are designed to avoid church-state entanglements. For example, the 1996 Charitable Choice provision specifies that government funds may not be used for "sectarian worship, instruction, or proselytization."[35] Likewise, although there is no specific legislative language involved in his proposal, President Bush has said that no government funds would be used "for proselytizing or other inherently religious activities."[36]

Stephen Burger, executive director of the International Union of Gospel Missions, points out the difficulty of defining terms like "proselytizing" and warns, "As well intentioned as Congress is in passing [Charitable Choice], it will be the government bureaucrats and civil-libertarian lawyers who enforce it."[37] Burger and others believe that the burden will be on charities to prove that the funds they receive are being correctly used. The Charitable Choice legislation contains provisions requiring charities receiving funds to submit to a government audit.[38] As a result, the government will have the right to snoop through a church's books.

116

Unfortunately, as Melissa Rogers of the American Baptist Convention notes, the audit language of the statute is "just the tip of the regulatory iceberg."[39] Acceptance of government funds subjects an organization to a wide range of federal regulations, chief among them federal civil rights laws. According to the 1988 Civil Rights Restoration Act, a private organization "will be covered by [federal nondiscrimination laws] in its entirety, if it receives federal financial assistance which is extended to it as a whole." Chief among the laws a private organization must now comply with are Title VI of the Civil Rights Act of 1964 (prohibiting discrimination on the basis of race, color, or national origin), sec. 504 of the Rehabilitation Act (barring discrimination on the basis of handicap), the Age Discrimination Act, and Title IX of the Educational Amendments of 1972 (prohibiting discrimination on the basis of sex and visual impairment in educational institutions and programs).

The Civil Rights Restoration Act does specify that the anti-discrimination laws will apply only to "the geographically separate plant or facility which receives the federal funds," but the legislative history makes it clear that geographically separate facilities are "facilities located in different localities and regions," not facilities that are part of a complex or proximate to each other in the same city.[40] Therefore, depending on how the courts or government agencies interpret the laws, the regulations could go well beyond the program receiving government funds and subject the entire church or organization to government oversight. Richard Hammar, author of *Pastor, Church & Law*, for one, suggests: "In most cases, church programs and activities are conducted in the church facility itself, not in a geographically separate facility. In such cases, [government regulation] will apply to the entire church and all of its programs and activities."[41]

The problem is not with a prohibition on discrimination (although if anti-discrimination language is extended to such areas as sex, sexual orientation, and religion, conflicts with church doctrine could very likely occur) but with the extensive compliance costs.

For example, under federal anti-discrimination statutes, organizations must do the following:

- "[K]eep such records and submit to the responsible Department official . . . timely, complete, and accurate compliance reports at such times, and in such form, and containing such information as the responsible Department official may determine to be necessary to enable him to ascertain whether the recipient has complied or is complying with [the regulation]." Recipients are specifically required to maintain "racial and ethnic data, showing the extent to which members of minority groups are beneficiaries of and participants in federally-assisted programs."[42]

- "[M]ake available to participants, beneficiaries, and other interested persons, such information regarding the provisions of [federal regulations] and its applicability to the program for which the recipient receives federal financial assistance."[43]

- Permit access by federal government officials to its "books, records, accounts, and other sources of information and its facilities as may be pertinent to ascertain compliance."[44]

Many large charities have avoided the worst of those regulatory intrusions by setting up separate, virtually secular, arms of their organizations to handle their social services. But that is not a tactic readily available to the small neighborhood churches that are among the most effective. The average church in the United States has a congregation of only 75 members. Fewer than 1 percent of churches have congregations of more than 900, and less than 10 percent have congregations exceeding 250 people. The average annual church budget is only $55,000.[45] Faith-based initiatives not associated with specific churches are also quite small, with budgets averaging around $120,000 annually. On average, they have only two full-time and two part-time employees.[46] For these smaller churches and organizations, compliance costs will be a terrible burden. As Michael Horowitz, senior fellow at the Hudson Institute, puts it, the leaders of those organizations are likely to end up spending more time reading the *Federal Register* than the Bible.[47]

Civil rights issues may be further extended because the courts have held that accepting government money can transform an organization from a private association into a "state actor," bringing the Fourteenth Amendment into play and imposing equal protection and due process obligations, which can frequently conflict with church doctrines.[48] For example, the courts have held that a religious foster home that receives substantial state funding may not prohibit foster children under its control from having access to contraceptives.[49] And, although Charitable Choice legislation contains language exempting faith-based organizations from civil rights prohibitions against discrimination on the basis of religion, the courts have said that accepting state funds can subject a church's hiring practices to scrutiny. In one case, the Salvation Army was prohibited from discharging an employee who was a Wiccan because the employee's position was largely paid for by public funds.[50] Whether the exemption contained in Charitable Choice will hold up in the face of litigation is questionable.

Additional "due process" regulations may give service recipients the right to a hearing, appeal, and legal challenges if their services are terminated.[51] Thus a homeless shelter that wishes to evict a client for, say, use of drugs or possessing a weapon, may not be able to do so without an extensive administrative and legal proceeding.[52]

Beyond civil rights issues, there are a host of labor, safety, licensing, staff training, and other regulations that come into play once a charity accepts public funds. For example, contractors may be required to pay prevailing union wages.[53] And because many federal funds are routed through state agencies, state regulations may also apply. Those can be as detailed and idiosyncratic as instructions on night-light placement and window-washing instructions.[54] States may also regulate the credentials of charitable workers and providers, requiring child-care workers or substance abuse counselors to meet certain educational requirements. For example, Missouri and South Carolina exempt church-run child-care facilities from most state child-care regulations, such as staffing level requirements and educational certification of child-care workers. However, in both states, that exemption does not apply if the "facility receives any state or federal funds for providing for children."[55]

Even the process of applying for federal funds can be costly and time-consuming, requiring detailed knowledge of the federal proposal process. Applications can run to dozens, even hundreds, of pages and require extensive supporting documentation. That, of course, gives an advantage in the competition for funding to large, established charities over the smaller, local organizations that are arguably more effective. At the very least, it is one more diversion of resources away from actually providing services to people.

Mission Creep

Even charities with the best of intentions will be tempted to subtly shift the emphasis of their mission to comply with the grant criteria.

119

In some cases that will mean becoming increasingly secular in orientation; in others it may simply mean the adoption of new missions and services that distract from the church's original goal. It is one thing for a church to open a soup kitchen because its congregation feels God has called them to do so. It is another to open that kitchen because someone dangles grant money in front of you.

The first of the two forms of mission creep, secularization, poses the clearest and most obvious threat to the nature of faith-based charities. Facing the threat of litigation or the loss of federal funding if they violate the First Amendment, many charities choose to err on the side of caution, virtually eliminating any religious component from their services.

Sen. Rick Santorum (R-Pa.) tells of the experience of a young priest who applied for a position as a counselor at a clinic sponsored by Catholic Charities. As part of his interview, he was asked about the advice he would provide under a number of scenarios involving such cases as a woman seeking an abortion, a man involved in a homosexual relationship, and a couple about to divorce. In each case, the priest provided an answer based on Catholic doctrine. As a result, he was not hired for the position. When he asked why, he was told bluntly, "We get government funds, so we are not Catholic."[56]

Similarly, Joe Loconte, William E. Simon Fellow in Religion and a Free Society at the Heritage Foundation, relates how the St. Francis House, a homeless shelter in Boston, once staffed largely by Franciscan brothers and nuns, now avoids hiring "overtly religious people." The St. Francis House receives 52 percent of its budget from state contracts.[57]

But why should faith-based charities eschew proselytizing and explicitly religious functions? There is a reason for the "faith" in "faith-based" charities. Those organizations believe that helping people requires more than simply food or a bed. It requires addressing deeper spiritual needs. It is, ultimately, about God. Yet, in the end, Bush's proposal may transform private charities from institutions that change people's lives to mere providers of services.

Amy Sheridan of the Hudson Institute has studied faith-based charities and found that "the most effective groups challenge those who embrace faith to live out its moral implications in every significant area of their lives, from breaking drug or alcohol addiction and repairing family relationships to recommitting themselves to the value of honest work." But Sheridan expresses concern that government social service contracts are not concerned with such outcomes. They measure success, not by whether a person has changed his life or embraced God, but by "the number of meals served, beds available, or checks cashed."[58]

Stephen Monsma, chairman of the Social Sciences Division at Pepperdine University, examined 766 religious nonprofit groups and concluded that there was an inverse relationship between religious practices and public funding. Grading the organizations on 15 indicative religious practices, such as having religious pictures or symbols in facilities, spoken prayers at meals, hiring practices in accordance with religious orientation, and "encouraging religious commitment by clients," Monsma found that 44 percent of those organizations scoring lowest on the religious practices scale received a high percentage of their annual budgets from public funds. Only 28 percent of those organizations with the highest scores received significant amounts of government funding.[59]

A second form of mission creep is more subtle but can also seriously distort a charity's purpose. In the chase for government funding, charities may adapt their programs to the federal grant process rather than to the needs of their clients. Jacquelin Triston of the Salvation Army puts it this way, "If you can't do it the way you want, then you'll take your program and fit it into whatever they'll give you money for."[60] As a result, charities may find themselves taking on tasks that have little to do with their original mission or for which they are untrained or ill equipped.

For example, Massachusetts subsidizes a large proportion of the charitable work undertaken by Catholic Charities in that state. Beginning in the mid-1990s, the state began to shift its funding priorities from other social services to substance abuse. As state funding shifted, so did the programs offered by Catholic Charities. Other programs, such as thrift shops, child-care programs, and soup kitchens, have been closed and alcohol and drug treatment programs opened. By 1995 the Massachusetts office of Catholic Charities was spending 80 percent of its funds on substance abuse programs that actually served only a quarter of its clients.[61]

That sort of change in direction can occur even on the smaller level of individual programs. Many government grants are highly prescriptive in the way they require government funds to be spent. For example, a government grant for substance abuse treatment may require that a specific percentage be spent on prevention, another amount on HIV, another amount on pregnant women, a certain percentage for overhead, and so on.[62] Charities attempting to meet all the grant conditions can find themselves completely redesigning their programs. As a result, a program that was once successful can become unrecognizable.

Stanley Carlson-Thies, director of social policy studies at the Center for Public Justice, refers to this mission creep as "vendorism," a process whereby government grants end up directing the activities of private charities, changing their direction, and turning them into mere "vendors" of government services, a government program wearing a clerical collar.[63]

Putting Charity on the Dole

There is an even more profound threat to the identity and mission of private charities. If the history of welfare teaches us anything, it is that government money is as addictive as any narcotic. "It becomes almost like heroin," says Ed Gotgart, president of the Massachusetts Association of Nonprofit Schools and Colleges. "You build your program around the assumption that you can't survive without government money."[64]

Ironically, therefore, given that many private charities are dedicated to fighting welfare dependency, government funding may quickly become a source of dependency for the charities themselves. Lobbying for, securing, and retaining that funding can quickly become the organization's top priority. As the Salvation Army's Triston says, "Most everyone is fighting for every penny they can get to run whatever program they have."[65]

Surely we do not want to put charities on the dole. There is no reason to believe that welfare for charities would be any less destructive than welfare for individuals.

In fact, one wonders what kind of message such charities would be sending to their clients. On the one hand, they would be trying to teach people to be responsible and independent, to find work rather than welfare, to take care of themselves. But at the same time, the organization would have its own hand out asking for a form of welfare. That seems as contradictory as an anti-smoking group investing in tobacco stocks.

In the previous chapter I spoke of the voluntariness of private charity as one of its strengths. As David Kelley explains, "Compassion and generosity are virtues . . . not a duty, but a value we choose to pursue."[66] It is the voluntariness of those virtues that makes them ennobling. But as Tibor Machan, professor of philosophy at Auburn University, points out, by turning generosity from a virtue to a legally compelled duty, government "limits the moral worth of generous conduct."[67] Over time, that can have a coarsening effect on society, diminishing people's desire to help, their charitableness. Instead of creating a more compassionate society, we could end up with a less compassionate one.

As evidence of that, studies show that, when charities receive government funds, there is a decrease in private donations, because potential donors perceive less need.[68] The crowding out effect is estimated to range from as little as 2 cents to as much as 53 cents in lost contributions for every dollar of government money received.[69]

In the end, charities come to rely more and more on government funds and less and less on true charitable contributions. As mentioned in the previous chapter, Catholic Charities now receives 62 percent of its funding from federal, state, and local governments.[70] Catholic Charities may indeed be an efficient and effective provider of government services, but at some point it becomes neither Catholic nor a charity.

Thus, the end result of these proposals will be the substitution of coercive government financing for compassion-based voluntary giving. That would mean the end of charity as we know it.

7. Getting Out of Poverty

It has been said that the surest ways to stay out of poverty are to (1) finish school; (2) not get pregnant outside marriage; and (3) get a job, any job, and stick with it. Yet too often the government not only fails to encourage such behavior, its policies actually discourage or stand in the way of exactly the actions people should be taking to escape poverty.

Both theory and experience show that government attempts to fight poverty or create prosperity will fail.[1] Government is unable to create prosperity for several reasons. First, the taxation or borrowing, or both, necessary to finance government programs tends to reduce the pool of funds needed for private investment and job creation. Second, because they are not market driven, government programs are not able to respond to the actual needs of the economy as those needs develop and change. Third, because they lack the discipline imposed by competition and markets, government programs tend to be less efficient than their private-sector counterparts.

In addition, whatever the intention behind government programs, they are soon captured by special interests. The nature of government is such that programs are almost always implemented so as to benefit those with a vested interest in them rather than to actually achieve the programs' stated goals.

As economists Dwight Lee and Richard McKenzie, among others, point out, the political power necessary to transfer income to the poor is power that can be used to transfer income to the nonpoor, and the nonpoor are usually better organized politically and more capable of using political power to achieve their purposes.[2] Among the nonpoor with a vital interest in anti-poverty programs are social workers and government employees who administer the programs and business people, such as landlords and physicians, who are paid to provide services to the poor. Thus, anti-poverty programs are usually more concerned with protecting the prerogatives of the bureaucracy than with fighting poverty.

125

Although government cannot *create* prosperity, wrongheaded government policies can inhibit economic growth. For example, almost everyone agrees that a job is better than any welfare program. Yet for years this country has pursued tax, regulatory, education, and other policies that seem almost perversely designed to discourage economic growth and reduce entrepreneurial opportunities.

Jobs and Economic Growth

Of all the ways to avoid poverty, the most obvious—and the most important—is to have a job. Critics often complain that low-wage jobs are insufficient to lift a family out of poverty. However, as columnist Walter Williams points out, a married couple, both working full-time at a minimum wage job that pays just $5.15 per hour, would earn an annual income of $20,600. Even with two children they would be living above the poverty level.[3] In addition, it is important to remember that few adults earn as little as the minimum wage, and those who do usually earn higher wages after a few months on the job.

In fact, very few working people are poor. Only 2.6 percent of full-time workers are poor. The "working poor" are a small minority of the poor population. Even part-time work makes a significant difference. Only 11.8 percent of part-time workers are poor, compared with 20.6 percent of adults who do not work.[4]

With the economy in decline and unemployment rising, there is a great deal of focus today on the need to create jobs. But for the poor, the need for good jobs is important even during periods of economic growth. National economic conditions may not adequately account for local economies. Specifically, economic conditions have deteriorated in inner-city areas regardless of national economic trends. Unemployment is higher in those areas and wages are lower.[5]

Perhaps one of the best studies of the interaction between economic conditions and other factors was conducted by the Rockefeller and Boston Foundations; they studied the poor in Boston between 1980 and 1988, a period when sustained economic growth reduced the unemployment rate in Massachusetts below 4 percent, a rate generally considered indicative of a "full-employment" economy.[6] The study found that improving economic conditions did reduce poverty. However, the reduction was uneven among different groups. For example, while the poverty rates for both blacks and whites declined at about the same rate, the percentage of African-American families below 125 percent of the poverty level remained a high 22.3 percent. The situation was even worse for Hispanics, who saw only a slight decline in poverty. Nearly 45 percent of Hispanics remained below the poverty level. Single persons with no children had the greatest decline in poverty in all ethnic groups, and female-headed households had the least.

Experience has shown that government can do very little to create genuine, long-lasting jobs. Not only are public works jobs usually temporary, but the government's efforts to finance them may destroy more jobs than are created. Richard Vedder of the University of Ohio estimates that for every additional 1 percent of gross domestic product devoted to government employment programs, unemployment *increases* by 1.3 percent.[7]

Although government cannot create jobs, poorly conceived government policies can reduce the number of jobs that the private sector can create. A good example of this can be found in our tax policies.

America's tax burden has both diverted capital from the productive economy and discouraged job-creating investment. Federal taxes now take 20.6 percent of the nation's GDP, the highest level since World War II.[8] When state and local taxes are added to the mix, in 1999 more than 30 percent of the national income was consumed by taxes, the largest tax burden in U.S. history.[9] Today, despite recent tax cuts, federal, state, and local taxes still total more than 25 percent of GDP (Figure 7.1).

The interaction of tax policy and economic growth should be readily apparent. Simply put, taxing an activity, any activity, will reduce the level of that activity.[10] That is the logic behind such policies as raising cigarette taxes to discourage smoking. But it applies equally to the impact of taxes on business decisions. Tax investment and you will get less investment. Tax employment and there will be fewer employees. Tax corporate profits to a point where businesses are unprofitable and there will be fewer businesses.

We can examine this thesis in two ways. First we can look at history, at past increases or decreases in taxes and what followed. Here, the Kennedy tax cuts of 1962 and the Reagan cuts of 1981 are perhaps the best examples.

As the 1950s came to a close, the boom years gave way to a prolonged period of economic stagnation. By April 1960 the country

Figure 7.1
FEDERAL AND STATE AND LOCAL TAXES AS A PERCENTAGE OF GDP, FISCAL YEARS 1947–2002

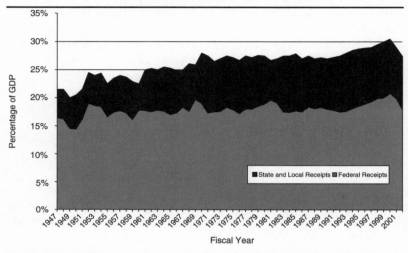

SOURCE: Congressional Research Service, "The Level of Taxes in the United States, 1940–2002," CRS RS20087, March 17, 2003, Figure 3.

was in a full-fledged recession that lasted more than 10 months. Even coming out of the recession, growth was remarkably sluggish, a situation very close to what we are seeing today. In 1962 President Kennedy reacted with a series of tax cuts, including slashing the top individual tax rate from 90 percent to 70 percent. Kennedy also reduced corporate income taxes and capital gains taxes.[11]

The result was a substantial increase in business investment and economic growth that spurred the longest peacetime economic expansion in U.S. history. Prior to the enactment of Kennedy's tax cuts, investment growth had been a modest 3 percent per year. But between the enactment of the cuts in 1962 and their repeal in 1969, investment growth more than doubled to an average annual rate of 6.1 percent. After the tax cuts were repealed, investment growth sank to 2.3 percent. Overall, the economy grew at 4.5 percent during the 1960s, compared to a pre–tax cut growth rate of just 2.5 percent.[12]

Inflation, the cost of the Vietnam War, and the massive government spending of the Great Society undid much of the economic gain of the 1960s. By the time Ronald Reagan was elected president in 1980, the U.S. economy was stuck in the doldrums of high inflation and high unemployment. Shortly after Reagan took office, the country slipped back into recession. Reagan reduced taxes, including across-the-board cuts in income tax rates and further reductions in capital gains and business taxes. Later in his term, Reagan would enact fundamental tax reform, lowering rates still further while simplifying the tax code and eliminating many special interest tax "loopholes."[13]

The results of Reagan's tax cuts were similar to those of Kennedy's. Investment shot up, growing throughout the 1980s at nearly double the postwar average. Of particular importance to the poor, employment grew at an annual rate of 2.4 percent. Not only was that faster than in the 1970s, it was twice as fast as during the Clinton presidency, a period we associate with an economic boom. In addition, the period of time that unemployed workers remained unemployed dropped significantly.[14] Income inequality declined throughout the period as all incomes rose.[15]

For further evidence of the nexus between taxes and jobs, we can look at the difference in taxation between states. For some time, economists have recognized that state and local governments provide an excellent laboratory for examining tax policy, since there are, in essence, 50 different tax systems to compare.[16] At least since Robert Genetski and Young Chin used a simple regression analysis in 1978 to demonstrate a relationship between high taxes and low economic growth, economists have known that state and local taxes do matter when it comes to creating growth and jobs.[17] Several state comparison studies show a direct impact of taxes on employment, with high taxes leading to high unemployment.[18] To some degree that is because the level of taxation is a factor used by both people and businesses in deciding where to relocate, but it also relates to the general tendency of high taxes to discourage economic activity.[19]

Different taxes affect economic growth in different ways and to different degrees. Business taxes clearly have a direct impact on business activity, especially capital formation and investment, although surprisingly there is some evidence that economic growth is less sensitive to the rates of business taxation than to individual income tax rates.[20]

Even more important than the rates of business taxation, though, is the cost to business of complying with our dizzyingly complex tax system. Those costs may exceed $194 billion every year. Businesses bear most of this burden, spending as much as $102.5 billion in compliance costs. In 2002 American workers and businesses were forced to spend more than 5.8 billion man-hours figuring out their taxes and filing the paperwork. To put that in perspective, the cost of complying with the federal tax code exceeds the entire annual revenue of Wal-Mart ($193 billion), the second largest corporation in America. And the burden is getting worse. By 2007 compliance costs are expected to surpass $350 billion.[21]

It is not just business taxes that hurt job creation. Small business in particular is impacted by personal income taxes, in part because many small businesses file taxes as individuals. In fact, the Internal Revenue Service reports that 49 percent of all individual income tax filers with adjusted gross incomes over $200,000 are limited partnerships or Subchapter S corporations and another 27 percent are sole proprietorships.[22] Thus many taxes designed to "soak the rich" actually fall heavily on small businesses. And even those taxes on the rich themselves may have at least an indirect impact on small business, since 40 percent of the income of the wealthiest 1 percent of Americans is derived from self-employment, entrepreneurship, and other small business activity.[23]

Not surprisingly, studies have shown that tax rates have a significant impact on small business profits, hiring, investment, and growth.[24] Increasing taxes reduces both capital investment spending and willingness to hire additional employees, and reducing taxes makes both investment and hiring more likely.[25]

Another tax that is especially hard on the poor is the capital gains tax. On the surface, that may seem surprising, since few poor people pay capital gains taxes. In fact, the capital gains tax is generally portrayed as a tax on the rich. However, it is also a tax on investment—investment that is needed to create jobs for poor people. As economist Jude Wanniski explains, "When the government puts a high tax on capital gains, the people who lose the most from a high rate are the poorest, the youngest, those at the beginning of their careers, those who are furthest from the sources of capital."[26]

When capital gains taxes are high, investment grows scarce. The areas that are the first to feel the lack of capital are areas where investments are most risky—inner-city neighborhoods with high crime rates, a poorly educated workforce, and high business bankruptcy rates.[27]

Historical evidence suggests that when capital gains taxes fall, investment seeps back into those neighborhoods. According to the U.S. Civil Rights Commission, after the capital gains tax was reduced from 49 percent to 28 percent in 1978, "the number of black-owned businesses increased in a five-year period by one-third." After the tax rate was cut again to 20 percent, the number of black-owned businesses increased by an additional 38 percent. But after the rate was raised back to 28 percent in 1986, the commission noted that the "expansion has slowed significantly."[28] That led the commission to conclude:

> The best hope for getting the critically needed seed money into Los Angeles and other tense urban areas is by cutting the capital gains tax. Just as the fruit of a tree contains the seeds for more trees, so the fruits of success—capital gains—contain the seeds that generate new investment and success for more people. Policies that punish success ultimately kill the seeds that promise enterprise and jobs to the poor. . . . Give us the seed for capital for inner-city jobs and investment, and we will use our rich potential to rebuild our city and transform America.[29]

As Jesse Jackson says, "Capitalism without capital is just an 'ism.'"[30] Yet America has one of the world's highest capital gains tax rates. In fact, many countries have no tax on capital gains at all.[31]

In addition to their negative impact on the economy, taxes also have a negative impact on the individual. After all, money paid in taxes is money no longer available for other purposes—whether for helping oneself or for helping others. As Frederic Bastiat wrote in his essay "What Is Seen and Not Seen" more than 200 years ago:

> [Money] spent by the state can no longer be spent as [it] would have been spent by the taxpayers. From all the benefits attributed to public spending we must deduct all the harm caused by preventing private spending. . . . [The taxpayer] would be better fed, better clothed; he would have had his sons better educated; he would have increased the dowry of his daughter, and he can no longer do so: *this is what is not seen. He would have joined a mutual aid society and can no longer do so.*[32]

Several alternatives have been suggested for making our income tax system fairer and simpler, including a flat tax and a national retail sales tax.[33] Regardless of the nature of tax reform, however, economic growth and prosperity require taxes to be one thing— lower.

Overregulation as well as taxes takes a tremendous toll on jobs and economic growth. Someone starting a business today needs a battery of lawyers just to comply with the myriad government regulations promulgated by a virtual alphabet soup of government agencies. It has been estimated that the current annual cost of government regulations is more than $1.1 trillion.[34] That is $1.1 trillion that cannot be used to create jobs and lift people out of poverty.

Although federal regulations are most damaging to the economy at large, state and local regulations are a particular hindrance to the poor. Zoning and occupational licensing laws, for example, are particularly damaging to the types of small businesses that may help people work their way out of poverty.

Given that impact, it is worth noting that many of the licensing requirements and other restrictions were originally developed to prevent African Americans from fully participating in the free market.[35] In the aftermath of slavery, plantation owners found themselves without their former supply of cheap labor, as blacks were able to enter the competitive labor market. Many former slaves had developed valuable skills as craftsmen and were setting up small businesses. Others began to contract their services to plantation owners. The available labor supply became increasingly scarce, and stiff competition drove up wages.

Many plantation owners tried to resist that trend. First, they attempted to form cartels, mutually agreeing to hold down wages. But, as is the case with all cartels, individual members soon began cheating, the cartels collapsed, and competition again began to force up wages. Unable to succeed on their own, the plantation owners turned to the power of government to enforce their will, seeking laws to restrict the economic freedom of African Americans. The first of those laws were explicitly based on race and were soon struck down by the courts. In addition, Congress passed federal legislation prohibiting the states from interfering with the right to contract.

Frustrated in their attempts to enact explicitly race-based restrictions, the plantation owners and their political allies turned to more subtle legislation that appeared neutral but, nonetheless, acted to restrict opportunities for African Americans. Enticement laws, for example, made it illegal for an employer to try to hire a worker already under contract to another employer. Vagrancy laws made it a crime to be unemployed, thus making it extremely difficult to quit a job in order to look for another one. Emigrant-agent laws made it illegal to entice people to move to other areas of the country.[36]

Near the beginning of the 20th century, as large numbers of blacks began to move into trades such as plumbing and carpentry, trade unions began to advocate occupational licensure laws to keep blacks out. Often those licensing laws contained testing and other requirements only tangentially related to the job in question. An examination of union journals and newspaper accounts at the time many of those laws were passed leaves little doubt as to their racist intent.[37]

Several studies have shown that although occupational licensing is no longer race based it continues to have a disproportionate impact on minorities.[38] Take, for example, cosmetology licensing in Missouri. As is the case in many states, in addition to fulfilling costly training requirements, potential hairstylists must pass both a practical examination—demonstrating their skill at hairdressing—and a written examination, which includes detailed esoteric questions about biology and chemistry. A study by economist Stuart Dorsey found that black candidates passed the practical examination at the same rate as white candidates but failed the written portion at vastly disproportionate rates.[39] The study concluded that "occupational licensing can restrict the labor market opportunities for groups of workers whose alternatives are already limited."[40]

We know that entrepreneurship is one major road out of poverty. Moreover, small businesses are the leading source of new jobs in businesses.[41] We are currently seeing both good news and bad in this regard. For example, African Americans own only 4 percent of small businesses in America.[42] Moreover, black-owned small businesses tend to be smaller than average. Approximately 80 percent are family-owned enterprises that employ no outside workers. About half of black-owned businesses have gross receipts of less than $5,000 per year. In addition, black-owned small businesses are disproportionately dependent on government contracts. Approximately 60 percent of their receipts come from government.[43]

One reason is that poor blacks lack the legal and financial resources to deal with the regulatory roadblocks to starting new businesses. Creating prosperity and helping the poor to become self-sufficient will therefore require the elimination of unnecessary rules and regulations that limit entrepreneurship.

Government regulations such as minimum wage laws and mandated benefits drive up the cost of employing additional workers. Minimum wage laws increase wages beyond the natural market rate, thereby increasing costs and prices, skewing the job market, and increasing unemployment. Of course, increasing the minimum wage benefits some low-wage workers. That is why its supporters advocate it. But those gains are more than offset by decreases in employment and hours worked, resulting in an overall decline in income.[44] A survey of labor economists by the *Journal of Economic Literature* found a strong consensus that increases in the minimum wage lead to higher unemployment.[45]

Other mandated benefits, from health insurance to family leave, have the same impact. By raising the cost of employment, they decrease the likelihood that a person will be hired. For a typical small business, the total tax and regulatory burden for hiring an additional worker is more than $7,000.[46] At best, that is $7,000 that is not going to the worker. At worst, the cost prevents the hiring of the worker. As a general rule, if we want poor people to work, we should avoid policies that punish employment.

Education

Our society is becoming more and more divided between those with the skills and education needed to function in the increasingly competitive global economy and those without such skills and education.

Lack of education is a critical determinant for poverty. High school dropouts are roughly three times more likely to end up in poverty than are those who complete at least a high school education.[47] If they do find jobs, their wages are likely to be low. Wages for high school dropouts have declined (in inflation-adjusted terms) by 23 percent over the past 30 years.[48] As the U.S. Department of Education warns, "In terms of employment, earnings, and family formation, dropouts from high school face difficulties in making the transition to the adult world."[49]

That situation is only going to grow worse as America enters a more competitive world of global competition and commerce, which requires advanced skills and technical knowledge.

Figure 7.2
POVERTY RATES OF CHILDREN UNDER AGE SIX BY EDUCATIONAL
LEVEL OF MORE EDUCATED PARENT, 1975–1997

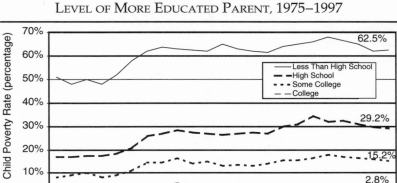

SOURCE: National Center for Children in Poverty, "Young Children in Poverty: A Statistical Update," New York, June 1999, Figure 9, p. 7.

Moreover, as Figure 7.2 shows, the impact is intergenerational. Children in families where parents have not completed high school are far more likely to be in poverty than children from families where the parents have more education. Simply put, the more education, the less poverty, a cause and effect that extends across all ethnic groups but is particularly pronounced for African Americans.[50]

A detailed discussion of education reform is well beyond the scope of this book, but there can be no serious attempt to solve the problem of poverty in America without addressing our failed government-run school system. Moreover, the "education gap" is growing steadily worse. Average annual earnings for high school dropouts have been declining in real terms, while incomes of college graduates have been increasing.

At the same time that education is becoming increasingly crucial, government schools are doing an increasingly poor job of educating children. The failures of public schools are well documented and need not be dwelled on at length here. Test scores plummeted throughout the 1960s and 1970s. There was a slight upturn in the 1980s, but scores have stagnated since.[51]

About 10 percent of girls and 12 percent of boys drop out of school.[52] These figures may understate the real problem, however, since black and Hispanic dropout rates are nearly three times higher than dropout rates for whites, and poor children are five times more likely to drop out.[53] Dropout rates in some inner cities can exceed 50 percent.[54]

Supporters of public education have long argued that the solution to our growing crisis in education lies in increased spending. However, there is no evidence that increasing the money spent on public schools will lead to increased educational performance. Education economist Eric Hanushek of the University of Rochester reviewed 147 studies of the relationship between spending on education and student performance and concluded that "there appears to be no systematic relationship between school expenditures and student performance."[55] Likewise, John Chubb and Terry Moe of the Brookings Institution concluded: "As for money, the relationship between it and effective schools has been studied to death. The consistent conclusion is that there is no connection between school funding and school performance."[56] Figure 7.3 shows how educational spending has been increasing, even as test scores have fallen.

The real problem lies not with the level of funding for education but with the very nature of the government-run education monopoly. As even Albert Shanker, the near-legendary president of the American Federation of Teachers, once admitted:

> It's time to admit that public education operates like a planned economy, a bureaucratic system in which everybody's role is spelled out in advance and there are few incentives for innovation and productivity. It is no surprise that our school system doesn't improve: it more resembles the communist economy than our own market economy.[57]

The problem is even worse among America's poor. Nearly 40 years after *Brown v. Board of Education*, America's schools are becoming increasingly segregated, on the basis not of race but of income. Wealthy and middle-class parents are able to send their children to private schools, or at least move to a district with better public schools. Poor families are trapped, forced to send their children to public schools that fail to educate.

It is time to break up the public education monopoly and give all parents the right to decide what schools their children will attend.

Figure 7.3
EDUCATIONAL SPENDING VS. SAT SCORES

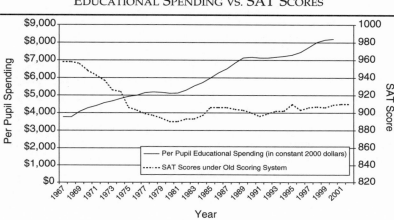

SOURCE: U.S. Department of Education, National Center for Education Statistics, *Digest of Education Statistics, 2001* (Washington: National Center for Education Statistics, 2002), Tables 135, 169; and The College Board, "10-Year Trend in SAT Scores Indicates Increased Emphasis on Math Is Yielding Results," News release NO179, August 27, 2002.

That can be done through a variety of mechanisms, from tuition tax credits to educational vouchers. Whatever the mechanics, educational control must be returned to parents.

Injecting competition, market forces, and parental choice into education will improve education for all Americans. But the greatest impact will be in the inner cities and among poor parents. Instead of being forced to send their children to the drug-infested, crime-ridden inner-city schools of today, poor parents will have the choice of a wide variety of competing schools—religious, Afrocentric, Montessori, traditional. Some children will still be born into poverty, but they will have a far better opportunity to get a good education, which has always been one of the best tickets out of poverty.[58]

Marriage and Family Formation

Jonathan Rauch calls marriage "America's new class divide," which may do more to divide Americans into haves and have-nots than race or income.[59] Certainly, as we have seen, the growing number of households headed by single women, either through divorce or single motherhood, is a significant predictor of poverty.

In the simplest terms, married couples have significantly higher family incomes than do single-parent families.[60] That is not hard to understand. Two individuals can generally bring in more income than one. As Adam Thomas and Isabel Sawhill of the Brookings Institution point out, the poverty threshold for a single mother with two children was $13,133 in 1998, while the poverty level for a two-parent family with the same number of children was $16,530. Therefore, to bring their income above the poverty level, the two-parent family needs to earn only $3,400 more than the single-parent family, but there are now two adults capable of working.[61]

That is especially important when the economy is in decline. Economic conditions worsen the income potential for female-headed families, but two-parent families have coped with economic changes by having a second wage earner in the family. Female-headed households simply do not have the option of a second wage earner.

However, there may be more indirect marital advantages as well. There is evidence, for example, that men's earnings increase as a result of marriage.[62] Different theories have been advanced for this "marriage wage premium." Robert Lerman of the Urban Institute postulates that the greater financial responsibilities of marriage spur men to greater diligence and productivity in the labor force.[63] Nobel prize–winning economist Gary Becker suggests that marriage allows for a more efficient allocation of household responsibilities, which in turn enhances a husband's labor force efficiency.[64] Linda Waite and Maggie Gallagher credit marriage with improving a man's general health and well-being, which leads to greater productivity and increased income.[65] Whatever the reason, the marriage premium seems to offer a substantial benefit.

In any case, the link between single parenthood and poverty is undeniable. Children growing up in single-parent families are five times more likely to be poor than children growing up in two-parent families.[66] Even more striking, white children growing up in a single-parent family are three times more likely to be poor than those growing up in a two-parent black family.[67] Roughly 62 percent of all poor children are in single-parent families.[68]

In fact, studies show that nearly all of the increase in poverty among children between 1970 and 1997 was associated with the growth in female-headed households[69] (Figure 7.4).

Figure 7.4
THE IMPACT OF CHANGES IN FAMILY STRUCTURE ON CHILD
POVERTY RATES, 1970–98

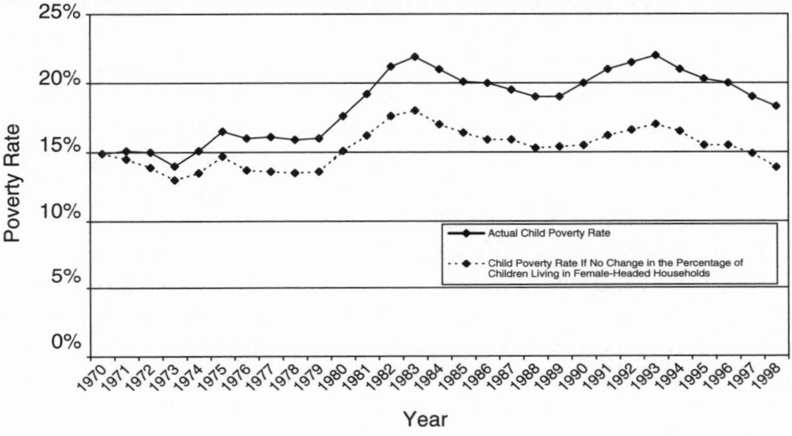

SOURCE: Isabel Sawhill and Adam Thomas, "Welfare Reform and Beyond,"
PowerPoint Presentation, Brookings Institution, Welfare Reform & Beyond
Initiative, July 2002, p. 65.

The trend may be even more pronounced for African-American
children. A study by David Eggebeen of the University of North
Carolina and Daniel Lichter of the University of Ohio found that,
if there had been no change in family structure between 1960 and
1988, the poverty rate for black children would have been only 28.4
percent rather than the actual 45.6 percent.[70]

A study by the Heritage Foundation's Center for Data Analysis,
using data from the National Longitudinal Survey of Youth, found
that nearly 80 percent of all long-term child poverty occurred among
children born out of wedlock (whether or not their mothers later
married) and children of divorced parents.[71]

Although all female-headed households suffer a high rate of poverty, the situation is even grimmer for women who give birth out
of wedlock. Only 6.7 percent of children from families with never-
married mothers will grow up without experiencing a single year
of poverty.[72] And children born and raised outside marriage will, on
average, spend more than half of their childhoods living in poverty.[73]

139

There is evidence that the impact of marital status may be so great, in fact, that it overrides other factors such as education in determining the likelihood of ending up in poverty.[74]

If one uses welfare as a surrogate for poverty, the results are the same. Approximately 30 percent of all welfare recipients go on welfare because they give birth out of wedlock.[75] The trend is even worse among teenage mothers. Half of all unwed teen mothers go on welfare within one year of the birth of their first child; 77 percent are on welfare within five years of the child's birth.[76] A child born to a single mother who does not subsequently marry will spend, on average, 71 percent of his life on welfare.[77]

Subsequent marriage alleviates but does not eliminate the problem. On average, children born out of wedlock, but whose mothers subsequently marry, spend only about half as much time in poverty as children whose mothers never marry.[78] However, women who have children out of wedlock may find it much more difficult to marry later. Daniel Lichter of Ohio State University finds that a woman who has a child out of wedlock is 40 percent less likely to marry than a woman without children. If subsequent marriage to the child's father is excluded, the likelihood of marriage is 51 percent lower than for women without children.[79] It is hardly surprising that young men seem to be unwilling to take responsibility for someone else's child.[80]

This has led to several proposals for the federal government to become directly involved in promoting marriage, especially among low-income men and women. Some states are already using Temporary Assistance for Needy Families funds to conduct small-scale demonstration projects in marriage education and promotion. The largest of those is in Arizona, which is spending just over $1 million on a program to create and distribute a marriage handbook for women and couples on welfare and the development of a community-based marriage and communication skills program. The program also offers vouchers to enable married or cohabiting couples to attend privately offered marriage skills training courses. Florida, Louisiana, Michigan, Oklahoma, and Utah offer similar, though much smaller programs. West Virginia has a $1.2 million program that pays two-parent couples on welfare an additional $100 per month for every month they remain married.[81]

The federal government is also directly funding some marriage initiatives. Health and Human Services secretary Tommy Thompson recently announced that the federal government would divert $2.2 million from child support enforcement services to religious, non-profit, and tribal organizations in 12 states to fund programs emphasizing the importance of healthy marriage.[82]

Recent proposals would go much further. For example, the proposed reauthorization of welfare reform includes provisions for $200 million in federal funds—to be matched by $100 million in state funds—to pay for educational and counseling programs that promote ways to make marriages work. Supporters say they would like to see the program eventually lead to an expansive outreach conducted through welfare and public health offices and schools.[83] Among the programs that might be funded under this proposal are public advertising campaigns to promote marriage, high school classes on the importance of marriage, marriage education and relationship skills for nonmarried pregnant women and the fathers of their children, premarital counseling for engaged couples, mentoring programs in which older married couples assist engaged couples, marriage counseling and enhancement programs, and divorce reduction programs.[84] Even that is not enough for Robert Rector of the Heritage Foundation, who wants to see at least 10 percent of all TANF funds used to promote marriage.[85]

However, before embarking on a massive new federally funded marriage program, we should consider several key problems with that approach. First, and most obvious, there is the question of just whom poor women, especially poor pregnant women or single mothers, are supposed to marry. William Julius Wilson and others have shown that in high-poverty areas, with their attendant crime and unemployment, there are relatively few marriageable men.[86] Several studies looked at the fathers of children born out of wedlock and found them quite unprepared to support a family. More than a third lacked a high school degree; 28 percent were unemployed; and 20 percent had incomes of less than $6,000 per year.[87] In addition, roughly 38 percent had criminal records.[88] That is a particular problem with young black men, nearly one-third of whom are in jail or on probation, primarily as a result of our ill-conceived war on drugs.[89] An examination of attempts to collect child support payments from low-income unwed fathers found that a substantial number of them faced serious employment barriers, including criminal records and poor health.[90] Many single mothers may find themselves

141

single precisely because they find their unemployed and undereducated potential partners unattractive marriage material.[91] Encouraging marriage to unsuitable partners may do more harm than good.

There is even some evidence that welfare reform itself may be making this problem worse. Because of its emphasis on work and education, welfare reform may be improving the prospects of women compared to their potential partners, thereby making them less likely to marry.[92]

Second, marriage may do less to increase family income than supposed. Despite the evidence cited above that marriage leads to increased family income, the impact on low-income single mothers may be less than on others. About half of unwed mothers are in fact already living with their child's father. Another third are romantically involved with the father but living separately.[93] There is some evidence that marrying the child's father, rather than cohabiting, leads to a greater sharing of resources and increased assistance from family and friends and may improve the mother and children's economic well-being.[94] However, the father can be presumed to already be providing at least some resources, so any increase would be marginal. Moreover, given the economic conditions of the fathers described above, they may have few additional resources to bring to a marriage.

It is also worth raising the caveat that there may be characteristics of unmarried mothers that contribute to their being both unmarried and poor. Poverty may be less a function of family structure than of other factors that affect both family structure and poverty. Or, as Theodora Ooms of the Center for Law and Social Policy asks, "Are single parents poor because they are not married, or are they not married because they are poor?"[95] The consensus of academic study currently gives more weight to family structure and nonmarital child bearing, but there are dissenting voices.[96]

Third, defining the issue as one of "marriage" may miss the real problem, that of out-of-wedlock births. Proponents of government marriage initiatives tend to lump all forms of single-parent families together, but there are significant differences between divorced families and families headed by never-married women. That is not to say that divorce makes no contribution to poverty. Divorced women are twice as likely to be poor as are women in intact marriages. But divorced women are only half as likely to be poor as are women who give birth out of wedlock.[97]

There are several reasons why poverty is worse for unwed mothers than for divorced women. Unwed mothers tend to be younger, have less education and fewer job skills, and be less likely to receive child support.[98] A woman who gives birth out of wedlock is more likely to drop out of school and less likely to work than are other women.[99] For example, only 59 percent of never-married mothers are high school graduates. Only 38 percent are working full-time.[100]

And if we think in terms of preventing out-of-wedlock birth, the question becomes slightly different: should we be promoting marriage or preventing pregnancy?

After all, despite conservative complaints, marriage is still the preferred family structure in America today. Most women eventually do marry, 90 percent by the time they reach age 45.[101] There has, however, been a strong societal trend toward later marriage. Between 1960 and 1999, the average age of first marriage for women increased from 20 to 25.[102] This has generally been beneficial, leading to greater educational and career achievement for women. On the down side, the greater interval between the onset of puberty and marriage has created a window that has led to increased out-of-wedlock pregnancy. As a result, up until their mid-20s, more women have babies than marry; afterwards the reverse is true.[103]

That means there are two ways to address the problem: reduce the age of marriage or delay pregnancy until after marriage. Trying to change the age of marriage promises to be extremely difficult in the face of prevailing cultural dynamics. It may also have unintended negative consequences. For example, teen mothers are more likely to have a rapid second birth if they marry, which brings with it a variety of economic and other concerns.[104] They are also more likely to leave school after they become pregnant and less likely to return to school later on.[105] In addition, marriages among younger men and women are far less stable than among people who delay marriage until they are older. Young people divorce more frequently and after a shorter period of marriage.[106]

Marriage subsequent to an out-of-wedlock birth is not a panacea. As we have seen, many if not most unwed mothers are already cohabiting with their child's father, and those fathers may be unsuitable marriage partners. Even if the mothers later marry men other than the child's father, the men they marry tend to be from the same disadvantaged circumstances.[107] As a result, research shows that subsequent marriage alleviates, but does not solve, the problems associated with unwed motherhood.[108]

It would make sense, therefore. to focus on pregnancy prevention rather than marriage itself—to delay childbearing until women have completed school, established themselves in the workplace, and married.[109]

Finally, even if marriage promotion is a good idea, one should ask whether the federal government is any more likely to be successful at this effort than it has been at promoting other desirable behavior. Although the Heritage Foundation and others are able to point to successful private-sector initiatives that encourage or sustain marriage, there is little evidence that government programs do so.[110]

That does not, of course, mean that there is nothing that the government can do. It can remove the incentives that currently act to penalize marriage and encourage out-of-wedlock birth. Since the Personal Responsibility and Work Opportunity Reconciliation Act was passed in 1996, states have made efforts to remove some of the most egregious disincentives to marriage in their welfare programs. For example, most states have removed the 100-hour rule that made low-income married couples, but not single-parent households, ineligible for welfare if one adult in the household worked more than 100 hours the previous month. Many states also have eliminated the Aid to Families with Dependent Children rule that required married households, but not single parents, to wait 30 days after the principal wage earner lost work before receiving benefits.[111] However, additional disincentives remain. Seventeen states still have different rules under TANF for two-parent than for one-parent families, even when both have similarly low incomes.[112]

There is also the problem—inherent in nearly all means-tested programs—that income-based phaseouts can penalize marriage. For example, a low-wage mother who marries a low-wage earner typically moves into an earnings range that reduces eligibility for the Earned Income Tax Credit.[113] In many cases, the financial loss can be significant. A mother earning $10,000 per year who marries a man with the same earnings could lose as much as $1,600 in EITC benefits.[114] And it's not just the EITC but the full range of means-tested programs. According to Eugene Steuerle of the Urban Institute, if a woman earning the minimum wage marries a man earning $8 per hour, she stands to lose more than $8,000 in total benefits.[115]

"Earnings-disregard" programs, such as the Minnesota Family Investment Program, have had some modest success in overcoming the financial disincentives of traditional welfare programs.[116] However, in the end it may be the elimination of welfare that does the most to make marriage a more attractive option for poor women and men.

State and local governments should also review the entire range of their laws regarding marriage to eliminate barriers and disincentives. In many cases, this can be as simple as lowering the fees for marriage licenses.[117]

Finally, government can pursue policies that increase the pool of marriageable men. The tax, regulatory, and education policies discussed above will increase employment among inner-city poor men, making them better marriage prospects. And ending the counterproductive war on drugs will mean fewer poor black men will be saddled with criminal records and diminished employment prospects.

Turning to the more important policy issue of reducing out-of-wedlock births, we again find relatively little that government can do in terms of a government program. Currently, the federal government spends more than $700 million per year on programs designed to combat out-of-wedlock births, most of which are focused on preventing teen pregnancies.[118] The largest part of this money funds traditional family planning and sex education programs, primarily through Medicaid Family Planning, Title X of the Health Services Act of 1970, Title XX of the Social Security Act, and CDC Community Partnership programs.[119] About $9 million is spent for "abstinence only" education under traditional pregnancy prevention programs such as Title XX, and PRWORA authorizes an additional $50 million for abstinence programs.[120] The $571 million figure also includes $120 million in TANF bonuses to states that meet out-of-wedlock birth reduction targets.[121]

There are also a number of state-funded and state-directed efforts to reduce out-of-wedlock births. Again the emphasis is on preventing teen pregnancies. Eighteen states and the District of Columbia make some form of sex education mandatory in their schools, and an additional 11 states provide content requirements for local school districts that choose to offer a sex education curriculum.[122] Overall, approximately 69 percent of school districts offer some form of sex education, although the nature and depth of what is taught vary widely.[123] In addition to school-based programs, states have also tried media campaigns, family planning clinics, youth conferences, father involvement programs, self-esteem programs, home visitation, and parental education programs, as well as mentoring, after-school programs, and similar efforts.[124]

Liberals and conservatives spar endlessly over the relative merits of those programs, with liberals touting comprehensive sex education and family planning services, including contraception, while conservatives prefer abstinence education. Both sides are able to cite a wide variety of studies supporting their contention. In reality, however, many of those studies are poorly designed, contain many biases, and offer a poor basis for determining the effectiveness of programs.[125] Many studies lacked sufficient sample size. Few included long-term follow-up. Many programs were conducted as demonstration projects, with a maximum of resources and support; and very few of those have been replicated in less ideal circumstances. A number of studies lacked an experimental design or independent evaluators, or they used improper statistical analysis. In addition, difficulty measuring behavior and a publishing bias toward positive outcomes limited what was known.[126]

In the end, there is little evidence that either approach significantly reduces either the sexual activity of teenagers or out-of-wedlock births. A detailed overview of the available literature says, "None of the programs have been shown to have large, sustained effects on adolescent sexual behavior, contraceptive use, pregnancy, and childbearing rates."[127]

The real solution to out-of-wedlock birth and teen pregnancy, therefore, lies not with more government programs but with changing the basic incentives encountered by young at-risk women. That means increasing the potential rewards for avoiding nonmarital pregnancy and the consequences of becoming pregnant out of wedlock.

One of the starkest illustrations of the current incentive climate can be seen in a survey of black, never-married girls under the age of 18 conducted by Ellen Freeman of the University of Pennsylvania. Only 40 percent of those surveyed thought that becoming pregnant in the next year would "make their situation worse."[128] Likewise, a study by Laurie Schwab Zabin and others in the *Journal of Research on Adolescence* found that "in a sample of inner-city black teens presenting pregnancy tests, we reported that more than 31 percent of those bringing the pregnancy to term told us, before their pregnancy was diagnosed, that they believed a baby would present a problem." In other words, 69 percent either did not believe having a baby out of wedlock would present a problem or were unsure.[129]

Until teenage girls, particularly those living in poverty, see real consequences to unmarried pregnancy, it will be impossible to gain control over out-of-wedlock births. But poor, inner-city teenagers have so little hope in their current circumstances that they are often unable to contemplate a future that could be disrupted by a baby. Surveys of women on welfare show that they have lower expectations of marriage and see little difference between married and nonmarried childbearing.[130] As University of Pennsylvania sociologist Elijah Anderson points out: "Most middle-class youths take a stronger interest in their futures and know what a pregnancy can do to derail it. In contrast, many [inner-city] adolescents . . . see little to lose by having a child out-of-wedlock."[131]

Therefore, any successful approach to reducing teen pregnancy and out-of-wedlock births should have two parts. First, governments should support those policies that are most likely to provide poor children with greater opportunities for the future, especially opportunities for education and employment.

Education is particularly important. We know, for example, that girls who drop out of school are far more likely to get pregnant out of wedlock than girls who complete at least a high school education.[132] In fact, educational failure is one of the strongest predictors of teen pregnancy.[133] This means that the proposals for education reform and school choice described above are more important than ever.

Likewise, the policies described above to strengthen economic growth and create jobs can have a positive impact on reducing out-of-wedlock birthrates. Poor people are poor; they are not stupid. Give poor women something to lose, and they are likely to reevaluate their behavior and react accordingly.

At the same time, we should remove the welfare safety net that insulates poor young women from the negative consequences of their childbearing decisions. In Chapters 3 and 5, I discussed at length the relationship between the availability of welfare benefits

and out-of-wedlock births. By eliminating welfare, we can significantly reduce the incidence of births to unmarried women, particularly if we combine this with the pro-opportunity, pro-hope policies
described above.

But even smaller steps toward limiting welfare appear to have a
positive effect on out-of-wedlock childbearing. Isabel Sawhill notes
that welfare reform is at least attempting to send a message to young
women that "they will receive much more limited assistance from
the government and that they will be expected to become self-sup-
porting."[134] They may well be getting the message. Surveys of women
on welfare in Delaware and Indiana found that they agreed that
welfare reform made them more likely to think about getting married, and significant numbers agreed that welfare reform made them
more likely to postpone or stop having additional children.[135] African-American women and women with low educational achievement were most likely to change their opinions as a result of welfare reform.[136]

Beyond a generalized message, PRWORA authorized states to
impose a "family cap," denying additional TANF benefits to women
on welfare who have more children, and 23 states have established
such caps.[137] A number of states also require that teen mothers stay
in school and continue living at home with their parents.

Research findings on the effectiveness of those approaches have
been mixed.[138] That is not terribly surprising; as Rebecca Blank notes,
changes in marriage and birth rates take a long time to show up.
Only a relatively small proportion of the population becomes pregnant each year, which means that any changes in behavior will
become clear only slowly over time. Moreover, it is reasonable to
assume that decisions about marriage and having children may react
more sluggishly to incentive changes than, say, work behavior.[139]
Still, in the long run, we may well see positive results from even
these incremental changes.

Charles Murray, among others, believes we should go much further. He has called for at least one state, possibly one with a small
caseload and a history of effective nongovernmental welfare, to cut
off all benefits to women under the age of 21. He believes that this
would provide a test of the responsiveness of young women to
welfare-based incentives for childbearing—that we would see a significant decline in out-of-wedlock births.[140]

In the long run, we should go still further. As I argued in Chapter 5, we should ultimately end government welfare entirely. That is likely to have a far greater impact on encouraging marriage and family formation, while discouraging unwed motherhood, than is any set of government marriage or sex education programs.

Savings, the Accumulation of Wealth, and Social Security Reform

To jobs, education, and marriage, we can add one more important stepping stone on the road out of poverty—savings and the accumulation of wealth. In many ways this runs contrary to the emphasis of current anti-poverty policy, which is heavily focused on increasing income. Certainly there is a logic to that: immediate needs for food, shelter, and so on must be met before other, more long-term, goals can be addressed. Yet, in the end, as Michael Sherraden of the Washington University in St. Louis has noted, "For the vast majority of households, the pathway out of poverty is not through consumption, but through saving and accumulation."[141]

Wealth, in this sense, is not just an amount of money that can be used to buy things; it is, as Melvin Oliver and Thomas Shapiro wrote in their seminal book, *Black Wealth/White Wealth,*

> used to create opportunities, secure a desired stature and standard of living, and pass class status on to one's children. . . . The command of resources that wealth entails is more encompassing than is income or education, and closer in meaning and theoretical significance to our traditional notions of economic well-being and access to life chances.[142]

Furthermore, as Sherraden notes:

> When people begin to accumulate assets, their thinking and behavior changes as well. Accumulating assets leads to psychological and social effects that are not achieved in the same degree by receiving and spending an equivalent amount of regular income. These behavioral effects are important for household "welfare" or well-being.[143]

For example, studies show that single mothers with savings are significantly more likely to keep their families out of poverty than are other single mothers, even after correcting for a variety of social and economic factors.[144] Not surprisingly, women with economic assets are far less likely to end up on welfare following divorce.[145] Other studies show that families with assets have greater household stability, are more likely to be involved in their community, demonstrate greater long-term thinking and planning, and provide increased opportunity for their children.[146]

Given the importance of asset ownership, recent news is not good. A report by the Federal Reserve reveals that the "wealth gap" in America may be the largest ever. According to the report, the difference in median net wealth between the wealthiest 10 percent of families and the poorest 20 percent jumped by nearly 70 percent between 1998 and 2001. The gap between whites and minorities grew by 21 percent.[147]

Some observers suggest that the whole definition of poverty should be revised to consider the accumulation of assets or the lack of them. One common definition of "asset poverty" would define people as asset poor if they lack sufficient savings or other assets to survive for three months at the poverty level. By that definition, more than 25 percent of the population would be considered asset poor, roughly double the official poverty rate.[148] Asset poverty is a particular problem for minorities, with as many as 61 percent of African Americans and 70 percent of Hispanics among the asset poor.[149] Indeed, a lack of assets may be the biggest single reason for economic inequality between whites and minorities.[150]

The problems caused by asset poverty are multigenerational. Studies show that the children of asset poor parents are far more likely to be poor themselves, even if income is held constant.[151] Other studies show that intergenerational differences in economic well-being between whites and blacks are far more a function of wealth than of income.[152]

The poor face many barriers to the accumulation of wealth, one of which is welfare itself. Most states still impose a limit on the amount of assets a family may accumulate while remaining eligible for TANF assistance.[153] Those limits are usually quite low ($2,000–$3,000), meaning that families who save, rather than spend, the assistance they receive are penalized.[154] At the same time, poor families who have some assets may be encouraged to spend those assets in order to qualify for government benefits.[155]

Public policy that is truly interested in helping people to escape from poverty should be encouraging rather than discouraging savings and asset accumulation. PRWORA took a small step in this direction by allowing states to assist in funding Individual Development Accounts on behalf of TANF recipients.

Those trust accounts may be set up for individuals who are eligible for assistance under TANF or other state welfare programs by the individuals themselves or their nonprofit sponsors. The individual funds must be used for the purposes of accumulating capital for postsecondary education, for a first-time home purchase, or to start up a business (section 404 (h) 2 (b)). Individuals on the welfare rolls can contribute to IDAs from earned income, from matching funds coming from 501(c)3 nonprofit organizations, or from state or local government agencies. Funds in an IDA will be disregarded for purposes of any asset tests for TANF or other forms of cash assistance.

Approximately 32 states have authorized IDAs as part of their state TANF plans, but only 15 have actually used their TANF funds for IDAs, and only 7 of those have allocated any significant amounts to IDAs.[156] States may also use a portion of the funds they receive for welfare-to-work programs aimed at the hardest to employ. Three states have taken advantage of this provision, as has New York City.[157] States may also have some form of IDA program unrelated to TANF, but again, relatively few of those programs are funded.[158]

The federal government became more directly involved in setting up IDAs under the Assets for Independence Act of 1998.[159] Although $125 million was appropriated for five years, Congress authorized only $10 million per year up to 2000; in 2001 Congress authorized the full $25 million appropriation. As of January 2000, IDA programs existed in approximately 250 communities, and another 100 were in development. More than 5,000 individuals held IDAs at that time, according to the Corporation for Enterprise Development in Washington.[160]

Although experience with IDAs has been limited, there is some evidence that the program does help increase savings rates for low-income individuals. Michael Sherraden's American Dream Demonstration Project is perhaps the largest IDA pilot project, operating in 13 communities in 12 states.[161] Nearly 10,000 people have IDAs under the program, which began in 1997 and works out of community organizations, social service agencies, housing organizations, and credit unions. Nearly 80 percent of participants are women, and half are single mothers. Nearly half (47 percent) are African

American, and 88 percent have incomes below 200 percent of the poverty level—21 percent have incomes equal to less than half the poverty level. Roughly 38 percent are receiving or have received AFDC or TANF benefits. According to a 2000 study examining a cross section of 2,378 program participants, they averaged monthly contributions of $25. While that does not sound like much, it represents a substantial increase in savings, especially for the lowest income participants. Counting matching funds (a 2:1 match under the American Dream Demonstration Project), the average participant was accumulating savings of roughly $900 per year.[162]

IDAs generate other positive benefits as well. According to Sherraden:

- Account participants perform better educationally, and 60 percent say they are more likely to make educational plans for their children because they are saving.
- Eighty-four percent of IDA participants feel more economically secure, and 57 percent say they are more likely to plan for retirement.
- Asset holding significantly improves long-term health and marital stability, even after controlling for income, race, and education. Half of account holders report improved relationships with family members, and one-third believes that holding assets increased their community involvement or made them more respected by their neighbors.
- Perhaps most important, 93 percent of individuals with IDA accounts feel more confident about the future, and 85 percent feel more in control of their lives because they are saving.[163]

Still, problems with IDAs remain. Most important, there is a limit to how much the lowest income individuals are able to save. Given the large proportion of fixed costs in the average household budget, low-income workers simply don't have much discretionary income. Evidence from employer-sponsored savings plans, such as 401(k)s, shows that even with fairly generous matching grants only a minority of those eligible can be induced to participate.[164]

Moreover, under the legislative provisions for IDA accounts, the amounts saved in an IDA can be withdrawn preretirement only for postsecondary education, first-time home purchases, or business start-ups, not really the type of activities pursued by the working poor. It cannot be used for the type of capital purchases ordinarily required by the working poor, for example, white goods, furniture, and job-related occupation certificate programs. As a result, those most actively participating in IDAs tend to be more educated, have more work experience, and have other advantages that make them atypical of the hard-core poor.[165]

Changing the withdrawal rules may help make IDAs more attractive to low-income workers. But the main problem—lack of disposable income—will remain. Fortunately, however, a solution may be available as part of another major economic reform—Social Security.

Most Americans today understand the need for Social Security reform. The national retirement program is facing irreversible economic and demographic pressures that make it unsustainable in its current form. Within just 15 years, the program will begin running a deficit, spending more on benefits than it takes in through taxes. The so-called Social Security Trust Fund represents not a real asset but a claim against future taxes, in essence an IOU.[166] Overall, Social Security is facing an unfunded liability of more than $25 trillion.[167]

Given this looming financial crisis, Social Security reform is definitely coming. It was former president Bill Clinton who identified the limited range of options available to restore Social Security to solvency: (1) raise taxes, (2) cut benefits, or (3) get a higher rate of return through investment in real capital assets.[168] Two of those options, raising taxes and cutting benefits, would substantially—and disproportionately—hurt low-income workers.[169]

However, the third option, private investment, actually provides an opportunity not only to solve Social Security's problems but to give low-income workers an opportunity to save, invest, and accumulate real assets.

The current Social Security system actually acts as a barrier to asset accumulation in two ways. First, workers are currently forced to pay 12.4 percent of their income into Social Security, despite the program's uncertain future and below-market rates of return. This regressive tax falls heaviest on low-income workers, depriving them of the income they need to save and invest privately. As we have seen, lack of discretionary income is one of the biggest barriers that the poor face in trying to save. In addition, the belief that Social Security will provide for their retirement, that the money they are paying into the system is buying them some form of retirement protection, may discourage people from saving on their own.[170] As Martin Feldstein puts it, low-income workers substitute "Social Security wealth" in the form of promised future Social Security benefits for other forms of savings.[171]

Unfortunately, "Social Security wealth" is not real wealth. It is not, in any sense, saved or set aside either by the worker or by the government on the worker's behalf. All the worker really has is the promise that a Congress 20 or 30 years from now will raise taxes on future workers and pay benefits. This is not even a legally binding promise. The Supreme Court has ruled in *Flemming v. Nestor* that workers and beneficiaries have no property or contractual right to Social Security benefits, even after a lifetime of paying Social Security taxes.[172]

Not only does Social Security contribute to asset poverty among current generations, it also helps perpetuate poverty for future generations. Social Security benefits are not inheritable. A worker can pay Social Security taxes for 30 or 40 years, but if that worker dies without children under the age of 18 or a spouse over the age of 65, none of the money paid into the system is passed on to his heirs.[173] As Jagadeesh Gokhale, an economist at the Federal Reserve Bank of Cleveland, has noted, Social Security essentially forces low-income workers to annuitize their wealth, preventing them from making a bequest of that wealth to their heirs.[174]

Moreover, because this forced annuitization applies to a larger portion of the wealth of low-income workers than high-income workers, it turns inheritance into a "disequalizing force," leading to greater inequality of wealth in America. The wealthy are able to bequeath their wealth to their heirs, while the poor cannot. Indeed, Gokhale and Boston University economist Laurence Kotlikoff estimate that Social Security doubles the share of wealth owned by the richest 1 percent of Americans.[175]

Feldstein reaches a similar conclusion. A greater proportion of a high-income worker's wealth is in fungible assets. Since fungible wealth is inheritable, while Social Security wealth is not, this has led to a stable concentration of fungible wealth among a small proportion of the population. Feldstein's work suggests that the concentration of wealth in the United States would be reduced by as much as half if low-income workers were able to substitute real wealth for Social Security wealth.[176]

This is especially significant for African Americans. At every age and every income level, African Americans have shorter life expectancies than do whites. Roughly one of every three African-American men will pay into Social Security but die before he can collect benefits. Think of this, again, in the context of forced annuitization. Jeffrey Brown of the Boston College Center for Retirement Research suggests that a college-educated white male would be best served by converting about 92 percent of his retirement savings into an annuity. On the other hand, an African-American man with less than a high school education should be annuitizing only about 69 percent of his retirement income. Yet, given the likelihood that Social Security will provide all, or nearly all, of his retirement income, he will effectively be forced to annuitize nearly 100 percent of his retirement funds.[177]

Therefore, millions of African Americans are being deprived of the opportunity to pass their wealth on to their children. If, as Darrell Williams of UCLA suggests, inheritance is "the single biggest factor that explains the [black-white] wealth gap," then the current situation becomes a civil rights issue as well as an anti-poverty one.[178]

Fortunately, there are several proposals currently being discussed to allow younger workers to privately invest all or part of their Social Security taxes through individual accounts.[179] Individual accounts would, by definition, belong to the individual. Like any other asset, they would be fully inheritable. They would allow the current generation of low-income workers to accumulate real wealth and to pass that wealth on to their children. In doing so, such accounts would help reduce long-term inequality and provide a host of social benefits.

Given the necessity for Social Security reform, the creation of individual accounts should be high on any anti-poverty agenda.

Conclusion

One government policy after another penalizes the poor. Agricultural price supports drive up the cost of milk, bread, and meat. The poor suffer. Trade barriers prevent the importation and sale of low-cost foreign goods.[180] The poor are hurt. The war on drugs has turned inner-city streets into war zones. And the poor must live in fear.

The largest part of getting out of poverty has to do with personal behavior—finishing school, avoiding pregnancy, getting a job. But few observers would deny that economic growth is an important factor in civil society's fight against poverty.

That means we must end those government policies—high taxes and regulatory excess—that inhibit economic growth and job creation. We must protect capital investment and give people the opportunity to start new businesses. We must reform our failed government school system to encourage competition and choice. We must encourage the poor to save and invest. In part, this means reforming Social Security to allow younger workers to privately invest a portion of their Social Security taxes through individual accounts.

Ending welfare is only the start. Creating prosperity is the rest of the story.

8. Conclusion: The Poverty of Welfare

Despite the government's having spent more than $8.3 trillion over the past 30 years on welfare programs, there are still nearly 33 million Americans living in poverty, including nearly 12 million children.[1]

One does not need statistics to see that the government's War on Poverty has failed. Simply drive through any inner-city slum, or the mountains of Appalachia, or the Mississippi delta area. You can see it in the faces of unemployed youths selling drugs in front of boarded-up storefronts. You can see it in the teenage mothers dropping out of school and raising children who will end up in poverty themselves. And you can see it in the children—abused, neglected, hungry.

We know that welfare is a failure. It has neither reduced poverty nor made the poor self-sufficient. It has torn at the social fabric of the country and been a significant factor in increasing out-of-wedlock births with all of their attendant problems. It has weakened the work ethic and contributed to rising crime rates. Most tragic of all, the pathologies it engenders have been passed on from parent to child, from generation to generation.

We also know that welfare "reform" is not the answer. The Personal Responsibility and Work Opportunity Reconciliation Act was successful in reducing welfare rolls, without increasing poverty or hardship among most former recipients, although we may have reached the limits of success in that regard. However, reform has not been successful in significantly reducing levels of out-of-wedlock births, nor has it enabled people to become truly self-sufficient.

It should be apparent, therefore, that true welfare reform will not be achieved through more small changes to the existing program. It is not a question of spending slightly more or less money or tinkering with the number of hours mandated by work requirements. It is not a question of funding childcare or fine-tuning education and training programs. And it is not a question of government-funded marriage promotion. Congress will undoubtedly debate all of those issues and will ultimately reauthorize welfare reform. But in the end, the poverty that is American welfare will remain largely intact.

We need a new debate, one that moves beyond the current system to focus on first principles. What should be the goal of U.S. welfare policy? In this author's opinion, it should be to create a society where every American can reach his or her full potential, where as few people as possible live in poverty, and where no one must go without the basic necessities of life. So far, government has not demonstrated that it can deliver even the material necessities of life. It certainly cannot deliver the less tangible things that make for a fulfilled and actualized life.

But there is an alternative. As Charles Murray explains: "A return to limited government should not be confused with ending communal efforts to solve social problems. In a free society, a genuine need produces a response. If government is not seen as a legitimate source of intervention, individuals and associations will respond."[2] In the absence of government welfare, civil society can be expected to rise to the occasion, as it always has, to address the needs of the poor in a way that is both more compassionate and more effective.

No government program can provide the degree of flexibility and diversity of private ones. But perhaps more important, voluntary, private charity treats both givers and recipients as individuals, fully respecting their worth and dignity. Unlike coercive government programs, private charity understands that true charity starts with the individual and the individual's choice to give out of his own conscience and virtue.

In many ways, this may actually demand more of us as individuals. We will no longer be able to ignore the poor, content with the notion that somehow government will solve the problem for us. We will have to become involved—we will have to give of ourselves, with genuine compassion.

Civil society will also value the individual worth of the poor, treating them like adults. It will accord them the dignity of holding them responsible for their actions. Poor people are poor—they are not stupid or lazy. They do not need the government to run their lives. They need to be given opportunity and responsibility, and they will respond.

At the same time, we must create the conditions that enable people to become self-sufficient and to lift themselves out of poverty. That means schools that educate and economic conditions that promote job growth and savings. We should encourage the formation of stable families and discourage out-of-wedlock births.

No one should pretend that this will be easy. Decades of the welfare state have undermined civil society and created too much of a sense of dependency and entitlement among the poor. The infrastructure of opportunity, schools and private enterprise, has withered under the weight of government control, taxes, and regulation. We have not arrived at our current situation overnight, and we will not turn it around overnight.

But given the suffering, despair, and, yes, poverty created by the current welfare system, how can we not take up the challenge? We cannot afford to continue a system that subsidizes a culture of long-term dependence. The longer we wait, the longer we tinker with and try to reform the current welfare system, the more people will be drawn into a cycle of poverty, welfare, illegitimacy, crime, and poverty. As in the case of other social pathologies, such as alcoholism or child abuse, we must break the cycle or watch the problem spread through succeeding generations. We should never forget that it is the children growing up in welfare-ravaged neighborhoods who are suffering under our current welfare policies.

We can do better. For the sake of our future, our society, and our children, we *must* do better.

Notes

Chapter 1

1. Barbara Vobejda, "Clinton Signs Welfare Bill Amid Division," *Washington Post*, August 23, 1996.

2. For two different but equally interesting accounts of the infighting behind the development of the Clinton welfare plan, see Ben Wattenberg, *Values Matter Most: How Republicans or Democrats or a Third Party Can Win and Renew the American Way of Life* (New York: Free Press, 1995), pp. 280–90; and R. Kent Weaver, *Ending Welfare As We Know It* (Washington: Brookings Institution, 2000).

3. Jason DeParle, "White House Memo Raises Price Tag of Welfare Plan," *New York Times*, April 5, 1994.

4. Ronald Suskind, "Scaled-Back Welfare-Reform Proposals Are Outlined by Clinton Administration," *Wall Street Journal*, March 3, 1995.

5. See Ed Gillespie and Bob Schellhas, eds., *Contract with America* (Washington: Times Books, 1994), pp. 74–75.

6. For a discussion of block grants and their relationship to welfare reform, see Howard Chernwick, "Fiscal Effects of Block Grants for the Needy: An Interpretation of the Evidence," *Tax and Public Finance* 5, no. 2 (1998): 205–33.

7. Judith Havemann and Barbara Vorbejda, "Advancing Welfare Bill Holds Compromises, Radical Changes," *Washington Post*, July 17, 1996.

8. Barbara Vobejda, "Senate Passes Tough Welfare Reform Measure," *Washington Post*, July 23, 1996.

9. Warren Strobel and Cheryl Wetztein, "Clinton Signs Reform of Welfare into Law; NOW Leads Protest outside of White House," *Washington Times*, August 23, 1996.

10. Deputy Assistant Secretary of Health and Human Services for Human Resources Wendell Primus, Assistant Secretary of Health and Human Services for Planning and Evaluation Peter Edelman, and Assistant Secretary of Health and Human Services for Families and Children Mary Jo Bane. Barbara Vobejda, "HHS Official Resigns in Protest of Decision to Sign Welfare Bill," *Washington Post*, August 18, 1996.

11. Francis X. Clines, "Clinton Signs Bill Cutting Welfare," *New York Times*, August 23, 1996.

12. For a detailed look at the welfare reform debate and Clinton's decision to embrace the issue, see Weaver.

13. Public Law 104-193.

14. Section 401(B) states, "No Individual Entitlement—This part shall not be interpreted to entitle any individual or family to assistance under any State program funded under this part." However, Kent Weaver of the Brookings Institution suggests that in some states an individual entitlement may still exist under state law. See Weaver, p. 328.

15. States may not use TANF funds to substitute for current state spending on teen pregnancy prevention efforts. TANF dollars may be used only to deliver special services over and above the programs generally available to other state residents without cost and regardless of income.

16. Robert Rector, "The Size and Scope of Means-Tested Welfare Spending," Testimony before the House Committee on the Budget, August 1, 2001.

17. Ibid., pp. A5–A6.

18. Ibid., Chart 1.

19. Ibid.

20. Ibid.

21. U.S. Department of Health and Human Services, *2002 TANF Annual Report to Congress,* sec. II, "Trends in Caseloads and Expenditures," March 2002, p. II-7.

22. Vee Burke, "Welfare Reform: TANF Trends and Data," Congressional Research Service, September 10, 2001.

23. Calculated from U.S. Department of Health and Human Services, *2002 TANF Annual Report to Congress,* sec. II, Tables 8–13.

24. White House, Office of the Press Secretary, "Fact Sheet: President Calls for Action on Welfare Reform," January 14, 2003.

25. U.S. Department of Health and Human Services, *2002 TANF Annual Report to Congress,* sec. X, "Characteristics and Financial Circumstances of TANF Recipients," p. X-184.

26. Nicholas Zill and Christine Moore, "The Life Circumstances and Development of Children in Welfare Families: A Profile Based on National Survey Data," Child Trends, Inc., Washington, 1991.

27. U.S. Department of Health and Human Services, *2002 TANF Annual Report to Congress,* sec. X, pp. X-185–86.

28. Ibid., p. X-184.

29. Ibid., p. X-186.

30. Ibid., p. X-191.

31. Ibid., p. X-186.

32. Stephen Dinan, "Immigrant Use of Welfare Increases," *Washington Times,* March 18, 2003.

33. U.S. House of Representatives, Committee on Ways and Means, *1996 Green Book: Background Material and Data on Programs within the Jurisdiction of the Committee on Ways and Means* (Washington: Government Printing Office, 1996), Table 43, p. 692.

34. Robert Rector, "Out of Wedlock Child-Bearing and Paternal Absence: Trends and Social Effects," *Familia et Vita* 2 (1999).

35. U.S. House of Representatives, p. 441.

36. U.S. Department of Health and Human Services, *2002 TANF Annual Report to Congress,* sec. X, p. X-185. For independent estimates of reasons for leaving welfare, see "Summary of State Surveys of Welfare Leavers since Passage of TANF," University of Missouri–Kansas City, Bloch School of Business and Public Administration, www.bloch.umkc.edu/wtw/matleaver.htm, accessed March 26, 2003.

37. U.S. House of Representatives, p. 504.

38. Ron Haskins, Isabel Sawhill, and Kent Weaver, "Welfare Reform Reauthorization: An Overview of Problems and Issues," Brookings Institution, Welfare Reform and Beyond Policy Brief no. 2, January 2001.

39. H.R. 4090, 2002.

40. Amy Goldstein and Juliet Eilperin, "House Passes GOP Welfare Plan," *Washington Post*, February 14, 2003.

41. White House.

42. As noted earlier, the new welfare reform law requires states to continue to spend state funds at a level equal to at least 80 percent of their fiscal year 1994 levels. If states meet the minimum work participation rates, the law also allows them to reduce their minimum spending requirement to 75 percent. In FY98, all states expended enough to meet the 75 percent MOE amount. Thirteen states reported state spending above 80 percent, and one state—West Virginia—exceeded 100 percent. U.S. Department of Health and Human Services, "State Spending under the New Welfare Program," Press release, March 8, 1999.

43. White House.

44. Ibid.

45. Bill Swindell, "Democrats Say Bush Welfare Reauthorization Plan Shortchanges Childcare, Asks Too Much Work," *CQ Today*, March 12, 2003. The main Democratic alternative in the House was sponsored by Rep. Ben Cardin (D-Md.). In the Senate, alternatives include proposals by Evan Bayh (D-Ind.) and Tom Carper (D-Del.), Max Baucus (D-Mont.), and a so-called tripartisan bill sponsored by John Breaux (D-La.), Jim Jeffords (I-Vt.), and Olympia Snowe (R-Maine).

46. Goldstein and Eilperin.

47. Robert Rector, "The Baucus 'WORK' Act of 2002: Repealing Welfare Reform," Heritage Foundation Backgrounder no. 1580, September 3, 2002.

48. Ibid.

49. The continued call for more child-care funding is especially puzzling given the lack of supporting evidence that unavailability of childcare is a significant barrier preventing women from moving off welfare. A 2000 study by Abt Associates found that states have sufficient funds to provide childcare to all families currently receiving TANF and to families leaving TANF for at least one year. Jean Layzer and Ann Collins, "National Study of Child Care for Low-Income Families," Abt Associates, Washington, November 2, 2000. Proponents of increased child-care subsidies frequently cite waiting lists for child-care programs, but those waiting lists are primarily for licensed, institutional daycare facilities. Studies consistently show that those are not the child-care facilities preferred by parents, who more often choose relatives or other informal—and unsubsidized—forms of childcare. Freya L. Sonenstein et al., "Findings from the 1999 Survey of American Families," Urban Institute, May 2002. That is not to say that localized shortages do not occur or to deny that some women may not be able to afford local child-care services. Still, in many cases, those problems may stem from a misdirection of resources, rather than a shortage of resources. It is notable, for example, that some states subsidize childcare for women earning up to 196 percent of the poverty level. For further discussion, see Jennifer Trice, "Is There a Childcare Crisis?" National Center for Policy Analysis Brief Analysis no. 432, March 12, 2003.

50. AAFRC Trust for Philanthropy, "Giving USA 2002," Indianapolis, Ind., June 20, 2002; and Independent Sector, "Giving and Volunteering in the United States 2002: Key Findings," Washington, November 2, 2002.

Chapter 2

1. *Annals of the Congress of the United States, 1789–1824* 4 (1794): 179.

2. Quoted in Charles Warren, *Congress as Santa Claus: Or National Donations and the General Welfare Clause of the Constitution* (1932; reprint, New York: Arno, 1978), pp. 62–63.

3. Michael Katz, *In the Shadow of the Poorhouse: A Social History of Welfare in America* (New York: Basic Books, 1986), pp. 13–14.

4. Ibid., p. 37.

5. Priscilla Clement, "The Philadelphia Welfare Crisis of the 1820s," *Pennsylvania Magazine of History and Biography* 2 (April 1981): 163.

6. Eric Monkkonen, "Nineteenth-Century Institutions: Dealing with the Urban Underclass," in *The Underclass Debate: Views from History*, ed. Michael Katz (Princeton, N.J.: Princeton University Press, 1993), p. 344.

7. Marvin Olasky, *The Tragedy of American Compassion* (Washington: Regnery, 1992), p. 11.

8. Monkkonen, p. 343.

9. Charles Burroughs, "A Discourse Delivered in the Chapel of the New Almshouse in Portsmouth, New Hampshire, December 15, 1834, on the Occasion of Its First Being Opened for Religious Service," in *The Jacksonians on the Poor: Collected Pamphlets*, ed. David Rothman (New York: Arno, 1971), pp. 49–50.

10. Quoted in Katz, *In the Shadow of the Poorhouse*, p. 23.

11. Ibid., p. 341.

12. J. V. N. Yates, "Report of the Secretary of State of New York on the Relief and Resettlement of the Poor," 1824, p. 952, cited in Olasky, p. 45.

13. Alexis de Tocqueville, *Democracy in America*, trans. George Lawrence (New York: Harper Collins, 1969), p. 219.

14. Olasky, pp. 6–24.

15. Clifford Thies, "Is It Time to End Welfare?" *St. Croix Review* 27, no. 5 (October 1994): 36–37.

16. Frederic Almy, "The Relation between Public and Private Charities," *Charities Review* 9 (1899): 65–71.

17. John Haynes Holmes, a Unitarian minister and religious writer, quoted in Paul T. Ringenbach, *Tramps and Reformers, 1873–1916: The Discovery of Unemployment in New York* (Westport, Conn.: Westport, 1973), p. 168.

18. Owen Lovejoy, "The Faith of a Social Worker," *Survey*, May 18, 1920, p. 209.

19. Warren, p. 92.

20. Ann Geddes, *Trends in Relief Expenditures, 1910–1935* (Washington: Government Printing Office, 1937), pp. 8–9.

21. Katz, *In the Shadow of the Poorhouse*, pp. 113–45.

22. Susan Tiffin, *In Whose Best Interest? Child Welfare in the Progressive Era* (Westport, Conn.: Greenwood, 1983), pp. 204–5.

23. Homer Folks, *The Care of Destitute, Neglected, and Delinquent Children* (New York: Macmillan, 1902), pp. 7–11.

24. Tiffin, pp. 205–10.

25. Monkkonen, p. 354.

26. Children's Bureau, *First Annual Report of the Chief*, 1914, p. 2.

27. Ibid., p. 122.

28. Ibid., p. 128–29.

29. *Proceedings of the Conference on Care of Dependent Children* (Washington: Government Printing Office, 1909), p. 721.

30. Olasky, p. 140.

31. Katz, *In the Shadow of the Poorhouse*, p. 128.

32. Sheila Rothman, *Woman's Proper Place: A History of Changing Ideals and Practices, 1870 to the Present* (New York: Basic Books, 1978), pp. 136–40.

33. Olasky, pp. 142–43.

34. Blanche Coll, *Safety Net: Welfare and Social Security, 1929–1979* (New Brunswick, N.J.: Rutgers University Press, 1995), p. 4.

35. Michael Katz, *Improving Poor People: The Welfare State, the Underclass, and Urban Schools as History* (Princeton, N.J.: Princeton University Press, 1995), p. 44.

36. Katz, *In the Shadow of the Poorhouse*, p. 63.

37. Ibid., p. 209.

38. Quoted in Olasky, p. 143.

39. I am particularly indebted to the pioneering work of David Beito in this field. Much of this chapter is drawn from his work, particularly David Beito, *From Mutual Aid to the Welfare State: Fraternal Societies and Social Services, 1890–1967* (Chapel Hill: University of North Carolina Press, 2000); and David Beito, "This Enormous Army: The Mutual Aid Tradition of American Fraternal Societies before the Twentieth Century," in *The Voluntary City: Choice, Community, and Civil Society*, ed. David Beito, Peter Gordon, and Alexander Tabarrok (Ann Arbor: University of Michigan Press, 2002), pp. 182–203.

40. See, for example, Robert Bremmer, *Children and Youth in America: A Documentary History* (Cambridge, Mass.: Harvard University Press, 1971), p. 301.

41. Mutual aid associations have deep historical roots dating back to medieval guilds. For centuries they were a primary source of charity until destroyed by the modern welfare state. For a good discussion of the history of mutual aid, see Otto Fredrich von Gierke, *Community in Historical Perspective*, ed. Anthony Black (Cambridge: Cambridge University Press, 1990).

42. Joe William Trotter, "Blacks in the Urban North: The Underclass Question in Historical Perspective," in *The Underclass Debate: Views from History*, ed. Michael Katz (Princeton N.J.: Princeton University Press, 1993), p. 64.

43. David Beito, "Mutual Aid, State Welfare, and Organized Charity: Fraternal Societies and the Deserving and Undeserving Poor, 1900–1930," *Journal of Policy History* 5, no. 4 (Fall 1993): 419–34.

44. Monroe Work, *Negro Year Book: Annual Encyclopedia of the Negro, 1916–17* (1918), p. 397, cited in Beito, "Mutual Aid, State Welfare, and Organized Charity," pp. 421–22.

45. John Hope Franklin and Alfred Moss Jr., *From Slavery to Freedom: A History of Negro Americans* (1947; reprint, New York: Alfred Knopf, 1988), pp. 93–95.

46. William Muraskin, *Middle-Class Blacks in White Society: Prince Hall Freemasonry in America* (Berkeley: University of California Press, 1975), p. 118, cited in Beito, "Mutual Aid, State Welfare, and Organized Charity," p. 422.

47. David Beito, "Mutual Aid for Social Welfare: The Case for American Fraternal Societies," *Critical Review* 4, no. 4 (Fall 1990): 712–13.

48. Harris Dickinson and Isidore Mantz, "Will the Widow Get Her Money? The Weaknesses in Fraternal Life Insurance and How It May Be Cured," *Everybody's Magazine* 22 (June 1910): 776, cited in Beito, "Mutual Aid for Social Welfare," p. 713.

49. Beito, "Mutual Aid, State Welfare, and Organized Charity," p. 423 n. 43.

50. Beito, "Mutual Aid for Social Welfare," pp. 718–19.

51. Illinois Health Insurance Commission, *Report of the Health Insurance Commission of the State of Illinois*, 1919, p. 22, cited in Beito, "Mutual Aid for Social Welfare," p. 720.

52. Sadie Tanner Mossell, "The Standard of Living among 100 Negro Migrant Families in Philadelphia," *Annals of the American Academy of Political and Social Sciences* 98 (November 1921): 200, cited in Beito, "Mutual Aid for Social Welfare," p. 719.

53. Trotter, pp. 65–66.

54. *History and Manual of the Colored Knights of Pythias* (Nashville: National Baptist Publishing Board, 1917), pp. 448–49, cited in Beito, "Mutual Aid, State Welfare, and Organized Charity," pp. 429–30.

55. Booker T. Washington, "Destitute Colored Children of the South," in *Proceedings of the Conference on the Care of Dependent Children* (Washington: Government Printing Office, 1909), pp. 114–17.

56. Beito, "Mutual Aid for Social Welfare." Mutual aid societies were also important sources of charity in other countries. See, for example, David Green, *Reinventing Civil Society: The Rediscovery of Welfare without Politics* (London: Institute for Economic Affairs, 1993); and David Green and Lawrence Cromwell, *Mutual Aid or Welfare State? Australia's Friendly Societies* (Sydney: George Allen & Unwin, 1984).

57. Beito, "Mutual Aid for Social Welfare," pp. 727–29.

58. David Beito, "The 'Lodge Practice Evil' Reconsidered: Medical Care through Fraternal Societies, 1900–1930," *Journal of Urban History* 23, no. 5 (July 1997): 569–600. Interestingly, the medical establishment in Britain pursued a similar course, attempting to destroy lodge-practice medicine. The ultimate result was the adoption of socialized medicine. David Green, *Working Class Patients and the Medical Establishment: Self-Help in Britain from the Mid-Nineteenth Century to 1948* (New York: St. Martin's, 1985).

59. Coll, pp. 1–3.

60. Josephine Chapin Brown, *Public Relief: 1929–1939* (New York: Octagon Books, 1940), p. 126.

61. James T. Patterson, *The New Deal and the States: Federalism in Transition* (Princeton, N.J.: Princeton University Press, 1969), p. 26.

62. Coll, p. 8.

63. William Bremer, *Depression Winters: New York Social Workers and the New Deal* (Philadelphia: Temple University Press, 1984), p. 65.

64. Quoted in Harry Hopkins, *Spending to Save: The Complete Story of Relief* (New York: W.W. Norton, 1936), p. 77.

65. David Schneider and Albert Deutsch, *The History of Public Welfare in New York State, 1867–1940* (Chicago: University of Chicago Press, 1941), pp. 307–414.

66. Coll, p. 9.

67. Brown, p. 85.

68. Katz, *In the Shadow of the Poorhouse*, p. 216.

69. Quoted in John McClaughry, *A Better Path: From Welfare to Work* (Concord, Vt.: Ethan Allen Institute, 1990), p. 20.

70. Coll, p. 2.

71. Quoted in Katz, *In the Shadow of the Poorhouse*, p. 218.

72. McClaughry, p. 21.

73. Coll, p. 13.

74. Katz, *In the Shadow of the Poorhouse*, pp. 215–16.

75. Warren, pp. 127–28.

76. Coll, pp. 15–16.

77. U.S. Senate Committee on Manufacturers, *Relief for Unemployed Transients: Hearings on S 5121 before a Subcommittee on Manufacturers*, 72d Cong., 2d sess., Legislation passed May 12, 1933.

78. Frances Fox Piven and Richard Cloward, *Regulating the Poor: The Functions of Public Welfare* (New York: Vintage Books, 1971), pp. 72–73.

79. Katz, *Improving Poor People*, p. 53.

80. Katz, *In the Shadow of the Poorhouse*, p. 228.

81. Ibid., p. 229.

82. Olasky, p. 154.

83. Piven and Cloward, p. 75.

84. For a discussion of the legislative history of ADC, see Coll, pp. 51–53.

85. Ibid., p. 104.

86. See Michael Tanner, "Social Security: 60 Years of Tinkering," *World & I*, November 1995, pp. 24–29.

87. Katz, *Improving Poor People*, pp. 55–56.

88. Ibid., p. 56.

89. William Brock, *Welfare, Democracy, and the New Deal* (New York: Cambridge University Press, 1986), p. 358.

90. Executive Office of the President, Office of Policy Development, *An Overview of the Current System*, vol. 1 of *The National Public Assistance System*, supplement 1 to *Up from Dependency: A New National Public Assistance Strategy* (Washington: Government Printing Office, 1986), p. 19.

91. Coll, p. 199.

92. Charles Murray, *Losing Ground: American Social Policy 1950–1980* (New York: Basic Books, 1984), p. 19.

93. Coll, p. 199.

94. See, for example, John Kenneth Galbraith, *The Affluent Society* (Boston: Houghton Mifflin, 1958); and Michael Harrington, *The Other America* (New York: Macmillan, 1962).

95. Quoted in McClaughry, p. 25.

96. Executive Office of the President, p. 19.

97. Coll, p. 241.

98. Executive Office of the President, p. 23.

99. McClaughry, pp. 25–26.

100. Katz, *In the Shadow of the Poorhouse*, p. 265.

101. James T. Patterson, *America's Struggle against Poverty* (Cambridge, Mass.: Harvard University Press, 1989), p. 171.

102. Olasky, p. 182.

103. Daniel Patrick Moynihan, *The Negro Family: The Case for National Action* (Washington: U.S. Department of Labor, 1965).

104. For a discussion of the Moynihan report and the reaction to it, see Lee Rainwater and William Yancey, *The Moynihan Report and the Politics of Controversy* (Cambridge, Mass.: Massachusetts Institute of Technology, 1967).

105. Quoted in Olasky, p. 177.

106. Doris Kearns Goodwin, *Lyndon Johnson and the American Dream* (New York: Harper & Row, 1976), p. 209.

107. Richard Cloward and Frances Fox Piven, *The Politics of Turmoil: Poverty, Race, and the Urban Crisis* (New York: Vintage Books, 1975), pp. 271–83.

108. 392 U.S. 309 (1968).

109. *Anderson v. Burson*, 300 F. Supp. 401 (1968).

110. 394 U.S. 618 (1969).

111. 397 U.S. 354 (1970).

112. Robert Rector and William Lauber, *America's Failed $5.4 Trillion War on Poverty* (Washington: Heritage Foundation, 1995), p. 11.

113. Ibid., pp. 12–13.

114. Richard McKenzie, *What Went Right in the 1980s* (San Francisco: Pacific Research Institute, 1994), Table 8.1, pp. 268–69.

115. General Accounting Office, "Welfare: Issues to Consider in Assessing Proposals for Reform," February 1987.

116. Rector and Lauber, p. 13.

117. Quoted in Bureau of National Affairs, *Daily Labor Report*, March 21, 1988, p. 2.

118. LaDonna Pavetti, "Creating a New Welfare Reality: Early Implementation of the Temporary Assistance for Needy Families Program," *Journal of Social Issues* 56, no. 4 (2000): 609.

119. Peter Hart Research Poll, cited in R. Kent Weaver, *Ending Welfare As We Know It* (Washington: Brookings Institution, 2000), p. 174.

120. Ann Rosewater, "Setting the Baseline: A Report on State Welfare Waivers," U.S. Department of Health and Human Services, Office of Planning and Evaluation, June 1997, sec. I, "Overview."

121. Ibid.

122. General Accounting Office, "Welfare Waivers Implementation: States Work to Change Welfare Culture, Community Involvement, and Service Delivery," GAO/HEHS-96-105, July 1996.

123. Council of Economic Advisers, "The Effects of Welfare Policy and the Economic Expansion on Welfare Caseloads: An Update," August 3, 1999.

124. For all means-tested programs, not just cash assistance programs.

125. Estimated from Rector and Lauber, Table 1; and Robert Rector, "The Size and Scope of Means-Tested Welfare Spending," Testimony before the House Committee on the Budget, August 1, 2001, Charts 1, 4.

126. Estimated from Rector and Lauber, Table 7; Rector, Charts 1, 4; and U.S. Bureau of the Census, *Statistical Abstract of the United States, 2002* (Washington: Government Printing Office, 2002), p. 441. This figure, like the one above for total spending, is for all means-tested programs. But even looking at TANF alone, the per recipient increase has been dramatic, increasing from about $7,000 to more than $17,000 since 1996. White House, Office of the Press Secretary, "Fact Sheet: President Calls for Action on Welfare Reform," January 14, 2003.

127. Paul Peterson and Mark Rom, *Welfare Magnets: A New Case for a National Standard* (Washington: Brookings Institution, 1990), pp. 100–103.

128. Rector, p. 3.

Chapter 3

1. The figure of $8.3 trillion represents total spending on "anti-poverty programs" since 1965, including all means-tested welfare programs, as well as a small number of federal programs targeted to economically distressed communities. Means-tested programs are those programs available only to low-income Americans. For example, food stamps is a means-tested program. Social Security is not. Robert Rector, "The Size and Scope of Means-Tested Welfare Spending," Testimony to the House Committee on the Budget, August 1, 2001, p. 6.

2. U.S. Bureau of the Census, "America's Families and Living Arrangements: March 2000," Current Population Reports, Series P20-537; U.S. Bureau of the Census, "Marital Status and Living Arrangements: March 1984," Series P20-399, p. 8; and U.S. Bureau of the Census, *1960 Census of the Population*, PC (2)-4B, "Persons by Family Characteristics," Tables 1, 19.

3. National Center for Health Statistics, cited in William Bennett, *The Index of Leading Cultural Indicators* (Washington: Empower America, March 1993), p. 16.

4. Centers for Disease Control, "Births: Final Data for 2001," *National Vital Statistics Report* 51, no. 2 (2001): 50, Table 19.

5. Elizabeth Terry-Humen, Jennifer Manlove, and Kristin Moore, "Births outside of Marriage: Myths and Reality," Child Trends Research Brief, Washington, April 2001, p. 2.

6. Charles Murray, *The Underclass Revisited* (Washington: American Enterprise Institute, 1998), pp. 19–20.

7. Federal Interagency Forum on Child and Family Statistics, *America's Children: Key Indicators of Well-Being* (Washington: U.S. Government Printing Office, 2001), p. 6.

8. See, for example, Robert Lerman, "The Impact of Changing U.S. Family Structure on Child Poverty and Income Inequality," *Economica* 63 (1999): 119–39; and Isabel Sawhill, "Families at Risk," in *Setting National Priorities: The 2000 Elections and Beyond*, ed. Henry Aaron and Robert Reischauer (Washington: Brookings Institution, 1999).

9. U.S. Department of Health and Human Services, "Indicators of Welfare Dependence: Annual Report to Congress, 2002," 2002, Table 11, p. II-35. Although this is the most recent study available, some of the data it uses are quite old, some even predating PRWORA. Other studies indicate that the actual welfare usage attributable to out-of-wedlock births could be as high as 40–50 percent. Jodie Levin-Epstein, Christine Grisham, and Myra Batchelder, "Regarding Teen Pregnancy Prevention and Teen Parenting Provisions in the Temporary Assistance for Needy Families (TANF) Block Grant," Center for Law and Social Policy, November 30, 2001.

10. Levin-Epstein, Grisham, and Batchelder.

11. Richard Wertheimer and Kristin Moore, "Childbearing by Teens: Links to Welfare Reform," Urban Institute, New Federalism Issues and Options for the States, Series A, no. A-24, August 1998.

12. Aimie Feijoo, "Teen Pregnancy: The Case for Prevention," Advocates for Youth, Washington, 1999.

13. Robert Rector, "Out of Wedlock Child-Bearing and Paternal Absence: Trends and Social Effects," *Familia et Vita* 2 (1999).

14. Deborah Dawson, "Family Structure and Children's Health and Well-Being: Data from the 1988 Interview Survey on Child Health," Paper presented at the Annual Meeting of the Population Association of America, Toronto, May 12, 1990.

15. M. Anne Hill and June O'Neill, "Underclass Behaviors in the United States: Measurement and Analysis of Determinants," Baruch College, City University of New York, August 1993.

16. Diana Zuckerman, "Welfare Reform in America: A Clash of Politics and Research," *Journal of Social Issues* 56 no. 4 (2000): 587–600.

17. Lee Shumow et al., "Risk and Resilience in the Urban Neighborhood: Predictors of Academic Performance among Low-Income Elementary School Children," *Merrill-Palmer Quarterly* 45 (Fall 1999): 309–31.

18. Sara McLanahan and Julien Teitler, "The Consequences of Father Absence," in *Parenting and Child Development in "Non-Traditional" Families*, ed. Michael Lamb (Mahwah, N.J.: Lawrence Earlbaum Associates, 1998); Deborah Dawson, *Family Structure and Children's Health: United States, 1998*, data from Centers for Disease Control, National Center for Health Statistics, National Health Survey, Series 10-178, June 1991; Maybeth Shinn, "Father Absence and Children's Cognitive Development," *Psychological Bulletin* 85, no. 2 (1978): 295–324; and Sheila Krein and Andrea Beller,

"Educational Attainment of Children from Single-Parent Families: Differences by Exposure, Gender, and Race," *Demography* 25 (May 1988): 288.

19. Dawson, *Family Structure and Children's Health.*

20. Nicholas Davidson, "The Daddy Dearth," *Policy Review*, no. 51 (Winter 1990): 43.

21. Jocelyn Brown et al. "A Longitudinal Analysis of Risk Factors for Child Maltreatment: Findings of a 17-Year Prospective Study of Officially Recorded and Self-Reported Child Abuse and Neglect," *Journal of Child Abuse and Neglect* 22 (1998): 1065–78.

22. Irwin Garfinkel and Sara McLanahan, *Single Mothers and Their Children: A New American Dilemma* (Washington: Urban Institute Press, 1986), p. 31.

23. Ibid.

24. In fact, a majority of children from single-parent families grow up without significant problems. Kristin Moore, Susan Jekielik, and Carol Emig, "Marriage from a Child's Perspective: How Does Family Structure Affect Children and What Can We Do about It?" *Child Trends*, June 2002.

25. Daniel Patrick Moynihan, *Family and Nation: The Godkin Lectures* (New York: Harcourt Brace Jovanovich, 1985), p. 8.

26. Charles Murray, "Restore Personal Responsibility," *Future of Welfare* 15, no. 12 (December 1992): 12.

27. Maine, Minnesota, North Dakota, as well as Washington, D.C. Kaiser Family Foundation, "Medicaid Coverage of Family Planning Services: Results of a National Survey," October 31, 2001, pp. 2, 34–35.

28. For a fairly detailed survey of the research leading up to welfare reform in 1996, see Robert Moffitt, "The Effect of Welfare on Marriage and Fertility: What Do We Know and What Do We Need to Know?" University of Wisconsin, Institute for Research on Poverty, Discussion Paper no. 1153–97, December 1997. For more recent discussions of the issue, see Jeff Groger and Stephen Bronars, "The Effect of Welfare Payments on Marriage and Fertility Behavior of Unwed Mothers: Results from a Twins Experiment," National Bureau of Economic Research Working Paper no. 6047, May 1997; Marianne Bitler et al., "The Impact of Welfare Reform on Marriage and Divorce," Federal Reserve Bank of Atlanta Discussion Paper no. 2002-9, May 2002; Francine Blau, Lawrence Kahn, and Jane Waldfogel, "The Impact of Welfare Benefits on Single Motherhood and Headship of Young Women: Evidence from the Census," National Bureau of Economic Research Working Paper no. 9338, November 2002; and Hilary Williamson Hoynes, "Does Welfare Play Any Role in Female Headship Decisions?" *Journal of Public Economics* 26, no 3 (1991): 545–61.

29. Ron Haskins, "Does Welfare Encourage Illegitimacy? The Case Just Closed. The Answer Is Yes," American Enterprise Institute, January 1996.

30. David Ellwood and Mary Jo Bane, "The Impact of AFDC on Family Structure and Living Arrangements," *Research in Labor Economics* 6 (1985): 137–207.

31. Charles Murray notes that a study of total welfare packages in 13 locations across the country by the General Accounting Office found that, taking into account local economies and the combined value of all benefits, there was little actual variation in the value of the benefits package. For example, the welfare package in San Francisco provided 66 percent of the median household income, while in New Orleans the package provided 65 percent of the median household income. Charles Murray, "Does Welfare Bring More Babies?" *Public Interest* 115 (Spring 1994): 17–30.

32. Michael Tanner, Stephen Moore, and David Hartman, "The Work vs. Welfare Trade-Off: An Analysis of the Total Level of Welfare Benefits by State," Cato Institute Policy Analysis no. 240, September 19, 1995.

33. Out-of-wedlock births have always been higher among African Americans than among whites at all income and education levels. For example, the out-of-wedlock birthrate among college-educated black women is seven times the rate among college-educated white women. Dinesh D'Souza, *The End of Racism* (New York: Free Press, 1995), p. 515, citing data from the Bureau of Health Statistics. The reasons have been subject to much debate. Robert Park, E. Franklin Frazier, Kenneth Stampp, and others point out that under slavery the only distinction between legitimate and illegitimate children was social, not legal. See, for example, E. Franklin Frazier, *The Negro Family in the United States* (New York: Free Press, 1979); Robert Park, *Race and Culture* (Glencoe, Ill.: Free Press, 1950); and Herbert Gutman, *The Black Family in Slavery and Freedom* (New York: Pantheon Books, 1976). W. E. B. DuBois observed that in 1900, a few decades after emancipation, the black out-of-wedlock birthrate was nearly 25 percent, compared to 2 percent among whites, and strongly argued that this represented a holdover of slave child-bearing patterns. W. E. B. DuBois, *The Negro American Family* (1908; reprint Cambridge, Mass.: MIT Press, 1970), pp. 151–52.

Recently some scholars have suggested additional reasons for the phenomenon, including black cultural traditions dating back to the custom of child fostering in Africa. Andrew Miller, "Social Science, Social Policy, and the Heritage of African-American Families," in *The Underclass Debate: Views from History*, ed. Michael Katz (Princeton, N.J.: Princeton University Press, 1993), pp. 252–93. Still others place the emphasis on the lack of economic opportunities for black men throughout much of this country's history. See, for example, William Julius Wilson, *The Truly Disadvantaged: The Inner City, the Underclass, and Public Policy* (Chicago: University of Chicago Press, 1987).

34. Murray, "Does Welfare Bring More Babies?"

35. Douglas Allen, "Welfare and the Family: The Canadian Experience," *Journal of Labor Economics* 7, no. 1 (January 1993): 202.

36. Charles Murray, *The Emerging British Underclass* (London: Institute for Economic Affairs, 1990).

37. P. Swan and Mikhail Bernstam, "Brides of the State," *IPA Review* 41 (May–July 1987): 22–25.

38. Marvin Olasky, *The Tragedy of American Compassion* (Washington: Regnery, 1992), p. 186.

39. Shelley Lundberg and Robert Plotnick, "Effects of State Welfare, Abortion, and Family Planning Policies on Premarital Childbearing among White Adolescents," *Family Planning Perspectives* 22, no. 6 (1990): 246–51.

40. Robert Hutchins, "Welfare, Remarriage and Marital Search," *American Economic Review* 69 (June 1989): 369–79.

41. Irwin Garfinkel and Sara McLanahan, *Single Mothers and Their Children* (Washington: Urban Institute, 1986); Sheldon Danziger et al., "Work and Welfare as Determinants of Female Poverty and Household Headship," *Quarterly Journal of Economics* 97 (August 1982): 519–34; and Robert Moffitt, "Incentive Effects of the U.S. Welfare System: A Review," *Journal of Economic Literature* 30, no. 1 (March 1992): 1–61.

42. Lee Rainwater, professor emeritus of sociology, Harvard University, Testimony to Senate Committee on Finance, October 31, 1993.

43. Charles Murray, "Family Formation," in *The New World of Welfare*, ed. Rebecca Blank and Ron Haskins (Washington: Brookings Institution, 2001), pp. 137–68.

44. U.S. Bureau of the Census, "Income in 1960 of Families and Persons in the United States," Current Population Reports, Series P60-80, 1961, p. 26.

45. U.S. Bureau of the Census, "Money Incomes in the United States: 2001," Current Population Reports, Series P60-80, 2002, p. 10.

46. See, for example, Leonard Goodwin, *Causes and Cures of Welfare* (Lexington, Mass.: Lexington Books, 1983); and Marta Tienda and Haya Stier, "Joblessness and Shiftlessness: Labor Force Activity in Chicago's Inner-City," in *The Urban Underclass*, ed. Christopher Jencks and Paul Peterson (Washington: Brookings Institution, 1991), pp. 135–54.

47. U.S. House of Representatives, Committee on Ways and Means, *1996 Green Book: Background Material and Data on Programs within the Jurisdiction of the Committee on Ways and Means* (Washington: Government Printing office, 1996), Table 1028, p. 404.

48. Several studies have shown that welfare acts as a disincentive to work. For a good review of the literature, see Sheldon Danziger, Robert Haveman, and Robert Plotnick, "How Transfers Affect Work, Savings, and Income Distribution," *Journal of Economic Literature* 19, no. 3 (September 1981): 975–1028; and Robert Moffitt, "Incentive Effects of the U.S. Welfare System: A Review," *Journal of Economic Literature* 30, no. 1 (March 1992): 1–61.

49. See, for example, Mary Jo Bane and David Ellwood, "The Dynamics of Dependence: The Routes to Self-Sufficiency," Report prepared for U.S. Department of Health and Human Services, assistant secretary for planning and evaluation, Office of Evaluation and Technical Analysis, Office of Income Security Policy, 1983; Greg Duncan, *Years of Poverty, Years of Plenty* (Ann Arbor: University of Michigan, Institute for Social Research, 1984); David Ellwood, "Targeting Would-Be Long-Term Recipients of AFDC," Mathematica Policy Research, Princeton, N.J., 1986; June O'Neill, Laurie Bassi, and Douglas Wolf, "The Duration of Welfare Spells," *Review of Economics and Statistics* 69 (1987): 241–49; and Robert Plotnick, "Turnover in AFDC Population: An Event History Analysis," *Journal of Human Resources* 18 (1983): 65–81.

50. Peter Brandon, "Jobs Taken by Mothers Moving from Welfare to Work and the Effects of Minimum Wages on This Transition," Employment Policies Institute, Washington, February 1995.

51. Governor's Commission on the Los Angeles Riots, *Violence in the City—An End or a Beginning?* (Los Angeles: state of California, 1966), p. 72.

52. Gregory Christiansen and Walter Williams, "Welfare Family Cohesiveness and Out-of-Wedlock Births," in *The American Family and the State* (San Francisco: Pacific Research Institute for Public Policy, 1986), p. 398.

53. Richard Vedder, Lowell Gallaway, and Robert Lawson, "Why People Work: An Examination of Interstate Variation in Labor Force Participation," *Journal of Labor Research* 12, no. 1 (Winter 1991): 47–59.

54. Sheldon Danziger, Robert Haveman, and Robert Plotnick, "How Income Transfers Affect Work, Savings, and Income Distribution: A Critical Review," *Journal of Economic Literature* 19 (September 1981): 996.

55. Moffitt, p. 17.

56. Richard Layte and Tim Callan, "Unemployment, Welfare Benefits, and the Incentive to Work," *Economic and Social Review* 32, no. 2 (July 2001): 103–29.

57. Terry Johnson, Daniel Klepinger, and Fred Dong, "Preliminary Evidence from the Oregon Welfare Reform Demonstration," unpublished paper, June 1990, cited in David Card, Philip Robins, and Winston Lin, "Would Financial Incentives for Leaving Welfare Lead Some People to Stay on Welfare Longer? An Experimental Evaluation of 'Entry Effects' in the Self-Sufficiency Project," National Bureau of Economic Research Working Paper no. 6449, March 1998.

58. Ibid.

59. Hill and O'Neill, pp. 82–83.

60. Jagadeesh Gokhale, Laurence Kotlikoff, and Alexi Sluchynsky, "Does It Pay to Work?" National Center for Policy Analysis Policy Research Report no. 258, March 2003, p. 16.

61. Ibid., p. 86.

62. Ken Auletta, *The Underclass* (New York: Random House, 1982).

63. Tienda and Stier, pp. 141–43.

64. John L. Wright, Marge Green, and Leroy Warren Jr., "An Assessment of Crime in Maryland Today," Maryland State Conference of Branches, NAACP, Annapolis, February 1994.

65. Mary Corcoran et al., "The Association between Men's Economic Status and Their Family and Community Origins," *Journal of Human Resources* 27, no. 4 (Fall 1992): 575–601.

66. Lao-Tzu, *Tao Te Ching,* trans. Stephen Mitchell (New York: Harper & Row, 1988), p. 57.

67. Wright, Green, and Warren, p. 7.

68. Hill and O'Neill, p. 73.

69. Douglas Smith and G. Roger Jarjoura, "Social Structure and Criminal Victimization," *Journal of Research in Crime and Delinquency* 25, no. 1 (February 1988): 27–52.

70. Barbara Dafoe Whitehead, "Dan Quayle Was Right," *Atlantic Monthly,* April 1993, p. 50

71. Cited in Tom Bethell, "They Had a Dream: The Politics of Welfare Reform," *National Review,* August 23, 1993, p. 33.

72. Robert Lerman, "Unwed Fathers: Who Are They?" *American Enterprise,* September–October 1993, pp. 32–37.

73. David Blankenhorn, *Fatherless America: Confronting Our Most Urgent Social Problem* (New York: Basic Books, 1995).

74. Alex Kotlowitz, *There Are No Children Here: The Story of Two Boys Growing Up in the Other America* (New York: Anchor Books, 1992).

75. Laurence Lynn Jr. and Michael McGeary, eds., *Inner-City Poverty in the United States* (Washington: National Academy Press, 1990), p. 26.

76. Daniel P. Moynihan, *Coping: Essays on the Practice of Government* (New York: Random House, 1961), p. 76.

77. Greg Duncan and Martha Hill, "Welfare Dependence within and across Generations," *Science,* January 29, 1988, pp. 467–71.

78. Martha Hill and Michael Ponza, "Does Welfare Beget Dependency?" Institute for Social Research, Ann Arbor, Mich., 1984.

79. Mwangi S. Kimenyi, "Rational Choice, Culture of Poverty, and the Intergenerational Transmission of Welfare Dependency," *Southern Economic Journal* 57, no. 4 (April 1991): 947–60.

80. William Fox et al., "Aid to Families with Dependent Children: 1995 Case Characteristics Study," University of Tennessee, Center for Business and Economic Research, December 1995, pp. 206–9.

81. Cited in Gertrude Himmelfarb, "True Charity: Lessons from Victorian England," in *Transforming Welfare: The Revival of American Charity,* ed. Jeffrey Sikkenga (Grand Rapids, Mich.: Acton Institute, 1996), p. 31.

Chapter 4

1. Katha Pollitt, "What We Know," *New Republic*, August 12, 1996, p. 3.

2. Sheila Zedlewski, "Potential Effects of Congressional Welfare Reform Legislation on Family Incomes," Urban Institute, 1996.

3. Daniel Lichter and Martha Crowley, "Poverty in America: Beyond Welfare Reform," Population Reference Bureau, 2002 (citing Census Bureau data), p. 5.

4. U.S. Bureau of the Census, "Poverty Status of People by Age, Race, and Hispanic Origin: 1959–2000," www.census.gov/hhes/poverty/histpov/histpov3.html.

5. Robert Rector and Sarah Youssef, *The Determinants of Welfare Caseload Decline* (Washington: Heritage Foundation, 1999), p. 1.

6. Committee for Economic Development, "Welfare Reform and Beyond: Making Work Work," Washington, 2000, p. 23. For the most part these numbers do not show the results of the recent economic slowdown. Presumably there will be some increase when future numbers are released, but the poverty rates should remain far below prereform levels.

7. Jason Fields and Lynne Casper, "America's Families and Living Arrangements," U.S. Bureau of the Census, Current Population Reports P20-537, June 2000; and U.S. Bureau of the Census, "Poverty Status of Families by Type of Family, Presence of Related Children, Race, and Hispanic Origin: 1959–2000," www.census.gov/hhes/poverty/histpov/histpov4.html.

8. Arloc Sherman et al., "Welfare to What? Early Findings on Family Hardship and Well-Being," Children's Defense Fund and National Coalition for the Homeless, Washington, December 1998.

9. U.S. Conference of Mayors, "Status Report on Hunger and Homelessness in American Cities," Washington, 2000.

10. Chris Schafer, Joel Emes, and Jason Clemens, "Surveying US and Canadian Welfare Reform," Fraser Institute Critical Issues Bulletin, August 2001.

11. Committee for Economic Development, p. 26.

12. Pamela Loprest, "Families Who Left Welfare: Who Are They and What Are They Doing?" Urban Institute, Washington, 1999, chart 3.

13. Joseph Dalaker, *Poverty in the United States, 1998* (Washington: Government Printing Office, 1999), p. 17.

14. June O'Neill and Anne Hill, "Gaining Ground? Measuring the Impact of Welfare Reform on Welfare and Work," Manhattan Institute, Center for Civic Innovation, New York, July 2001.

15. Robert Rector, "Welfare Reform and the Decline of Dependence," Testimony before the Subcommittee on Post-Secondary Education, Training, and Life-Long Learning of the House Committee on Education and Workforce, September 9, 1999.

16. Sheldon Danziger et al., "W2: Converting to Wisconsin Works: Where Did Families Go When WAFDC Ended in Milwaukee?" Hudson Institute and Mathematica Policy Research, Indianapolis, 1999.

17. Lichter and Crowley, p. 8.

18. Ibid.

19. Megan DeBell, Hsiao-Ye Yi, and Heidi Hartmann, *Single Mothers, Jobs, and Welfare: What the Data Tell Us* (Washington: Institute for Women's Policy Research, 1997), p. 7.

20. National Campaign for Jobs and Income Support, "Leaving Welfare, Left Behind: Employment Status, Income, and Well-Being of Former TANF Recipients," Washington, September 13, 2001, p. 4.

21. Loprest.

22. U.S. Department of Health and Human Services, Office of the Assistant Secretary for Planning and Evaluation, "'Leavers' and Diversion Studies: Summary of Research on Welfare Outcomes Funded by ASPE," 1999, aspe.hhs.gov/hsp/leavers99/ombsum.htm.

23. For example, the Committee for Economic Development reports that approximately 23 percent of those leaving welfare for work initially receive health insurance benefits through their employers. After one year that rises slightly to approximately 25 percent; after three years, it has risen to 38 percent. Committee for Economic Development, p. 5. Cynthia Miller of the Manpower Demonstration Research Corporation provides slightly more optimistic numbers. Approximately half of former recipients are offered health insurance by their employers, but because of the cost of employee contributions, etc., only about one-third accept it. Cynthia Miller, "Leavers, Stayers, and Cyclers: An Analysis of the Welfare Caseload," Manpower Demonstration Research Corporation, November 2002.

24. Richard Vedder and Lowell Gallaway, "The War on the Poor," Institute for Policy Innovation, Lewisville, Tex., June 1992.

25. Cynthia Fagnoni, Statement before the Subcommittee on Human Resources of the House Committee on Ways and Means, May 27, 1999, in General Accounting Office, "Welfare Reform: States' Implementation Progress and Information on Former Recipients," GAO/T-HEHS-99-116, May 1999, p. 7.

26. Miller.

27. See Lisa Oliphant, "Four Years of Welfare Reform: A Progress Report," Cato Institute Policy Analysis no. 378, August 22, 2000.

28. Sheldon Danziger, "Welfare Reform: A Fix for All Seasons?" *Milken Institute Review* (Fall 2002): 29.

29. 1996 dollars. Cited in ibid., p. 29. Ellwood may well have been underestimating the total value of welfare benefits. See Michael Tanner, Stephen Moore, and David Hartman, "The Work vs. Welfare Trade-Off: An Analysis of the Total Level of Welfare Benefits by State," Cato Institute Policy Analysis no. 240, September 19, 1995. See also Michael Tanner and Naomi Lopez, "The Value of Welfare: Cato vs. the CBPP," Cato Institute Briefing Paper no. 27, June 12, 1996.

30. Sandra Danziger, "Women's Employment Survey," University of Michigan Program on Poverty and Social Welfare, 2001.

31. Loprest, p. 14.

32. General Accounting Office, *Welfare Reform: Information on Former Recipients' Status* (Washington: Government Printing Office, 1999), p. 18.

33. Gregory Acs, Pamela Loprest, and Tracy Roberts, "Final Synthesis Report of Findings from ASPE Leavers Grants," Urban Institute, Washington, November 27, 2001.

34. State of Wisconsin, Department of Workforce Development, "Survey of Those Leaving AFDC or W2, January to March, 1998, Preliminary Report," January 13, 1999, p. 10.

35. Sara McLanahan, Irwin Garfinkel, and Ronald Mincy, "Fragile Families, Welfare Reform, and Marriage," Brookings Institution Policy Brief no. 10, November 2001.

36. For example, a study of welfare recipients in Chicago in 1990 found that welfare payments accounted for only about 57 percent of recipients' income. The remainder came from gifts from family, friends, and absent fathers; unreported work; other

government programs; and illegal activities. Christopher Jencks and Kathryn Edin, "The Real Welfare Problem," *American Prospect* (Spring 1990).

37. David Stoesz, *A Poverty of Imagination: Bootstrap Capitalism, Sequel to Welfare Reform* (Madison: University of Wisconsin Press, 2000).

38. Quoted in Kathy Kiely and William Welch, "Welfare Reform's Success Isn't Unquestioned," *USA Today*, September 22, 2001.

39. Diana Zuckerman, "Welfare Reform: Research Findings Contradict the Aura of Success," National Center for Policy Research for Women and Families, October 1999.

40. Arloc Sherman, "Extreme Child Poverty Rises Sharply in 1997," Children's Defense Fund, 1999.

41. Committee for Economic Development, p. 23.

42. Rebecca Blank and Robert Schoeni, "Changes in the Distribution of Children's Families Income over the 1990s," Paper prepared for the American Economics Association, January 2003.

43. Nicholas Zill et al., "The Life Circumstances and Development of Children in Welfare Families: A Profile Based on National Survey Data," Child Trends, Inc., Washington, 1991.

44. U.S. Department of Health and Human Services, Administration for Children and Families, "U.S. Welfare Caseloads Information," www.acf.dhhs.gov/news/stats/newstat2.shtml. However, looking solely at federal caseload numbers may overstate the actual caseload reductions. Many states, most notably California and New York, continue to use their own funds to provide cash assistance to tens of thousands of families. In California, for example, nearly 50,000 families are receiving state-funded welfare benefits, a population greater than the entire caseload in many states. Trends in this regard are difficult to track since HHS only recently required states to provide information on separate state programs. General Accounting Office, "Welfare Reform: With TANF Flexibility, States Vary in How They Implement Work Requirements and Time Limits," GAO-02-770, July 2002, p. 8.

45. U.S. Department of Health and Human Services, "Average Monthly Families and Recipients for Calendar Years 1936–2001," May 2002, www.dcf.dhhs.gov/news/stats/3697.htm.

46. O'Neill and Hill, p. 18.

47. Council of Economic Advisers, "The Effects of Welfare Policy and the Economic Expansion on Welfare Caseloads: An Update," August 3, 1999, Executive Summary.

48. Rector and Youssef, p. 6.

49. Michael New, "Welfare Reform That Works: Explaining the Welfare Caseload Decline, 1996–2000," Cato Institute Policy Analysis no. 435, May 7, 2002, pp. 7–8.

50. Douglas Besharov, "The Past and Future of Welfare Reform," *Public Interest* 150 (Winter 2003).

51. Ibid.

52. General Accounting Office, "Welfare Reform: State Sanction Policies and Number of Families Affected," March 2000, pp. 44–47.

53. Rector and Youssef.

54. New, pp. 6–7.

55. Ibid., p. 6.

56. U.S. Department of Health and Human Services, "Characteristics and Financial Circumstances of TANF Recipients, FY1998," www.acf.dhhs.gov/programs/opre/characteristics/fy98.sum.htm.

57. Jan Kaplan, "The Use of Sanctions under TANF," Welfare Information Network, April 1999.

58. Dan Bloom, "The Cross-State Study of Time-Limited Welfare, Welfare Time-Limits: An Interim Report Card," New York, Manpower Demonstration Research Corporation, April 1999.

59. Sandra Danziger et al., "Barriers to the Employment of Welfare Recipients," Institute for Research on Poverty, Discussion Paper no. 1193–99, June 1999, p. 7.

60. William Niskanen, "Welfare and the Culture of Poverty," *Cato Journal* 16, no. 1 (Spring–Summer 1996).

61. Charles Murray, *Losing Ground: American Social Policy 1950–1980* (New York: Basic Books, 1984).

62. New, p. 8.

63. Besharov, p. 18.

64. See, for example, Marta Tiendra and Haya Stier, "Joblessness and Shiftlessness: Labor Force Activity in Chicago's Inner-City," in *The Urban Underclass*, ed. Christopher Jencks and Paul Peterson (Washington: Brookings Institution, 1991), pp. 135–54.

65. According to a survey in the mid-1990s, only about 35 percent of recipients had applied for a job within the previous three months. U.S. House of Representatives, Committee on Ways and Means, *1996 Green Book: Background Material and Data on Programs within the Jurisdiction of the Committee on Ways and Means* (Washington: Government Printing office, 1996), p. 404.

66. Tanner, Moore, and Hartman; and Tanner and Lopez.

67. Blank and Schoeni.

68. U.S. Department of Health and Human Services, "Characteristics and Financial Circumstances of TANF Recipients, FY 1998."

69. U.S. Department of Health and Human Services, *2001 TANF Annual Report to Congress*, sec. II, "Trends in Caseloads and Expenditures," Table 2.4, pp. II-34–35.

70. U.S. Department of Health and Human Services, "TANF Total Number of Families and Recipients," November 2002, www.acf.dhhs.gov/news/stats/jan_mar2002_rev.htm; and U.S. Department of Health and Human Services, *2001 TANF Annual Report to Congress*. More recent, but incomplete, data indicate that as many as 36 states have now seen increases in the number of recipients. See Danzinger, "Welfare Reform," p. 27.

71. David Ellwood, "Targeting Would-Be Long-Term Recipients of AFDC," Mathamatica Policy Research, Princeton, N.J., 1986.

72. Sandra Danziger et al.

73. Frank Bennici, "Final Report: Managing Expectations for Welfare to Work: The Realities of Serving Those Hardest to Serve," National Center on Education and the Economy, Rochester, N.Y., August 1999, p. 1. See also Loprest.

74. Charles Murray, *The Underclass Revisited* (Washington: American Enterprise Institute, 1999).

75. Katherine Allen and Maria Kirby, "Unfinished Business: Why Cities Matter to Welfare Reform," Brookings Institution, July 2000.

76. Sandra Danziger et al.

77. Ibid.

78. Amy Johnson and Alicia Meckstroth, "Ancillary Services to Support Welfare to Work: Multiple Barriers," U.S. Department of Health and Human Services, Office of the Assistant Secretary for Planning and Evaluation, June 22, 1998, p 1.

79. Sheila Zedlewski, "Work-Related Activities and Limitations of Current Welfare Recipients," Urban Institute, Assessing the New Federalism Program, Discussion Paper, November 1999, pp. 11–12.

80. U.S. Department of Health and Human Services, "TANF Report to Congress," 1998, introduction, pp. 2–5, www.acf.dhhs.gov/news/welfare/congress/tanfintr.htm.

81. State of Wisconsin, Department of Workforce Management.

82. Ibid.

83. Ellen Scott, Andrew London, and Kathryn Edin, "Looking to the Future: Welfare-Reliant Women Talk about Their Job Aspirations in the Context of Welfare Reform," *Journal of Social Issues* 56, no. 4 (2000): 727–46.

84. Ibid., p. 731

85. P. Lindsay Chase-Lansdale et al., "Mothers' Transition from Welfare to Work and the Well-Being of Preschoolers and Adolescents," *Science* 299 (March 7, 2003): 1548–52.

86. General Accounting Office, "Welfare Reform: States' Implementation Progress and Information on Former Recipients," p. 11.

87. Martha Zaslow et al., "Welfare Reform and Children: Possible Implications," Urban Institute, Assessing the New Federalism Program, Issues and Options for the States no. A-26, September 1998, p. 5.

88. Kristin Shook, "Assessing the Consequences of Welfare Reform for Child Welfare," Joint Center for Poverty Research, *Poverty Research News* 2, no 1 (Winter 1998): 5.

89. Kaplan, p. 7.

90. Jane Kitzner et al., "Enhancing the Well-Being of Young Children and Families in the Context of Welfare Reform: Lessons from Early Childhood, TANF, and Family Support Programs," U.S. Department of Health and Human Services, June 1999, p. 33.

91. Judith Havemann and Barbara Vobejda, "Children of Welfare Parents Feel Reform's Help, Hurt," *Washington Post*, December 27, 1998.

92. Mwangi Kimenyi, "Rational Choice, Culture of Poverty, and the Intergenerational Transmission of Welfare-Dependence," *Southern Economic Journal* 57 (1991).

93. Mary Corcoran et al, "The Association between Men's Economic Status and Their Community Origins," *Journal of Human Resources* (Fall 1992): 575–601.

94. Martha Zaslow et al., "Maternal Employment and Measures of Children's Health Development among Families with Some History of Welfare Receipt," *Research in the Sociology of Work* 7 (1999).

95. Anne Hill and June O'Neill, "Family Endowments and the Achievements of Young Children with Special Reference to the Underclass," *Journal of Human Resources* (Fall 1994): 1090–91.

96. Sandra Hofferth et al., "Achievement and Behavior among Children of Welfare Recipients, Welfare Leavers, and Low-Income Single Mothers," *Journal of Social Issues* 56, no. 4 (2000): 747–74.

97. K. A. Moore and A. Driscoll, "Low-Wage Maternal Employment and Outcomes for Children: A Study," *Future of Children* 7, no. 1 (1997): 122–27.

98. Hofferth et al.

99. Ibid.

100. Pamela Morris et al., "How Welfare and Work Policies Affect Children: A Synthesis of Research," Manpower Demonstration Research Corporation, 2001.

101. Quoted in Kiely and Welch.

102. Personal Responsibility and Work Opportunity Reconciliation Act of 1996, Title I, Part A, sec. 401.

103. See, for example, Charles Murray, "Does Welfare Bring More Babies?" *Public Interest* 115 (1994): 17–30. In addition, see Charles Murray, "Family Formation Issues and Welfare Reform," in *The New World of Welfare*, ed. Rebecca Blank and Ron Haskins (Washington: Brookings Institution, 2001).

104. The legislation did appropriate $50 million for abstinence education. In addition, it directed the U.S. Department of Health and Human Services to develop a national strategy to prevent teen pregnancy. Specifically HHS is required to report to Congress on its efforts to develop a comprehensive approach to combating teen pregnancy and its efforts to assist state initiatives in this regard.

105. Cited in Paul Offner, "Reducing Non-Marital Births," Brookings Institution Welfare Reform & Beyond, Policy Brief no. 5, August 2001.

106. Joyce Martin et al., "Births: Final Data for 2001," Centers for Disease Control and Prevention, National Center for Health Statistics, *National Vital Statistics Report* 51, no. 2 (December 18, 2002).

107. Rebecca Blank, "Evaluating Welfare Reform in the United States," *Journal of Economic Literature* 40, (December 2002): 1154–55.

108. Allen Dupree and Wendell Primus, "Declining Share of Children Living with Single Mothers in the Late 1990s," Center for Budget and Policy Priorities, 2001.

109. Martin et al.

110. Richard Wertheimer and Kristen Moore, "Childbearing by Teens: Links to Welfare Reform," Urban Institute, Assessing the New Federalism Project, Issues and Options for the States no. A-24, 1999, p. 1.

111. Cheryl Wetzstein, "Teen Birthrates Drop in U.S. As Unwed Mother Totals Rise," *Washington Times*, January 18, 2000.

112. Ibid.

113. Ibid.

114. Murray, "Family Formation Issues and Welfare Reform," p. 157.

115. U.S. Department of Health and Human Services, *2001 TANF Annual Report to Congress*, sec. VIII, "Out-of-Wedlock Pregnancies and Births," Table 8.7, pp. 166–67.

116. Anna Lovejoy and Shayna Strom, "State Teen Pregnancy and Abstinence Education Efforts: Survey Results on the Use of TANF and Title V Funds," American Public Human Services Association, July 1999.

117. Marianne Bitler, Jonah Gelbach, and Hilary Hoynes, "The Impact of Welfare Reform on Living Arrangements," unpublished manuscript, University of California, Davis, cited in Blank, "Evaluating Welfare Reform in the United States," p. 1155; John Fitzgerald and David Ribar, "The Impact of Welfare Waivers on Female Headship Decisions," Northwestern University Joint Center on Poverty Research Working Paper no. 247, 2001; and Robert Schoeni and Rebecca Blank, "What Has Welfare Reform Accomplished? Impacts on Welfare Participation, Employment, Income, and Family Structure," National Bureau of Economic Research Working paper no. 7627, 2000.

118. Isabel Sawhill, "What Can Be Done to Reduce Teen Pregnancy and Out-of-Wedlock Births?" Brookings Institution Welfare Reform & Beyond Policy Brief no. 8, October 2001.

119. The requirement for single-parent families increased to 50 percent in 2002, but data are not yet available on state compliance.

120. U.S. Department of Health and Human Services, *2001 TANF Report to Congress*, pp. 81–82.

121. Ibid.

122. Ibid., p. XIII-18.

123. Ibid., p. III-1.

124. U.S. Department of Health and Human Services, *2001 TANF Annual Report to Congress*, Table 13.3.

125. LaDonna Pavetti, "Creating a New Welfare Reality: Early Implementation of the Temporary Assistance for Needy Families Program," *Journal of Social Issues* 56, no. 4 (2000): 609.

126. Ibid.

127. General Accounting Office, "Welfare Reform: With TANF Flexibility, States Vary in How They Implement Work Requirements and Time Limits," pp. 11–12.

128. Center for Law and Social Policy, State Policy Documentation Project, "State Policy Regarding TANF Work Activities and Requirements," June 2000, p. 2.

129. Author's calculations, based on U.S. Department of Health and Human Services, *2001 TANF Annual Report to Congress*, Tables 3.4a, 3.4b, 3.5, pp. 96–99, 102–3.

130. Ibid.

131. See, for example, Paul Street, "Only Work Should Pay: A Short History of Welfare Reform in Six Midwestern States," Northern Illinois University, Office for Social Policy Research, 1997.

132. U.S. Department of Health and Human Services, "HHS Releases Evaluation of Welfare-to-Work Strategies," Press release, November 7, 2001. The press release summarizes 26 separate studies. A complete list of those studies can be found at aspe.hhs.gov/hsp/NEWWS.

133. Bruce Meyer and Dan Rosenbaum, "Welfare, the Earned Income Tax Credit, and the Labor Supply of Single Mothers," *Quarterly Journal of Economics* (August 2001): 1064–1114.

134. However, some studies indicate that gains do show up seven to nine years out. Joseph Holtz, Guido Imbens, and Jacob Klerman, "The Long-Term Gains from GAIN: A Reanalysis of the Impacts of the California GAIN Program," National Bureau of Economic Research, paper no. 8007, 2000.

135. The 20 percent federal exemption may actually be much larger than 20 percent. As mentioned below, child-only families are exempt from time limits under other provisions of PRWORA. However, in calculating the 20 percent, all recipients including child-only cases are considered. Therefore, the number of adults exempted can vastly exceed 20 percent. In Wyoming, for example, it is estimated that 77 percent of adult welfare recipients fall under the federal exemption, 53 percent do so in Wisconsin, 49 percent in Florida, and so on. Given the dynamics of welfare usage, few if any recipients in those states will ever face time limits. General Accounting Office, "Welfare Reform: With TANF Flexibility States Vary in How They Implement Work Requirements and Time Limits,"Appendix VII, pp. 35–36.

136. Indeed, as of early 2002, in 22 states TANF had not been in effect for long enough for anyone to reach the time limit. Ibid., p. 19.

137. Blank, pp. 1113–14.

138. LaDonna Pavetti and Dan Bloom, "Sanctions and Time Limits: State Policies, Their Implementation, and Outcomes for Families," in *The New World of Welfare*, pp. 245–69.

139. General Accounting Office, "Welfare Reform: With TANF Flexibility States Vary in How They Implement Work Requirements and Time Limits," pp. 16–18.

140. Ibid., p. 18.

141. Ibid., pp. 19–20.

142. Dan Bloom, *Welfare Time Limits: An interim Report Card* (New York: Manpower Demonstration Research Corporation, 1999).

143. See, for example, Barbara Vobejda and Judith Havemann, "States' Welfare Shift: Stop It before It Starts, *Washington Post*, August 12, 1998.

144. I focus here solely on TANF and the other programs covered by PRWORA, as well as the programs funded by states with TANF-connected funds. There are more than 70 other federal, and numerous state, programs that may justifiably be considered welfare, in that they are means-tested programs designed to provide assistance to poor and low-income individuals. Spending on most of those programs has also continued to rise.

145. Vee Burke, "Welfare Reform: TANF Trends and Data," Congressional Research Service, September 10, 2001, p. 3.

146. Ibid.

147. White House, Office of the Press Secretary, "Fact Sheet: President Calls for Action on Welfare Reform," January 14, 2003.

148. Ibid.

149. U.S. Department of Health and Human Services, *2001 TANF Annual Report to Congress*, chap. 2.

150. Burke.

151. U.S. Department of Health and Human Services, *2001 TANF Annual Report to Congress*, chap. 2.

152. Chris Edwards, Stephen Moore, and Phil Kerpen, "States Face Fiscal Crunch after 1990s Spending Surge," Cato Institute Briefing Paper no. 80, February 12, 2003.

153. Personal Responsibility and Work Opportunity Reconciliation Act of 1996, Title I, Part A, sec. 401.

154. White House, Office of the Press Secretary.

155. See Oliphant.

156. Quoted in Janet Schrader, "Lost on the Road to Reform," *Washington Post*, May 11, 1997.

157. Loprest, p. 18.

158. Maria Cancian et al., "Work, Earnings, and Well-Being after Welfare: What We Know," University of Wisconsin, Institute for Research on Poverty, Madison, January 1999, pp. 19–23.

159. Pamela Friedman, "Community Work Experiences and Publicly Funded Jobs—Helping the Hardest-to-Save Meet Work Requirements," *Welfare Information Network Issue Notes* 3, no. 5 (July 1999). See also Loprest, p. 19.

160. "The New Welfare Trap," *Detroit News*, January 13, 2000.

161. Miller.

162. Ibid. See also Amy Johnson and Alicia Meckstroth, "Ancillary Services to Support Welfare to Work: Lack of Health Insurance," U.S. Department of Health and Human Services, Office of the Assistant Secretary for Planning and Evaluation, June 22, 1998, http://aspe.os.dhhs.gov/hsp/isp/ancillary/hi.htm.

163. Miller.

164. Johnson and Meckstroth.

165. Bowen Garrett and John Holahan, "Welfare Leavers, Medicaid Coverage, and Private Health Insurance," Urban Institute, Assessing the New Federalism Program, National Survey of American Families no. B-13, March 2000.

166. Because our health-care system links health insurance to employment, those who are unemployed or who work for businesses that do not provide insurance are left at a disadvantage in trying to purchase insurance on their own. Cato Institute studies have recommended the creation of a universal health-care tax credit to enable individuals to purchase health insurance outside the workplace. See Sue Blevins, "Restoring Health Freedom: The Case for a Universal Tax Credit for Health Insurance," Cato Institute Policy Analysis no. 290, December 12, 1997.

167. General Accounting Office, "Food Stamp Program: Various Factors Have Led to Declining Participation," GAO/RCED-99-185, July 1999, pp. 1–2.

168. Sheila Zedlewski and Sarah Brauner, "Decline in Food Stamp and Welfare Participation: Is There a Connection?" Urban Institute, Assessing the New Federalism Program, Discussion Paper, October 1999, pp. 24–26.

169. Ibid., p. 6.

170. Zedlewski and Brauner, p. 3.

171. Victoria Wegener, "Food Stamp Education and Outreach: Working to Provide Nutrition Benefits to Eligible Households," *Welfare Information Network Information Note*, no. 3, December 1999.

172. Acs, Loprest, and Roberts. See also Tamar Lewin, "Study Finds Welfare Changes Lead a Million into Child Care," *New York Times*, February 4, 2000.

173. Johnson and Meckstroth.

174. State of Wisconsin, Department of Workforce Development, pp. 1–2.

175. Acs, Loprest, and Roberts.

176. Meyer and Rosenbaum. Although the work incentive is positive for those first leaving the welfare rolls, there may well be negative work incentives for those earning slightly more, especially those in the program's phase-out range. Edgar Browning, "Effects of the Earned Income Tax Credit on Incomes and Welfare," *National Tax Journal* 45, no. 2 (March 1995): 23–45. The General Accounting Office found that the EITC increases work effort among the lowest paid workers, but in the phase-out range reduces the number of hours worked by 7 percent. General Accounting Office, "Earned Income Tax Credit: Design and Administration Could Be Improved," GAO/GGD-93-145, September 1993, pp. 51–52. The GAO report also suggests that the EITC may act as a disincentive to marriage.

177. John Merline, "The Democrats' Taxing Rhetoric, Claims on Working Poor Tax Credit Strain Belief," *Investor's Business Daily*, October 24, 1995.

178. For a detailed description of the program, see Cynthia Miller et al., *Reforming Welfare and Rewarding Work: Final Report on the Minnesota Family Investment Program* (New York: Manpower Resources Demonstration Corporation, 2000).

179. Blank, "Evaluating Welfare in the United States," pp. 1149–50.

180. Charles Michalopoulos and Christine Schwartz, "What Works Best and for Whom: Impacts of 20 Welfare-to-Work Program Subgroups," U.S. Department of Health and Human Services, National Evaluation of Welfare-to-Work Strategies, 2001. There is also evidence that income-disregard programs may have a positive impact on the children of recipients as well. Pamela Morris et al., *How Welfare-to-Work Policies Affect Children: A Synthesis of Research* (New York: Manpower Resources Demonstration Corporation, 2001).

181. Blank and Schoeni.

182. Tanner, Moore, and Hartman.
183. Meyer and Rosenbaum.
184. Besharov, "The Past and Future of Welfare Reform," p. 20.

Chapter 5

1. Christine Hall, "Welfare Reform Could Get Weakened in Senate," *CNS News,* March 6, 2003.
2. In many cases this devolution occurs more on paper than in reality. However, California, Colorado, Maryland, North Carolina, Ohio, and Wisconsin have seriously pursued continued devolution. Jack Tweedie et al., *Meeting the Challenges of Welfare Reform: Programs with Promise* (Denver: National Council of State Legislatures, 1998), pp. 88–89.
3. Keith Watson and Steven Gold, *The Other Side of Devolution: Shifting Relationships between State and Local Governments* (Washington: Urban Institute, 1997).
4. Tweedie et al., p. 88.
5. Scott Logan, Jacqueline Byers, and Marilana Sanz, "America's Counties: Making Welfare Reform Work," National Association of Counties, Washington, March 2001.
6. Jack Tweedie, "Building a Foundation for Change in Welfare," *State Legislatures,* February 1998.
7. Christine Kelleher and Susan Webb Yackee, "Second-Order Devolution: A Focus on the Opinions of County-Level Officials." *Policy Currents* 11, no. 3 (2002).
8. Richard Nathan and Thomas Gais, "Implementing the Personal Responsibility Act of 1996: A First Look," State University of New York, Nelson Rockefeller Institute of Government, 2000.
9. Rebecca Blank, "Evaluating Welfare Reform in the United States," *Journal of Economic Literature* (December 2002): 1114.
10. Although more states have authorized lump sum payments than any other type of diversion program, the U.S. Department of Health and Human Services reports that those programs are rarely used in practice. Kathleen Maloy et al., "Diversion as a Work-Oriented Welfare Reform Strategy and Its Effect on Access to Medicaid: An Examination of the Experience of Five Local Communities," U.S. Department of Health and Human Services, Office of the Assistant Secretary for Planning and Evaluation, March 1999, pp. 8–9. Utah, Virginia, and Montana appear to have the most extensive experience with the concept.
11. U.S. Department of Health and Human Services, Office of the Assistant Secretary for Planning and Evaluation, "A Description and Assessment of State Approaches to Diversion Programs and Activities," August 1998, Executive Summary, p. 2, http://aspe.os.dhhs.gov/hsp/isp/diverzn/execsum.htm.
12. Maloy et al., p. 9.
13. U.S. Department of Health and Human Services, Office of the Assistant Secretary for Planning and Evaluation.
14. Ibid.
15. Ibid.
16. Exceptions are Alabama, Georgia, Kansas, Maryland, Nevada, New York, and Oklahoma.
17. U.S. Department of Health and Human Services, Office of the Assistant Secretary for Planning and Evaluation.
18. Ibid., p. 2.

19. Ibid., p. 6.4

20. Ibid., p. 6.5.

21. Barbara Vobejda and Judith Havemann, "States' Welfare Shift: Stop It before It Starts," *Washington Post*, August 12, 1998.

22. General Accounting Office, "Welfare Reform: States' Implementation Progress and Information on Former Recipients," GAO/T-HEHS-99-116, May 1999, p. 15.

23. Rep. David Heaton (D-Iowa), Statement before the Senate Finance Committee, Field Hearing on Welfare Reauthorization, Des Moines, Iowa, February 20, 2003.

24. U.S. Department of Health and Human Services, Office of the Assistant Secretary for Planning and Evaluation.

25. June O'Neill, Testimony before the Subcommittee on Human Resources of the House Committee on Ways and Means, 106th Cong., 1st sess., May 27, 1999.

26. Charles Murray, "Family Formation," in *The New World of Welfare*, ed. Rebecca Blank and Ron Haskins (Washington: Brookings Institution, 2000).

27. Robert Haveman et al., "Do Teens Make Rational Choices? The Case of Teen Nonmarital Childbearing," University of Wisconsin, Institute for Research on Poverty, Discussion Paper no. 1137–97, July 1997.

28. For a discussion of this research, see Murray, "Family Formation."

29. Chief among the needed changes is the removal of all restrictions on transracial adoptions. Nearly every state prohibits or delays the adoption of minority children on the basis of the race of the adoptive parents. Yet there is no evidence that transracial adoption has any adverse impact on a child's development. See Rita J. Simon, Howard Altstein, and Marygold Melli, *The Case for Transracial Adoption* (Washington: American University Press, 1994).

30. Robert Kaestner and June O'Neill, "Has Welfare Reform Changed Teenage Behaviors?" National Bureau of Economic Research Working Paper no. W8932, May 2002.

31. Richard Vedder and Lowell Gallaway, *The War on the Poor* (Lewisville, Tex.: Institute for Policy Innovation, June 1992), pp. 21–24.

32. John 12:8.

33. According to the American Association of Fund Raising Council Trust for Philanthropy, $161 billion was contributed by individuals in 2001. AAFRC Trust for Philanthropy, "Giving USA 2002," New York, June 20, 2002.

34. Based on a Gallup poll cited in John Goodman, Gerald Reed, and Peter Ferrara, "Why Not Abolish the Welfare State?" National Center for Policy Analysis Policy Report no. 187, Dallas, Tex., October 1994.

35. American Association of Fund Raising Council Trust for Philanthropy.

36. Independent Sector, "Giving and Volunteering in the United States, 2002: Key Findings," Washington, November 2, 2002.

37. Glenn C. Loury, "Values and Judgments: Creating Social Incentives for Good Behavior," in *Transforming Welfare: The Revival of American Charity*, ed. Jeffrey Sikkenga (Grand Rapids, Mich.: Acton Institute, 1996), p. 24.

38. Quoted in Marvin Olasky, *The Tragedy of American Compassion* (Washington: Regnery, 1992), p. 191.

39. M. Bateman, "Administration of AFDC in Illinois: A Description of Three Local Efforts," Abt Associates, Cambridge, Mass., July 1990.

40. Theresa Funiciello, *Tyranny of Kindness: Dismantling the Welfare System to End Poverty in America* (New York: Atlantic Monthly Press, 1993). Funiciello has some dubious proposals regarding welfare reform, notably her call for a guaranteed national

income. However, her book remains must reading for anyone interested in the failures of the welfare system.

41. Bureau of the Census data cited in Goodman, Reed, and Ferrara, p. 25.

42. Robert Wuthnow, Conrad Hackett, and Becky Yang Hsu, "Effectiveness and Trustworthiness of Faith-Based and Other Service Organizations: A Study of Recipients' Perceptions," Paper presented at a conference on the Role of Faith-Based Organizations in the Social Welfare System, Washington, March 6–7, 2003.

43. Goodman, Reed, and Ferrara.

44. David Kelley, *A Life of One's Own: Individual Rights and the Welfare State* (Washington: Cato Institute, 1998), p. 116.

45. Robert Woodson, "Is the Black Community a Casualty of the War on Poverty?" Heritage Foundation Lecture, February 6, 1990. It is important to note that the 70 percent figure is not solely government administrative overhead. That figure also includes government payments to the nonpoor on behalf of the poor. For example, Medicaid payments go to doctors. Housing subsidies are frequently paid directly to landlords. Woodson bases his estimate on figures provided in Executive Office of the President, Office of Policy Development, *An Overview of the Current System*, vol. 1 of *The National Public Assistance Strategy* (Washington: Government Printing Office, 1986). Several local studies have shown a similar 70/30 split. See, for example, "New York's Poverty Budget," Community Service Society of New York, 1984; and "The Cook County, Illinois, Welfare System," Northwestern University, Center for Urban Affairs and Policy Research, 1991.

46. For an excellent discussion of the religious and spiritual dimensions of fighting poverty, see Marvin Olasky, *Renewing American Compassion* (New York: Free Press, 1996); and Joseph Loconte and Lia Fantuzzo, "Churches, Charity, and Children," University of Pennsylvania, Center for Research on Religion and Urban Civil Society, 2002. However, there are serious problems with quantitative analyses of the outcomes of faith-based interventions. As a result, while there is an overwhelming perception of success by these organizations, there is little scientific evaluation on the subject. See, for example, Robert Fisher, "The Devil Is in the Details: Implementing Outcome Measurement in Faith Based Organizations," Paper presented to a conference on the Role of Faith-Based Organizations in the Social Welfare System, Washington, March 6–7, 2003.

47. Robert Sirico, "Restoring Charity," in *Transforming Welfare*, p. 6.

48. James Payne, *The Promise of Community* (Indianapolis: Philanthropy Roundtable, 1994), p. 13.

49. Ibid., p. 15.

50. James Strong, *Strong's Exhaustive Concordance of the Bible* (Lynchburg, Va.: Old Time Gospel Hour, 1986).

51. Gertrude Himmelfarb, *Poverty and Compassion* (New York: Alfred Knopf, 1991), p. 3.

52. Robert Thompson, *Manual for Visitors among the Poor* (Philadelphia: Lippincott, 1879), p. 246, cited in Olasky, *The Tragedy of American Compassion*, p. 224.

53. Cited in Gertrude Himmelfarb, "True Charity: Lessons from Victorian England," in *Transforming Welfare*, pp. 31–32.

54. Quoted in Sirico, "Restoring Charity," p. 7.

55. Brian O'Connell, "Private Philanthropy and the Preservation of a Free and Democratic Society," in *Philanthropy: Four Views*, ed. Robert L. Payton (New Brunswick, N.J.: Transaction Books, 1988), p. 32.

56. Lisa Montiel, "The Use of Public Funds for Delivery of Faith-Based Human Services," Roundtable on Religion and Social Welfare Policy, Albany, N.Y., Table 2, p. 10.

57. Ibid.

58. Laurie Goldstein, "Churches May Not Be Able to Patch Welfare Cuts," *Washington Post*, February 22, 1995.

59. Robin Karman and Steve Malanga, "Nonprofits: NY's New Tammany Hall," *Cain's*, October 31, 1994.

60. Payne, pp. 11–12.

61. Ibid., p. 11.

62. Ibid.

63. For a discussion of Aramony's tenure at United Way, see John S. Glaser, *The United Way Scandal: An Insider's Account of What Went Wrong and Why* (New York: John Wiley & Sons, 1994).

64. Payne, p. 39.

65. Ibid.

66. Kimberly Dennis, "Some Philanthropists Turn Their Backs on Voluntarism," *The Freeman*, October 1994, p. 565.

67. www.millionairclub.org. See also *Guide to Effective Compassion* (Grand Rapids, Mich.: Acton Institute, 1998), p. 40.

68. Steve Tappan, "A New York Charity Challenges the Conventional Wisdom," *Philanthropy Magazine*, March–April 2002.

69. http://members.tripod.com/barbspad/stmartindeporres.html.

70. Evan Gahr, "She Gives Them Shelter," *Wall Street Journal*, November 26, 1999.

71. Quoted in Robert Sirico, "Putting Private Charity Back into Welfare," *Detroit News*, May 28, 1995.

72. Robert Sirico, "Charities on the Dole," *Wall Street Journal*, March 31, 1995.

73. Amy Sherman, "The Seven Habits of Highly Effective Charities," *Philanthropy Magazine*, March–April 2002.

74. Quoted in Amy Sherman, "How Sharon Baptist Discovered Welfare Ministry," *Christianity Today*, June 14, 1999.

75. Ibid., pp. 40–43.

76. Quoted in ibid, p. 41.

77. Sen. Daniel Coats, *Congressional Record* 141, no. 123 (July 27, 1995): 510823.

78. Quoted in Lawrence Reed, "The Right Direction for Welfare Reform," *The Freeman* 45, no. 5 (May 1995).

79. Jim Gittings, "Churches in Community: Places to Stand," *Christianity and Crisis*, February 2, 1997.

80. Quoted in Thomas McCardle, "Tools of Success for the Poor," *Investor's Business Daily*, November 11, 1993.

81. Charles Murray, *What It Means to Be a Libertarian: A Personal Interpretation* (New York: Broadway Books, 1997), p. 59.

82. See, for example, Russell Roberts, "A Positive Model of Private Charity and Public Transfers," *Journal of Political Economy* 92 (1984): 136–48; and B. A. Abrams and M. D. Schmitz, "The Crowding Out Effect of Government Transfers on Private Charitable Contributions," *Public Choice*, no. 1 (1978): 28–40.

83. AAFRC Trust for Philanthropy, "Giving USA 2002," Indianapolis, Ind., June 20, 2002.

84. Only about 9.1 percent of all charitable giving goes to social service agencies. Don Eberly, "Use Tax Credits to Spur Charity," in *Mandate for Charity: Policy Proposals for the Bush Administration*, ed. Robert Huberty and Christopher Yablonski (Washington: Capital Research Center, 2001), p. 7.

85. Ibid.

86. Ralph Kramer, *Voluntary Agencies in the Welfare State* (Berkeley: University of California Press, 1981), pp. 57–76; and AAFRC Trust for Philanthropy, "Giving USA," various years.

87. Ned Lees, "Boom or Bust: The Dow and Charitable Giving," *Marts and Lundy Newsletter* 1 (Winter 1998–99).

88. Christopher Horne, David Van Slyke, and Janet Johnson, "Attitudes for Public Funding for Faith-Based Organizations and the Potential Impact on Private Giving," Paper presented to a conference on the Role of Faith-Based Organizations in the Social Welfare System, Washington, March 7–8, 2003.

89. Frederic Almy, "The Relation between Public and Private Charities," *Charities Review* 9 (1899): 65–71.

90. Stephen Ziliak, "The End of Welfare and the Contradiction of Compassion," *Independent Review* 1 (Spring 1996): 56.

91. Legislation to this effect, "The Charity Aid, Relief, and Empowerment Act of 2003," has been introduced by Sens. Rick Santorum (R-Pa.) and Joseph Lieberman (D-Conn.).

92. PricewaterhouseCoopers, "Incentives for Nonitemizers to Give More: An Analysis," Independent Sector White Paper, January 2001.

93. Goodman, Reed, and Ferrara, pp. 28–31.

94. James Angelini, William O'Brien Jr., and David Tuerck, "The Next Step toward Welfare Reform: A Manual for Enacting Tax Credits for Charitable Contributions," Beacon Hill Institute, Boston, 1998.

95. "Rallying the Armies of Compassion," January 2001, p. 11, www.whitehouse.gov/news/reports/faithbased.pdf.

96. This book is focused on programs affecting the poor because the poor suffer the most at the hands of the current welfare system. But, just to be clear, dismantling the welfare state should also end subsidies to the middle class and business. Corporate welfare is just as illegitimate as individual welfare.

Chapter 6

1. Portions of this chapter were previously published in Michael Tanner, "Corrupting Charity: Why Government Should Not Fund Faith-Based Charities," Cato Institute Briefing Paper no. 62, March 22, 2001.

2. Marvin Olasky, *The Tragedy of American Compassion* (Washington: Regnery, 1992).

3. Veto Message of February 27, 1811. Quoted in Gene Garman, "Separation of Church and State," *Liberty Magazine*, May–June 1996.

4. Douglas Laycock, "The Underlying Unity of Separation and Neutrality," *Emory Law Journal* 46 (Winter 1997): 2.

5. One odd exception was federal funding of missionaries to the Indians.

6. Joseph Loconte, *Seducing the Samaritan: How Government Contracts Are Reshaping Social Services* (Boston: Pioneer Institute for Public Policy Research, 1997), p. 2.

7. Carl Esbeck, *The Regulation of Religious Organizations as Recipients of Government Assistance* (Washington: Center for Public Justice, 1996).

8. George F. Will, "Keeping Faith behind Initiatives," *Washington Post*, January 28, 2001.

9. Stanley Carlson-Thies, "Faith-Based Institutions Cooperating with Public Welfare: The Promise of the Charitable Choice Provision," in *Welfare Reform and Faith-Based Organizations*, ed. D. Davis and B. Hankins (Houston, Tex.: Baylor University, 1999), p. 38.

10. U.S. Department of Housing and Urban Development, Emergency Shelter Grants Program, 51 *Fed. Reg.* 45277 (1986).

11. PL 104–193 sec. 104a(1)(a).

12. Ibid.

13. White House, "Agency Responsibilities with Respect to Faith-Based and Community Initiatives," News release, January 29, 2001.

14. Statement of President George W. Bush, January 29, 2001, www.whitehouse.gov/news/releases/20010129.5.htm.

15. Courtney Jarchow, "Faith-Based Initiatives in Welfare Reform," National Conference of State Legislatures, May 2002.

16. Much of the discussion in this chapter concerns faith-based or religious charities, because that is the focus of the current debate and a relatively new innovation in government policy. But many of the same arguments would apply to secular charities as well. In short, government funding of *any* private charitable program is not a good idea.

17. I set aside for the moment the question of whether there is constitutional authority for the federal government to fund any social welfare services, no matter who administers them. For a discussion of this question, see Robert Levy, "The Federalist Case against Faith-Based Initiatives," *American Spectator Online*, February 14, 2001.

18. 403 U.S. 602 (1971), as cited in William Van Alstyne, *First Amendment Cases and Materials* (Westbury, N.Y.: Foundation Press, 1995), pp. 909–15.

19. 175 US 291 (1899), as cited in Melissa Rogers, "The Wrong Way to Do It Right: Charitable Choice and Churches," in *Welfare Reform and Faith-Based Organizations*, pp. 61–88.

20. 426 U.S. 736 (1976), as cited in Jim Castelli and John McCarthy, "Religion-Sponsored Social Services: The Not-So-Independent Sector," Aspen Institute Nonprofit Sector Research Fund, March 1998, p. 3.

21. 487 U.S. 589 (1988), as cited in Esbeck, *The Regulation of Religious Organizations as Recipients of Government Assistance*.

22. 413 U.S. 734 (1973), as cited in ibid.

23. Diana Etindi, "Charitable Choice and Its Implications for Faith-Based Organizations," Hudson Institute, September 28, 1999.

24. *Lemon v. Kurtzman*, p. 912.

25. Karen DeYoung, "Abortion Aid Ban's Global Impact Debated," *Washington Post*, January 26, 2001.

26. See, for example, Luis Lugo, *Equal Partners: The Welfare Responsibility of Governments and Churches* (Washington: Center for Public Justice, 1998).

27. John DiIulio, "Know Us by Our Works," *Wall Street Journal*, February 14, 2001.

28. 115 S. Ct. 2510., as cited in Carl Esbeck, "A Constitutional Case for Governmental Cooperation with Faith-Based Social Service Providers," *Emory Law Journal* 46 (Winter 1997).

29. For an excellent discussion of the difficulties in sorting out government's ability to impose conditions on its contracts and grants, see Richard Epstein, *Bargaining with the State* (Princeton, N.J.: Princeton University Press, 1993).

30. 111 S. Ct. 1759, as cited in Alstyne.

31. *NEA v. Finley*, 524 U.S. 569 (1998).

32. House Committee on Banking and Financial Oversight, Hearings, March 2, 1995.

33. Quoted in Joseph Conn and Robert Boston, "President Bush and Faith-Based Initiatives: AU Report and Answers to Frequently Asked Questions," Americans United for the Separation of Church and State, January 29, 2001.

34. Steven Carter, *God's Name in Vain: The Wrongs and Rights of Religion in Politics* (New York: Basic Books, 2000).

35. 42 U.S.C. sec. 609a(j) (Supp. 1998).

36. Statement of President George W. Bush.

37. Stephen Burger, "New Hope for Gospel Missions: The Devil's in the Details," *USA Today*, September 3, 1996.

38. 42 U.S.C. sec. 609a(h) (Supp. 1998).

39. Rogers, pp. 61–88.

40. Ibid., note 18.

41. Richard Hammar, *Pastor, Church & Law*, 5th ed. (Matthews, N.C.: Christian Ministry Resources, 1991), p. 592.

42. 45 C.F.R., sec. 80.6(b)(1997).

43. 45 C.F.R., sec. 80.7(a)(1997).

44. 45 C.F.R., sec. 80.6(c)(1997).

45. Mark Chaves, "Religious Congregations and Welfare Reform," *Social Science and Modern Society* 38 (January–February 2001): 26.

46. Castelli and McCarthy, p. 4.

47. Michael Horowitz, "Subsidies May Cost Churches Their Souls," *Wall Street Journal*, December 16, 1999.

48. Esbeck, *The Regulation of Religious Organizations as Recipients of Governmental Assistance*, pp. 45–47.

49. *Arneth v. Gross*, 699 F. Supp. 450 (S.D. N.Y. 1988), as cited in ibid., p. 46.

50. *Dodge v. Salvation Army* U.S. Dist. Lexis 4797 (S.D. Miss. 1989), as cited in Rogers.

51. Esbeck, *The Regulation of Religious Organizations as Recipients of Governmental Assistance*, pp. 34–35.

52. For example, the HUD "Safe Havens for Homeless Individuals Program" specifically requires a hearing before benefits may be terminated. 42 USC sec. 11396.

53. 40 U.S.C. secs. 276(a)–276(a)-5 (Supp. 1994.)

54. Loconte, Appendix B.

55. Mo. Rev. Stat. sec. 210.211.1(5)(1984); and S.C. Code Ann. sec. 20-7-2700(b)(10)91976). Both cited in Esbeck, *The Regulation of Religious Organizations as Recipients of Governmental Assistance*.

56. Rick Santorum, "But Are They Catholic?" *National Review*, June 2, 1997.

57. Loconte, pp. 78–79.

58. Amy Sheridan, "Cross Purposes: Will Conservative Welfare Reform Corrupt Religious Charities?" *Policy Review* 74 (Fall 1995): 58.

59. Stephen Monsma, *When Sacred and Secular Mix: Religious Non-Profit Organizations and Public Money* (Lanham, Md.: Roman & Littlefield, 1997).

60. Quoted in Loconte, p. 41.

61. Robert Sirico, "Charities on the Dole," *Wall Street Journal*, March 31, 1995.

62. Loconte, pp. 34–35.

63. Carlson-Thies, p. 36.

64. Quoted in Loconte, p. 41.

65. Quoted in ibid.

66. David Kelley, *A Life of One's Own: Individual Rights and the Welfare State* (Washington: Cato Institute, 1998), p. 118.

67. Tibor Machan, *Generosity: Virtue in Civil Society* (Washington: Cato Institute, 1998), p. 70.

68. Arthur Brooks, "Public Subsidies and Charitable Giving: Crowding Out, Crowding In or Both?" *Journal of Policy Analysis and Management* 19, no. 3 (2000): 451–64.

69. Christopher Horne, David Van Slyke, and Janet Johnson, "Attitudes for Public Funding for Faith-Based Organizations and the Potential Impact on Private Giving," Paper presented to a conference on the Role of Faith-Based Organizations in the Social Welfare System, Washington, March 7–8, 2003.

70. Lisa Montiel, "The Use of Public Funds for Delivery of Faith-Based Human Services," Roundtable on Religion and Social Welfare Policy, Albany, N.Y., September 2002, Table 2, p. 10.

Chapter 7

1. This is not necessarily to say that there is no role for government. Government can and should defend people's rights, including property rights, so that people can coordinate their behavior in ways that will create wealth and prosperity.

2. Dwight R. Lee and Richard B. McKenzie, *Failure and Progress: The Bright Side of the Dismal Science* (Washington: Cato Institute, 1993), pp. 120–22.

3. Walter Williams, "Poverty in the Nation," *Washington Times*, February 20, 2003.

4. U.S. Bureau of the Census, "Poverty in the United States: 2001," Current Population Reports, Series P60–219, 2002, p. 8.

5. Paul Jargowsky and Mary Jo Bane, "Ghetto Poverty: Basic Questions," in *Inner-City Poverty in the United States*, ed. Laurence E. Lynn and Michael McGeary (Washington: National Academy Press, 1990), pp. 28–31.

6. Paul Osterman, "Impact of Full Employment in Boston," in *The Urban Underclass*, ed. Christopher Jencks and Paul Peterson (Washington: Brookings Institution, 1991), pp. 122–34.

7. Richard Vedder, "Why Government Job Training Fails," *Investor's Business Daily*, January 10, 1996.

8. David Brumbaugh, "The Level of Taxes in the United States, 1940–2000," Congressional Research Service, 2001.

9. Ibid., p. 5.

10. Joint Economic Committee, "Taxes and Long-Term Economic Growth," February 1997.

11. Institute for Policy Innovation, "Another Look at the Kennedy Tax Cut," September 20, 1996.

12. Ibid. See also Joint Economic Committee, "The Mellon and Kennedy Tax Cuts: A Review and Analysis," September 1982.

13. Joint Economic Committee, "Taxes and Long-Term Economic Growth."

14. David Henderson, "The Truth about the 1980s," Hoover Institution Essays in Public Policy, 1994. See also William Niskanen, "Myths about the 1980s," *Wall Street Journal*, November 5, 1996.

15. Joint Economic Committee, "Taxes and Long-Term Economic Growth." Of course, critics point to the rising deficits of the 1980s and early 1990s as a consequence of tax cutting. However, government revenue actually increased during this period. The deficits resulted from Congress's inability to control spending.

16. Richard Vedder, "Do Taxes Matter?" The Taxpayers Network, September 2001.

17. See Robert Genetski and Young Chin, "The Impact of State and Local Taxes on Economic Growth," Harris Bank, Chicago, 1978; and Richard Vedder, "State and Local Taxation and Economic Growth: Lessons for Federal Tax Reform," Joint Economic Committee, 1996.

18. Michael Wasylenko and Therese McGuire, "Jobs and Taxes: The Effect of Business Climates on the States' Unemployment Growth Rates," *National Tax Journal* (December 1985); Thomas Plaut and Joseph Pluta, "Business Climate, Taxes and Expenditures, and State Industrial Growth in the United States," *Southern Economic Journal* (July 1983); Ernest Goss, Phillips Preston, and Joseph Phillips, "State Employment Growth: The Impact of Taxes and Economic Development Agency Spending," *Growth and Change* (Summer 1994); and Richard Vedder and Lowell Gallaway, "Spatial Variations in U.S. Unemployment," *Journal of Labor Research* (Summer 1996).

19. Vedder, "Do Taxes Matter?"

20. Ibid.

21. Scott Moody, "The Cost of Tax Compliance," Tax Foundation, February 2002.

22. Internal Revenue Service, *Statistics of Income Bulletin*, Winter 2000–2001.

23. Edward Wolff, "Who Are the Rich?" in *Does Atlas Shrug? The Economic Consequences of Taxing the Rich*, ed. Joel Slemrod (New York: Russell Sage Foundation, 2000).

24. Robert Carroll et al., "Personal Income Taxes and the Growth of Small Firms," National Bureau of Economic Research Working Paper no. 7980, October 2000.

25. Robert Carroll et al., "Income Taxes and Entrepreneurs' Use of Labor," *Journal of Labor Economics*, October 1999.

26. Jude Wanniski, Testimony before the Senate Committee on Finance, Hearing on Tax Treatment of Capital Gains, 104th Cong., 1st sess., February 15, 1995, p. 102.

27. Stephen Moore and John Silvia, "The ABCs of the Capital Gains Tax," Cato Institute Policy Analysis no. 242, October 4, 1995, p. 34.

28. Cited in Arthur Fletcher et al., "Help the Poor, Cut the Cap Gains Tax," *Wall Street Journal*, August 25, 1993.

29. Quoted in ibid.

30. Quoted in Dick Armey, "The GOP's Fiscal Challenge," *Washington Post*, October 25, 1995.

31. Moore and Silvia, p. 18.

32. Frederic Bastiat, *Selected Essays on Political Economy*, trans. Seymour Cain (Irvington-on-Hudson, N.Y.: Foundation for Economic Education, 1964), p. 39. Emphasis added.

33. For a discussion of the national sales tax, see Laurence J. Kotlikoff, "The Economic Impact of Replacing Federal Income Taxes with a Sales Tax," Cato Institute Policy Analysis no. 193, April 15, 1993. For a discussion of the flat tax, see Robert Hall and Alvin Rabushka, *The Flat Tax* (Stanford, Calif.: Hoover Institution Press, 1995).

34. Government Regulatory Compliance Cost Report, April 2003, http://mwhodges.home.att.net/regulation.htm.

35. For an excellent discussion of the history of occupational licensing and minorities, see Clint Bolick, *Unfinished Business: A Civil Rights Strategy for America's Third Century* (San Francisco: Pacific Research Institute, 1990).

36. Ibid.

37. Typical was this letter in the January 1905 edition of the *Plumbers, Gas, and Steam Fitters Official Journal:* "There are about 10 Negro skate plumbers working around here [Danville, Va.], doing quite a lot of jobbing and repairing, but owing to the fact of not having an examination board it is impossible to stop them, hence the anxiety of men here to organize." Quoted in Walter E. Williams, *The State against Blacks* (New York: McGraw-Hill, 1982), pp. 91–92.

African Americans were not the only targets of discriminatory laws. Regulations were also used to limit the access of other minorities to the economy. For example, one of the nation's earliest zoning laws was an 1885 Modesto, California, ordinance aimed at Chinese immigrants: "[It is] unlawful for any person to establish, maintain, or carry on the business of a public laundry . . . within the City of Modesto, except that part of the city which lies west of the railroad track south of G street." Cited in Michael Goldberg and Peter Horwood, *Zoning: Its Costs and Relevance for the 1980s* (Vancouver: Fraser Institute, 1980), p. 11.

38. See, for example, Susan Michalik and Louise G. Trubek, "Regulating Occupations: Legal Challenges to Licensing Examinations in Wisconsin," Center for Public Representation, Madison, 1988; Simon Rottenberg, ed., *Occupational Licensure and Regulation* (Washington: American Enterprise Institute, 1980); and S. David Young, *The Rule of Experts: Occupational Licensing in America* (Washington: Cato Institute, 1987).

39. Stuart Dorsey, "The Occupational Licensing Queue," *Journal of Human Resources* 15, no. 3 (1980): 424–34.

40. Ibid., p. 424.

41. Personal communication from the Small Business Administration, Office of Advocacy, February 15, 1996.

42. U.S. Small Business Administration, Office of Advocacy, "Minorities in Business, 2001," November 2001, p. 8.

43. National Urban League, *The State of Black America, 1993* (New York: AG Publishing, 1993), pp. 94, 101.

44. David Neumark, "The Effects of Minimum Wage throughout the Wage Distribution," National Bureau of Economic Research Working Paper no. 7519, February 2000.

45. Victor Fuchs, Alan B. Krueger, and James M. Poterba, "Economists' Views about Parameters, Values, and Policies: Survey Results in Labor and Public Economics," *Journal of Economic Literature* 36 (September 1998). It is also worth noting that at least some minimum wage laws, like occupational licensing laws, were originally intended to discriminate against minorities. For example, the Davis-Bacon Act, which requires prevailing wages (in practice, usually standard union wages) to be paid on all government contracts, was originally promoted to keep black workers, who were generally not allowed to join unions, from competing with unionized whites. One of the law's early supporters, the notorious racist Rep. Clay Allgood (D-Miss.), candidly explained that the law would put an end to "cheap colored labor . . . that is in competition with white labor throughout the country." Quoted in Williams, *The State against Blacks*, p. 122.

46. U.S. Small Business Administration, Office of Advocacy, "The Impact of Regulatory Costs on Small Firms," 2001, p. 9.

47. Annie E. Casey Foundation, *Children at Risk: State Trends 1990–2000* (Baltimore: Annie E. Casey Foundation, 2001), citing Census Bureau data.

48. Larence Mishel, Jared Bernstein, and John Schmidt, *The State of Working America, 2000–2001* (Ithaca, N.Y.: Cornell University Press, 2001), p. 153.

49. U.S. Department of Education, National Center for Education Statistics, "National Dropout Rates in the United States," 2000, p. viii.

50. Uri Bronfenbrenner et al., *The State of Americans* (New York: Free Press, 1996), pp. 176–77.

51. Samuel Brunelli, ed., *Report Card on American Education 1994: A State-by-State Analysis* (Washington: American Legislative Exchange Council, 1994).

52. U.S. Department of Education, National Center for Education Statistics, "National Dropout Rates in the United States."

53. U.S. Department of Education, National Center for Education Statistics, "Student Dropout Rates by Race/Ethnicity," 2001.

54. Chicago may have the nation's highest dropout rate, nearly 65 percent. William Murray, "Christo Rey School Puts Students to Work, New Philanthropic Model Supports High School Education," Heartland Institute, January 1, 2002.

55. Eric Hanushek, "The Economics of Schooling: Production and Efficiency in Public Schools," *Journal of Economic Literature* 24 (September 1986): 1161–62.

56. John E. Chubb and Terry M. Moe, *Politics, Markets, and America's Schools* (Washington: Brookings Institution, 1990), p. 193.

57. Quoted in "Reding, Wrighting & Erithmatic," *Wall Street Journal*, October 2, 1989.

58. For a discussion of how educational choice will benefit the poor, see Clint Bolick, *Voucher Wars: Waging the Legal Battle over School Choice* (Washington: Cato Institute, 2003).

59. Jonathan Rauch, "The Widening Marriage Gap: America's New Class Divide," *National Journal*, May 23, 2001.

60. Federal Reserve Board, *Survey of Consumer Finance*, 1998.

61. Adam Thomas and Isabel Sawhill, "For Richer or Poorer: Marriage as an Antipoverty Strategy," *Journal of Policy Analysis and Management* (2001).

62. Hyunbe Chun and Injae Lee, "Why Do Married Men Earn More: Productivity or Marriage Selection?" *Economic Inquiry* 39 (2001): 307–19; and K. Daniel, "The Marriage Premium," in *The New Economics of Human Behavior*, ed. M. Tommasi and K. Ierulli (Cambridge: Cambridge University Press, 1995).

63. Robert Lerman, "The Impact of the Changing U.S. Family Structure on Poverty and Income Inequality," *Economica* 63 (1996): 119–39.

64. Gary Becker, *A Treatise on the Family* (Cambridge, Mass.: Harvard University Press, 1981).

65. Linda Waite and Maggie Gallagher, *The Case for Marriage: Why Married People Are Happier, Healthier, and Better-Off Financially* (New York: Doubleday Books, 2000), pp. 97–109.

66. Federal Interagency Forum on Child and Family Statistics, *America's Children: Key Indicators of Well-Being* (Washington: Government Printing Office, 2001).

67. Isabel Sawhill, "Welfare Reform and the Marriage Movement," Brookings Institution, October 2001.

68. U.S. Bureau of the Census, Current Population Survey, March 2000. www.bls.census.gov/cps.

69. Adam Thomas and Isabel Sawhill, "For Richer or for Poorer: Marriage as an Antipoverty Strategy," *Journal of Policy Analysis and Management* (2001). See also Lerman, "The Impact of the Changing U.S. Family Structure on Poverty and Income

Inequality"; and Isabel Sawhill, "Families at Risk," in *Setting National Priorities: The 2000 Elections and Beyond*, ed. Henry Aaron and Robert Reischauer (Washington: Brookings Institution, 1999).

70. David Eggebeen and Daniel Lichter, "Race, Family Structure, and Changing Poverty among American Children," *American Sociological Review* 56 (1991): 801–17. More recent studies have found less clearly defined but similar results for both black and white children. See, for example, Maria Cancian and Deborah Reed, "Trends in Family Structure and Behavior and the Poverty Problem," Paper presented to the conference on Understanding Poverty in America: Progress and Problems, University of Wisconsin, Madison, May 2000; Peter Gottschalk and Sheldon Danziger, "Family Structure, Family Size, and Income: Accounting for Changes in the Economic Well-Being of Children," in *Uneven Tides: Rising Inequality in America*, ed. Sheldon Danziger and Peter Gottschalk (New York: Russell Sage Foundation, 1997), pp. 167–93; and Lerman, "The Impact of the Changing U.S. Family Structure on Poverty and Income Inequality."

71. Robert Rector and Kirk Johnson, "The Effects of Marriage and Maternal Education in Reducing Childhood Poverty," Report of the Heritage Center for Data Analysis no. CDA02-05, August 2, 2002, p. 1.

72. David Ellwood, "Poverty through the Eyes of Children, " Harvard University, 1989, p. 78.

73. Patrick Fagan et al., "The Positive Effects of Marriage: A Book of Charts," Heritage Foundation, 2002, chart 6, p. 6, using data from the National Longitudinal Study on Youth.

74. Rector and Johnson, Table 1, p. 6.

75. U.S. House of Representatives, Committee on Ways and Means, *1996 Green Book: Background Material and Data on Programs within the Jurisdiction of the Committee on Ways and Means* (Washington: Government Printing office, 1996), Table 10–50, p. 451.

76. Douglas Besharov, "Escaping the Dole," American Enterprise Institute, Washington, December 12, 1993.

77. Fagan et al., chart 7, p. 12.

78. Ibid., chart 6, p. 6.

79. Daniel Lichter and Deborah Roempke Graefe, "Finding a Mate? The Marital and Cohabitation Histories of Unwed Mothers," in *Out of Wedlock: Trends, Causes, and Consequences of Nonmarital Fertility*, ed. Lawrence Wu and Barbara Wolfe (New York: Russell Sage Foundation, 2001).

80. Isabel Sawhill, "Is Marriage the Real Problem?" *American Prospect*, April 8, 2002.

81. National Conference of State Legislatures, "TANF-Funded Marriage Initiatives," Denver, 1998.

82. "Government Awards Grants to Promote Marriage," *USA Today*, January 3, 2003.

83. Bill Swindell, "Republicans Eye $200 Million to Promote Marriage," *Congressional Quarterly Today*, February 3, 2003.

84. Patrick Fagan, Robert Patterson, and Robert Rector, "Marriage and Welfare Reform: The Overwhelming Evidence That Marriage Education Works," Heritage Foundation Backgrounder no. 1606, October 25, 2002.

85. Robert Rector, "Using Welfare Reform to Strengthen Marriage," *American Experiment Quarterly* 4 (2001): 64.

86. See, for example, William Julius Wilson, *When Work Disappears: The World of the Urban Poor* (New York: Alfred Knopf, 1996); William Julius Wilson and Kathleen Neckerman, "Poverty and Family Structure: The Widening Gap between Evidence and Public Policy Issues," in William Julius Wilson, *The Truly Disadvantaged: The Inner City, the Underclass, and Public Policy* (Chicago: University of Chicago Press, 1987); and Kathryn Edin, "Few Good Men: Why Poor Mothers Don't Marry or Remarry," *American Prospect*, June 2, 2000.

87. Sara McLanahan et al., "The Fragile Families and Child Well-Being National Baseline Report," Princeton University, 2001; and Irwin Garfinke et al., *Fathers under Fire: The Revolution in Child-Support Payments* (New York: Russell Sage Foundation, 1998).

88. McLanahan et al.

89. "Young Black Americans and the Criminal Justice System," The Sentencing Project, Washington, October 1995.

90. Cynthia Miller and Virginia Knox, "The Challenge of Helping Low-Income Fathers Support Their Children: Final Lessons from Parents Fair Share," Manpower Demonstration Research Corporation, New York, 2001.

91. Theodora Ooms, "Marriage and Government: Strange Bedfellows," Center for Law and Social Policy, Policy Brief no. 1, August 2002, p. 3.

92. Marianne Bitler et al., "The Impact of Welfare Reform on Marriage and Divorce," Federal Reserve Bank of Atlanta, Working Paper no. 2002–9, June 2002.

93. Sara McLanahan, Irwin Garfinke, and Ronald Mincy, "Fragile Families, Welfare Reform, and Marriage," Brookings Institution, Welfare Reform and Beyond, Briefing Paper no. 10, November 2001.

94. Robert Lerman, "Marriage as a Protective Force against Economic Hardship," Paper presented at the 23rd Annual Research Conference of the Association for Public Policy and Management, Washington, November 1, 2001.

95. Ooms, p. 3.

96. See, for example, Mary Jo Bane, "Household Composition and Poverty," in *Fighting Poverty: What Works and What Doesn't*, ed. Sheldon Danziger and Daniel Weinberg (Cambridge, Mass.: Harvard University Press, 1986).

97. Ooms.

98. V. Joseph Hotz et. al., *The Costs and Consequences of Teenage Childbearing for Mothers* (Chicago: University of Chicago Press, 1995).

99. Neil Gilbert, "The Unfinished Business of Welfare Reform," *Society* 24, no. 3 (March–April 1987): 5–11.

100. Suzanne Bianchi, "Children of Poverty: Why Are They Poor?" in *Child Poverty and Public Policy*, ed. Judith Chafe (Washington: Child Welfare League of America, 1993), Table 4.2, p. 100.

101. Sawhill, "Welfare Reform and the Marriage Movement."

102. Ibid., p. 4.

103. U.S. Bureau of the Census, "Fertility of American Women: June 1998," Current Population Reports Series P20-526, 2000.

104. Deborah Kalmuss, "Subsequent Childbearing among Teenage Mothers: The Determinants of a Closely-Spaced Second Birth," *Family Planning Perspectives* 26, no. 4 (July 1994): 149–53.

105. Stephen McLaughlin et al., "The Effects of Sequencing of Marriage and First Birth at Adolescence," *Family Planning Perspectives* 18, no. 1 (January–February 1986).

106. Naomi Seiler, "Is Teen Marriage a Solution?" Center for Law and Social Policy, Washington, April 2002.

107. Sawhill, "Welfare Reform and the Marriage Movement," p. 7.

108. Daniel Lichter, Deborah Roemke Graefe, and J. Brian Brown, "Is Marriage a Panacea? Union Formation among Economically-Disadvantaged Unwed Mothers," Ohio State University, April 2001.

109. I am setting aside the entire question of whether marriage is desirable in and of itself. However, there is certainly evidence that both the left and the right have allowed their views of marriage, the roles of women in society, and the propriety of sex outside marriage to color their views of the economic impact of marriage and the desirability of the federal government's promotion of it.

110. See Fagan, Patterson, and Rector for a detailed list of the literature on various marriage initiatives.

111. Wade Horn, "Wedding Bell Blues: Marriage and Welfare Reform," *Brookings Review* (Summer 2001): 39–42.

112. Karen Gardner et al., "State Policies to Promote Marriage," submitted to U.S. Department of Health and Human Services, September 2002, Exhibit 2, http://asps.hhs.gov/hsp/marriageolf.

113. Wade Horn and Isabel Sawhill, "Fathers, Marriage, and Welfare Reform," in *The New World of Welfare*, ed. Rebecca Blank and Ron Haskins (Washington: Brookings Institution, 2001), pp. 429–31.

114. David Ellwood and Isabel Sawhill, "Fixing the Marriage Penalty in the EITC," Brookings Institution Children's Roundtable Working Paper, 2000.

115. Eugene Steuerle, "The Effects of Tax and Welfare Policies on Family Formation," Paper presented at a Family Impact Seminar conference on Strategies to Strengthen Marriage, Washington, February 1997.

116. Virginia Knox, Cynthia Miller, and Lisa Gennetian, "Reforming Welfare and Rewarding Work: A Summary of the Final Report on the Minnesota Family Investment Program," Manpower Demonstration Research Corporation, New York, 2000.

117. Mary Parke and Theodora Ooms, "More Than a Dating Service? State Activities Designed to Strengthen and Promote Marriage," Center for Law and Social Policy, Couples and Marriage Series Policy Brief no. 2, October 2002.

118. For a detailed description and discussion of federal, state, and local programs designed to combat out-of-wedlock birth and teen pregnancy, see U.S. Department of Health and Human Services, "A National Strategy to Prevent Teen Pregnancy: Annual Report 2000."

119. www.cdc.gov/needphp/teen/htm.

120. http://aspe.hhs.gov/hsp/teenp/97-98rpt.htm; and http://opa.osophs.dhhs.gov/titlexx/oapp-funding-history.html.

121. U.S. House of Representatives, Committee on Ways and Means, 2000 *Green Book: Background Material and Data on Programs within the Jurisdiction of the Committee on Ways and Means* (Washington: Government Printing Office, 2000), pp. 371–72.

122. Sexuality Information and Education Council of the United States, "Sexuality Education in the Schools: Issues and Answers," 2000, www.siecus.org/pubs/fact/fact0007.html.

123. Helen Lippman, "What Are We Teaching in Sex Ed These Days?" *Medical Economics*, April 24, 2000, pp. 2–3.

124. Anna Lovejoy and Shayna Strom, "State Teen Pregnancy Prevention and Abstinence Education Efforts: Survey Results on the Use of TANF and Title V Funds," American Public Human Services Association, July 1999.

125. Douglas Kirby, "Do Abstinence-Only Programs Delay the Initiation of Sex among Young People and Reduce Teen Pregnancy?" U.S. Department of Health and Human Services, National Campaign to Prevent Teen Pregnancy, October 2002.

126. Sharon Lovick Edwards and Renee Freedman Stern, "Building and Sustaining Community Partnerships for Teen Pregnancy Prevention," Cornerstone Consulting Group, June 1998. See also Douglas Kirby, "No Easy Answers: Research Findings on Programs to Reduce Teen Pregnancy," U.S. Department of Health and Human Services, National Campaign to Reduce Teen Pregnancy, 1997.

127. Edwards and Stern.

128. Ellen Freeman et al., "Adolescent Contraceptive Use: Comparisons of Male and Female Attitudes and Information," *American Journal of Public Health* 70, no. 8 (August 1980): 790–97.

129. Laurie Schwab Zabin, Nan Marie Astone, and Mark Emerson, "Do Adolescents Want Babies? The Relationship between Attitudes and Behavior," *Journal of Research on Adolescence* 3 (1993): 77. The authors reported that fully 77 percent of teens who chose an abortion believed that having a baby would pose a problem. But as Douglas Besharov points out, "That is exactly the point: the more inconvenient unwed motherhood seems to a teenager, the less likely it is that she will become a mother." Douglas Besharov, Letter to the editor. *Wall Street Journal*, April 27, 1994.

130. Jane Mauldon et al., "What Do They Think? Welfare Recipients' Attitudes toward Marriage and Childbearing," Abt Associates, Welfare Reform and Family Formation Project, Research Brief no. 2, November 2002.

131. Quoted in Douglas Besharov, "Escaping the Dole," American Enterprise Institute, December 12, 1993.

132. J. Manlove, "The Influence of High School Dropout and School Disengagement on the Risk of School-Age Pregnancy," *Journal of Research on Adolescence* 8, no. 2 (1998): 187–220.

133. Kristin Moore et al., "Adolescent Sex, Contraception, and Childbearing: A Review of Recent Research," Child Trends, Inc., Washington, 1995.

134. Sawhill, "Welfare Reform and the Marriage Movement."

135. Mauldon et al., p. 5.

136. Ibid.

137. U.S. Department of Health and Human Services, "State Implementation of Major Changes to Welfare Policies," http://aspe.hhs.gov/hsp/Waiver-Policies99/W2JOBSexmp.htm.

138. See Rebecca Blank, "Evaluating Welfare Reform in the United States," *Journal of Economic Literature* 40 (December 2002), Table 9, for an excellent and detailed review of the available literature.

139. Ibid., p. 1155.

140. Charles Murray, "Family Formation," in *The New World of Welfare*, ed. Rebecca Blank and Ron Haskins (Washington: Brookings Institution, 2000).

141. Michael Sherraden, *Assets and the Poor: A New American Welfare Policy* (Armonk, N.Y.: M.E. Sharpe, 1991).

142. Melvin Oliver and Thomas Shapiro, *Black Wealth/White Wealth* (New York: Rutledge, 1996), p. 32.

143. Michael Sherraden, "Assets and the Poor: Implications for Individual Accounts and Social Security," Testimony to the President's Commission to Strengthen Social Security, October 18, 2001.

144. Cynthia Rocha, "Factors That Contribute to Economic Well-Being in Female Headed Households," *Journal of Social Service Research* 23, no. 1 (1997): 1–17.

145. Esther Cho, "The Effects of Assets on the Economic Well-Being of Women Following Marital Disruption," Washington University in St. Louis, Center for Social Development Working Paper no. 99-6, 1999.

146. Deborah Page-Adams and Michael Sherraden, "What We Know about the Effects of Asset-Holding: Implications for Research on Asset-Based Anti-Poverty Initiatives," Washington University in St. Louis, Center for Social Development Working Paper no. 96-1, 1996.

147. Federal Reserve Board of Governors, "2001 Survey of Consumer Finances," January 2003.

148. Robert Havemann and Barbara Wolfe, "Who Are the Asset Poor? Levels, Trends, and Composition, 1983–1998," Paper presented to the Symposium on Asset Building: Research and Policy, Washington University in St. Louis, Center for Social Development, 2000.

149. Ibid.

150. Dalton Conley, *Being Black, Living in the Red: Race, Wealth and Social Policy in America* (Berkeley: University of California Press, 1999).

151. Russell Cheng, "Asset Holding and Intergenerational Poverty Vulnerability in Female-Headed Families," Paper presented at the Seventh International Conference of the Society for the Advancement of Socio-Economics, Washington, April 7–9, 1995.

152. Rukmalie Jayakody, "Race Differences in Intergenerational Financial Assistance: The Needs of Children and the Resources of Parents," *Journal of Family Issues* 19 (1999): 508–34.

153. Ray Boshara, "The Rationale for Assets, Asset-Building Policies, and IDAs for the Poor," in *Building Assets: A Report on the Asset Development and IDA Field*, ed. Ray Boshara (Washington: Corporation for Enterprise Development, 2001), p. 18.

154. Many states have been raising their asset limits for TANF, but strict limits remain for food stamps, SSI, and Medicaid.

155. Boshara, p. 14.

156. Ibid., p. 102.

157. Ibid.

158. There are also limited IDA-style programs available using sec. 8 housing funds. Sherraden, *Assets and the Poor*.

159. PL 105-285, 1998; and 42 U.S.C. 604.

160. See www.cfed.org/individual_assets/ida/ida.overview.html.

161. Rene Bryce-Laporte, "The American Dream Demonstration," in *Building Assets*.

162. Mark Schreiner et al., "Savings and Asset Accumulation in IDAs: Downpayments on the American Dream Policy Demonstration, a National Demonstration of Individual Development Accounts," Washington University in St. Louis, Center for Social Development, 2001.

163. Michael Sherraden, cited in Andrew Biggs, "Fringe Benefits," *American Enterprise Magazine*, July–August, 2002, p. 32.

164. William Bassett, Michael Flemming, and Anthony Rodriguez, "How Workers Use 401(k) Plans: The Participation, Contribution and Withdrawal Decisions," *National Tax Journal* 11, no. 2 (June 1998): 275.

165. For example, 85 percent of account holders have completed high school; 61 percent have attended at least some college. Colleen Daily, "IDA Practice," in *Building Assets*.

166. As President Clinton's 2000 Federal Budget explained, "These [Trust Fund] balances are available to finance future benefit payments and other Trust Fund expenditures—but only in a bookkeeping sense. . . . They do not consist of real assets that can be drawn down in the future to pay benefits. Instead, they are claims on the Treasury that, when redeemed, will have to be financed by raising taxes, borrowing from the public, or reducing benefits or other expenditures. The existence of large Trust Fund balances, therefore, does not, in itself, have any impact on the government's ability to pay benefits." Office of Management and Budget, *Budget of the United States Government, Fiscal Year 2000* (Washington: Government Printing Office, 2000), Analytic Perspectives, p. 337.

167. Andrew Biggs, "Social Security: Is It 'A Crisis That Doesn't Exist'?" Cato Institute Social Security Paper no. 21, October 5, 2000.

168. William Jefferson Clinton, Speech to the Great Social Security Debate, Albuquerque, N.M., July 27, 1998.

169. Jagadeesh Gokhale, "The Impact of Social Security Reform on Low-Income Workers," Cato Institute Social Security Paper no. 23, December 6, 2001.

170. Congressional Budget Office, "Social Security and Private Saving: A Review of the Evidence," July 1998.

171. Martin Feldstein, "Privatizing Social Security: The $10 Trillion Opportunity," Cato Institute Social Security Paper no. 7, January 31, 1997.

172. 363 U.S. 603 (1960).

173. Survivors' benefits may be extended to age 21 if the child is enrolled in college.

174. Gokhale, "The Impact of Social Security Reform on Low-Income Workers." See also, Jagadeesh Gokhale et al., "Simulating the Transmission of Wealth Inequality via Bequests," *Journal of Public Economics* (2000).

175. Jagadeesh Gokhale and Laurence Kotlikoff, "The Impact of Social Security and Other Factors on the Distribution of Wealth," National Bureau of Economic Research, October 1999.

176. Martin Feldstein, "Social Security and the Distribution of Wealth," *Journal of the American Statistical Association* 71 (December 1976): 800–807.

177. Jeffrey Brown, "Redistribution and Income: Mandatory Annuitization with Mortality Heterogeneity," Boston College Center for Retirement Research Working Paper no. 2001-02, April 2001, p. 26.

178. Quoted in Eric Smith, "Prescription for Wealth," *Black Enterprise*, January 2000, p. 87.

179. See, for example, The President's Commission to Strengthen Social Security, *Strengthening Social Security and Creating Wealth for All Americans* (Washington: Government Printing Office, December 2000). For more discussion of the proposals put forward by the president's bipartisan commission, see Andrew Biggs, "Perspectives on the President's Commission to Strengthen Social Security," Cato Institute Social Security Paper no. 27, August 22, 2002. For a discussion of other proposals for individual accounts, see Peter Ferrara and Michael Tanner, *A New Deal for Social Security* (Washington: Cato Institute, 1998).

180. See Edward Gresser, "Toughest on the Poor: America's Flawed Tariff System," *Foreign Affairs* 81, no. 6 (November–December 2002).

Chapter 8

1. Robert Rector, "The Size and Scope of Means-Tested Welfare Spending," Testimony to the House Committee on the Budget, August 1, 2001, p. 6; and Bernadette Proctor and Joseph Dalaker, "Poverty in the United States, 2001," U.S. Bureau of the Census, September 2002, Table 1, p. 3.

2. Charles Murray, *What It Means to Be a Libertarian: A Personal Interpretation* (New York: Broadway Books, 1997), p. 59.

Index

About the Author

Michael Tanner is director of health and welfare studies at the Cato Institute in Washington, D.C., as well as director of the Institute's Project on Social Security Choice. He is the author of several books on health and welfare, including *The End of Welfare: Fighting Poverty in the Civil Society* (1996) and *A New Deal on Social Security* (1998). Tanner's writing has been published in the *Washington Post*, the *Los Angeles Times*, the *Wall Street Journal*, and *USA Today*, and he has appeared on *ABC World News Tonight*, *CBS Evening News*, *NBC Nightly News*, NPR, *PBS NewsHour with Jim Lehrer*, the Fox News Channel, MSNBC, CNBC, and Voice of America.

Cato Institute

Founded in 1977, the Cato Institute is a public policy research foundation dedicated to broadening the parameters of policy debate to allow consideration of more options that are consistent with the traditional American principles of limited government, individual liberty, and peace. To that end, the Institute strives to achieve greater involvement of the intelligent, concerned lay public in questions of policy and the proper role of government.

The Institute is named for *Cato's Letters*, libertarian pamphlets that were widely read in the American Colonies in the early 18th century and played a major role in laying the philosophical foundation for the American Revolution.

Despite the achievement of the nation's Founders, today virtually no aspect of life is free from government encroachment. A pervasive intolerance for individual rights is shown by government's arbitrary intrusions into private economic transactions and its disregard for civil liberties.

To counter that trend, the Cato Institute undertakes an extensive publications program that addresses the complete spectrum of policy issues. Books, monographs, and shorter studies are commissioned to examine the federal budget, Social Security, regulation, military spending, international trade, and myriad other issues. Major policy conferences are held throughout the year, from which papers are published thrice yearly in the *Cato Journal*. The Institute also publishes the quarterly magazine *Regulation*.

In order to maintain its independence, the Cato Institute accepts no government funding. Contributions are received from foundations, corporations, and individuals, and other revenue is generated from the sale of publications. The Institute is a nonprofit, tax-exempt, educational foundation under Section 501(c)3 of the Internal Revenue Code.

CATO INSTITUTE
1000 Massachusetts Ave., N.W.
Washington, D.C. 20001